Modern Foreign Languages

This accessible and thought-provoking book considers what beginner teachers need to know about learning, teaching, assessment, curriculum and professional development, in the context of teaching modern foreign languages. This book will prove an invaluable resource to those on PGCE courses, those in their induction year, and those in the early years of their teaching career. It is also suitable for subject leaders with mentor responsibilities and Advanced Skills teachers undertaking specialist inset and teaching support.

It explores issues to do with subject knowledge in learning to teach, based on the premise that an essential element of a secondary teacher's identity is tied up with the subject taught. The authors show how MFL teachers can communicate their own enthusiasm for their subjects and inspire their pupils to learn and enjoy learning.

The book is divided into three sections:

- Framing the subject – which defines subject knowledge and raises questions about MFL as a school subject;
- Teaching the subject – which looks at pedagogical, curricular and pupil knowledge;
- MFL within the professional community – which focuses on the place of MFL within the wider curriculum and the teaching community.

This book aims to provide stimulating assistance to subject specialists by helping them to find ways of thinking about their specialism, how to teach with it and how to engage with what pupils learn through it.

Norbert Pachler is Reader in Education and Co-Director of the Centre for Excellence for Work-based Learning for Education Professionals at the Institute of Education, University of London, UK. **Michael Evans** is Senior Lecturer in Education, University of Cambridge, UK. **Shirley Lawes** is Lecturer in Education at the Institute of Education, University of London, UK.

Teaching School Subjects 11–19 Series

Series Editors: John Hardcastle and David Lambert

Mathematics
Candia Morgan, Anne Watson and Clare Tikly

English
John Hardcastle

Geography
David Lambert and John Morgan

Science
Edited by Vanessa Kind and Keith Taber

Modern Foreign Languages
Norbert Pachler, Michael Evans and Shirley Lawes

Business, Economics and Enterprise
Edited by Peter Davies and Jacek Brant

Modern Foreign Languages

Teaching School Subjects 11–19

Norbert Pachler, Michael Evans
and Shirley Lawes

Routledge
Taylor & Francis Group

LONDON AND NEW YORK

First published 2007
by Routledge
2 Park Square, Milton Park, Abingdon, Oxon OX14 4RN

Simultaneously published in the USA and Canada
by Routledge
270 Madison Avenue, New York, NY 10016

Routledge is an imprint of the Taylor & Francis Group, an informa business

© 2007 Norbert Pachler, Michael Evans and Shirley Lawes

Typeset in Sabon and Bell Gothic by
Florence Production Ltd, Stoodleigh, Devon
Printed and bound in Great Britain by
TJ International Ltd, Padstow, Cornwall

British Library Cataloguing in Publication Data
A catalogue record for this book is available from
the British Library

Library of Congress Cataloging in Publication Data
Pachler, Norbert.
   Modern foreign languages: teaching school subjects 11–19/
   Norbert Pachler, Michael Evans and Shirley Lawes.
      p. cm.
      Includes bibliographical references.
   1. Languages, Modern – Study and teaching. 2. Languages,
   Modern – Study and teaching (Secondary) I. Evans, Michael,
   1951–, May 12. II. Lawes, Shirley, 1950–. III. Title.
   PB35.P133 2007
   418.0071′2–dc22   2007028514

ISBN10: 0–415–37342–5 (hbk)
ISBN10: 0–415–34284–8 (pbk)
ISBN10: 0–203–93279–X (ebk)

ISBN13: 978–0–415–37342–5 (hbk)
ISBN13: 978–0–415–34284–1 (pbk)
ISBN13: 978–0–203–93279–7 (ebk)

Contents

About the authors

Dr Norbert Pachler is Reader in Education and Co-Director for the Centre of Excellence in Work-based Learning for Education Professionals at the Institute of Education, University of London. As former Subject Leader for two Secondary PGCEs in Modern Foreign Languages and as Course Leader for an MA in Modern Languages in Education, Norbert has extensive experience in foreign language (FL) teacher education and development. His research interests include FL pedagogy and policy, teacher education and development as well as new technologies. He supervises and has published widely in these fields. Norbert is Joint Editor of the *Language Learning Journal* and of *German as a Foreign Language*.

Dr Michael Evans is Senior Lecturer in Education at the University of Cambridge. He co-ordinates the Modern Languages Secondary PGCE course at the Faculty of Education as well as the taught MPhil course entitled 'Research in Second Language Education'. He has extensive experience of supervision of PhD and Masters students engaged in research in different aspects of FL education. His research publications include work on the impact of school exchange visits on FL proficiency, analysis of online pupil bilingual discourse, the role of ICT in FL education, the politics of second language education and the European dimension in education. Until recently Michael was Editor of *Vida Hispanica*, the language-specific journal for Spanish of the Association for Language Learning.

Dr Shirley Lawes is Lecturer in Education at the Institute of Education, University of London and subject leader for the secondary PGCE in MFL.

She is the Editor of *Francophonie,* the language-specific journal for French of the Association for Language Learning. Among her publications are numerous articles and papers as well as several contributions to books on foreign language teaching.

For many years Shirley worked as a teacher of French in secondary schools, further and adult education, and in industry. She has worked on various PGCE MFL courses, and developed and led a PGCE/Maîtrise FLE dual certification programme in partnership with the Université du Littoral, Côte Opale. She also worked on an Economic and Social Research Council (ESRC)-funded research project in the Department of Educational Studies at Oxford University.

Editors' preface

This series aims to make sense of school subjects for new teachers at a moment when subject expertise is being increasingly linked to the redefinition of teachers' responsibilities (Whitty *et al.*, 2000). We start from the common assumption that teachers' passion for their subject provides the foundation for effective teaching. But we also take the view that effective teachers develop complicated understandings of students' learning. Therefore we also aim to offer subject specialists a picture of students' learning in their chosen field.

The central argument of the series as a whole is that teachers' professional development in subject specialism turns on their growing appreciation of the complexities of learning. In essence, the subject knowledge that new teachers bring from their experiences in higher education has to be reworked before it can be taught effectively to children. Our contention is that it is the sustained engagement with the dynamics of students' learning that uniquely sheds light on the way that existing subject knowledge has to be reconfigured locally if it is to be taught successfully in schools. What teachers know about their subject has to be reworked on site. And such is teachers' agency that they will always have a key role in shaping curriculum subjects.

Teaching involves a critical re-engagement with existing subject knowledge. This occurs chiefly through contact with children and communities. All new teachers have to learn how to make complicated judgements about the selection, ordering and presentation of materials with particular learners, real children, in mind. Teachers, then, are learners too. So as well as giving a picture of students' learning, the series aims to offer a sufficiently complicated account of professional development for new teachers to recognise themselves as learners as they take on new responsibilities in their schools. Thus we aim to offer insights into the kind of thinking – intellectual work – that teachers at the early stages are going to have to do.

This series is aimed chiefly at new teachers in their years of early professional development. This includes teachers in their initial training year, their induction year and those in years two and three of a teaching career. In addition to PGCE students and newly qualified teachers (NQTs) working toward the induction standards, the Series therefore also addresses *subject leaders* in schools, who have mentor responsibilities with early career teachers, and advanced skills teachers (ASTs) undertaking subject specialist Inset and teaching support.

The books in the series cover the training standards for NQT status and the induction standards. They use both the training terminology and the structure of the official standards in a way that enables readers to connect the arguments contained in the books with their obligation to demonstrate achievement against performance criteria. And yet the series as a whole has the ambition to take readers further than mere 'compliance'. It openly challenges teachers to acknowledge their own agency in interpreting 'competence' and to see their role in developing the subject, thus shaping their professional identities.

A distinctive feature of the series as a whole is its concern with how the *particular school subjects* haves been 'framed'. Thus the books offer a contrast with much that has been published in recent times, including the well-known *Learning to Teach* series also published by Routledge Falmer. They include substantial material on how school subjects connect with wider disciplines. They are also alert to broad social and cultural realities. They form a response, therefore, to what has been identified as a major weakness in training and teacher support in recent years, namely its preoccupation with generic matters of teaching competence at the expense of paying adequate attention to particular issues associated with subject specialism. The *Teaching School Subjects* series aims to redress the balance.

Those who believe that there is a general 'science' of teaching have been especially influential in recent years. There is no denying that the Key Stage Three Strategy, for instance, has had an impact on the preparedness of teachers generally. Further to this, the identification and recommendation of specific teaching approaches and techniques have enhanced new teachers' technical proficiency generally. Recently, much has been made of teaching 'thinking skills', and such initiatives have raised teachers' all-round performance as well as their professional self-esteem. But when push comes to shove, teaching cannot be sustained in this way. Pupils cannot be taught simply to think. They have to have something to think *about*. If this 'something' is trivial, irrelevant or out of date then the education process will be devalued, and students will quickly become disaffected.

The Secretary of State recognised something of this in 2003 when he launched his *Subject Specialisms Consultation*:

> Our very best teachers are those who have a real passion and enthusiasm for the subject they teach. They are also deeply committed to the learning of their students and use their enthusiasm for their subject to motivate them, to bring their subject alive and make learning an exciting, vivid and enjoyable experience.
>
> It is teachers' passion for their subject that provides the basis for effective teaching and learning. These teachers use their subject expertise to engage students in meaningful learning experiences that embrace content, process and social climate. They create for and with their children opportunities to explore and build important areas of know-ledge, and develop powerful tools for learning, within a supportive, collaborative and challenging classroom environment.
>
> (DfES, 2003a, Paras 1–2)

The *Teaching School Subjects* series aims to make practical sense of such assumptions by fleshing them out in terms of teachers' experiences. So, as well as looking at the histories of particular school subjects and current national frameworks, we shall also be looking at practical matters through case studies and teachers' narratives. We have noted how new teachers sometimes feel at a loss regarding the very subject knowledge they carry forward from their previous educational experiences into teach-ing. This feeling may be due to their entering a highly regulated profession where it appears that choices concerning what to teach (let alone how to teach it) are heavily constrained. However, much will be lost that could sustain creative and healthy classrooms if the system cuts off a primary source of energy, which is teachers' enthusiasm for their subject. Good teachers connect such enthusiasm with the students' interests. The series, *Teaching School Subjects*, engages with just this issue. If it has a single, clear mission it is to encourage the thought in teachers that they do not merely 'deliver' the curriculum in the form of prefigured subject knowledge, but they have an agentive role in making it.

What does it mean, to 'make' a curriculum? This is a huge question, and we do not aim to provide a definitive curriculum theory. However, we note that current accounts of curriculum and pedagogy (e.g. Moore, 2000) tend to emphasise the role of competing interests in deciding the educational experience of students. They offer a complicated picture of curriculum construction by taking in societal, economic and cultural influences. Plainly, no single interest wholly determines the outcome. Additionally, there is a growing agreement among educationists in England and Wales that 'central government control of the school curriculum must be loosened' to release teachers' energies (White, 2003, p. 189). We adopt a position similar to John White's, which is to 'rescue' the curriculum from central prescription and 'to see teachers having a greater role than now in . . . decisions on the curriculum . . .' (ibid., pp. 189–90).

This is not to say that the government has no role at all. Few would want to return fully to the arrangements before the 1988 Education Reform Act, when the curriculum experience of students was almost entirely in the hands of teachers and other interest groups. It is surely right that the elected government should regulate what is taught – but not that it should prescribe the curriculum in such an inflexible manner that it stifles teachers' initiative. Teachers play an active role in shaping the curriculum. They make professional decisions given, as White puts it, their 'knowledge of the pupils on whom the curriculum will be inflicted'. We argue that it is here, in deciding what to teach and how to teach it, that teachers' knowledge and creativity are of cardinal value. Teaching is quintessentially a practical activity, and teachers' performance matters. But we also know that behind the creativity in teaching lies a form of intellectual work. Our starting position is that intellectual effort is required at every stage of teaching and learning if it is to be worthwhile.

Knowledge of the pupils is a fundamental component of curriculum design. Effective teachers are in secure possession of just this kind of knowledge of their pupils where it informs their decisions about the selection of content and the choice of methods. However, the Series also makes it plain that knowledge of the pupils on its own is an insufficient basis for working out what to teach and how to teach it. Secure subject knowledge is equally important. Further to this, we take the view that an essential element of a secondary teacher's professional identity is tied up with a sense of their subject specialism. It is generally true that effective teaching requires a deeper grasp of subject than that specified by the syllabus. What is more, pupils frequently admire teachers who 'know their stuff'. What 'stuff' means is usually larger than a particular topic or a set of facts. Indeed, the way that an effective teacher makes a particular topic accessible to the pupils and enables them to progress often relies on their having a good grasp of the architecture of the subject, what the main structures are and where the weaknesses lie. You can't mug this up the night before the lesson.

It is widely recognised that PGCE students and early career teachers frequently turn to school textbooks to fill the gaps. This is fine, inevitably there will be aspects of the subject that the specialist has not covered. Many now use the internet proficiently as a rich source of information, data, images and so on. Also, fine. But what teachers also need to do is to make sense of the material, organise it and sift it for accuracy, coherence and meaning. The Series helps new teachers to do this by taking you into the relevant subject debates. The authors introduce you to the conceptual struggles in the subject and how these impinge on the making of the school subject. Through debating the role of the school subject, and showing how it hangs together (its 'big concepts'), they also show how it contributes to wider educational aims. Such a discussion takes place in the context of renewed debate about the future of school subjects and the subject-based curriculum. Though the Series serves the needs of subject specialists, it does not take as given the unchanging status of school subjects, and the authors will take up this debate explicitly.

Current notions of subjects, as inert 'contents' to be 'delivered' grate against learning theories, which foreground the role of human agency (teachers and pupils) in the construction of knowledge. For the teacher, good subject knowledge is not about being 'ahead of the students', but being aware of the wider subject. Teachers might ask themselves what kinds of knowledge their subject deals with. And, following on from this they might also ask about the kinds of difficulty that students often encounter. Note that we are not concerned with 'correcting' pupils' 'misconceptions' about what they get in lessons, but with what they actually make of what they get.

The Series has a broad, theoretical position that guides the way that the components of the individual books are configured. These components include lesson planning, classroom organisation, learning management, the assessment of/for learning and ethical issues. However, there is no overarching prescription, and the various volumes in the series take significantly different approaches. Such differences will depend on the various priorities and concerns associated with particular specialist subjects. In essence, the books aim to develop ways of thinking about subjects – even before readers set foot inside the classroom.

We doubt the adequacy of any model of teaching and learning that reduces the role of the teacher to that of the technician. Teachers mediate the curriculum for their students. Further to this, there is an urgent justification for this series of books.

It is the ambition of the series to restate the role of subjects in schools, but not in a conservative spirit that fails to engage with substantial change and developments. For some commentators, the information explosion, together with the still-quickening communications revolution, spells the death of subjects, textbooks and the rest of the nineteenth century school apparatus. We do not share this analysis. But we acknowledge that the *status quo* is not an option. Indeed, subject teachers may need to become less territorial about curriculum space, more open to collaboration across traditional subject boundaries and more responsive to what have been called 'unauthorised subject stories' – student understandings, media representations and common-sense views of the world. In such an educational environment, we would argue, the role of disciplinary knowledge is even *more* important than it was a decade ago, and teachers need to engage with it creatively.

Teaching School Subjects aims to support new teachers by helping them discover productive ways of thinking about their specialism. The specialist authors have tried to maintain an optimistic, lively and accessible tone, and we hope you enjoy them.

John Hardcastle and David Lambert
London, January 2004

About this book

Over the last ten or fifteen years there has been a significant growth in books aimed at supporting the initial and early professional development of foreign language (FL) teachers. Most of these books have taken as their framework of reference the competences or standards imposed by government for the award of qualified teacher status (QTS), the requirements of the National Curriculum for modern foreign languages and a growing number of other government initiatives ostensibly aimed at improving the quality of FL teaching and learning. This approach has necessarily prescribed the nature of the content and, to some extent, the assumptions and principles upon which such books are premised. What we have set out to do is to put to one side, although not entirely ignore, government requirements and to consider FL teaching and learning and FL teacher professionalism in a scholarly way. We seek to engage critically but constructively with prevailing orthodoxies in the field as well as with national policies and prescriptions. The book draws on findings from international research into second language acquisition (SLA) and foreign language learning (FLL). We aim to promote a principled and evidence-informed approach to FL pedagogy that, despite references to the English context, addresses a much wider audience beyond our national borders.

In this book we have taken on the task of trying to distil into one volume what we consider to be areas of professional knowledge that are essential to the FL teacher who is seeking to know more than what to do in the classroom and how to do it, but who wants to begin to understand the theories and principles that inform practice. This book might, therefore, be seen as an advanced introduction to the field of FLs in education for readers who have some knowledge both of practical FL teaching and learning as well as of the professional and pedagogical literature in the field.

In the face of an increase in the UK in central prescription of FL content and methodology under the banner of school effectiveness policies, the book explores alternative ways of conceptualising the knowledge bases involved in FL teaching, not, of course, in deliberate juxtaposition to government-endorsed interpretations of subject knowledge and related fields, but in order to present contesting views and to encourage our readers to see both policy and practice as open to critical discussion and debate and not merely conformist implementation. We would argue that the true professional does not adopt unquestioningly government policy – or any other methodological or pedagogical approaches for that matter, but seeks to make informed judgements based on a firm foundation of theoretical and conceptual knowledge, carefully thought-out professional principles and values as well as practical experience. Among other things, we seek to initiate new teachers into the spirit of critical engagement and debate of competing ideas about FL teaching and learning in the firm belief that this approach to teacher professional development is the hallmark of FL teacher excellence.

Norbert Pachler (London), Michael Evans (Cambridge)
and Shirley Lawes (London), June 2007

Abbreviations

ALL	Association for Language Learning
ASTs	Advanced Skills Teachers
BECTA	British Educational Communications and Technology Agency
BERA	British Educational Research Association
BPRS	Best Practice Research Scholarships
CALLA	Cognitive academic language learning approach
CBI	Content-based instruction
CEF	Common European Framework
CILT	National Centre for Languages/(Centre for Information on Language Teaching and Research)
CLT	Communicative language teaching
CMC	Computer-mediated communication
CORI	Concept-orientated reading instruction
CPD	Continuing Professional Development
CPS	Centre for Policy Studies
DCSF	Department for Children, Schools and Families
DfES	Department for Education and Skills
EEC	European Economic Community
ESRC	Economic and Social Research Council
FIPF	Fédération internationale des professeurs de français
FL	Foreign language
FL2	Second foreign language
FLA	Foreign language assistant
(F)LAC	(Foreign) languages across the curriculum

FLL	Foreign language learning
GCSE	General Certificate in Secondary Education
GTC	General Teaching Council
GTP	Graduate Teacher Programme
HE	Higher education
HEI	Higher Education Institution
ICT	Information and communications technology
IDV	Der Internationale Deutschlehreruerband
INSET	In-service training
IPPR	Institute of Public Policy Research
ITE	Initial Teacher Education
IWB	Interactive whiteboard
KAL	Knowledge about language
KS3	Key Stage Three
KS4	Key Stage Four
LEAs	Local Education Authorities
LLS	Language learning strategies
MFL	Modern Foreign Language
NC	National Curriculum
NFER	National Foundation for Educational Research
NQT	Newly qualified teachers
NVQs	National Vocational Qualifications
PCK	Pedagogical Content Knowledge
PGCE	Post-graduate Certification in Education
PoS	Programme of Study
PPD	Postgraduate Professional Development
PPP	Presentation–practice–production
PSHE	Personal, social and health education
QAA	Quality Assurance Agency
QCA	Qualifications and Curriculum Authority
QTS	Qualified teacher status
SLA	Second language acquisition
TBLT	Task-Based Language Teaching
TDA	Teacher Development Agency for Schools
TL	Target language
UCET	Universities Council for the Education of Teachers

Introduction: foreign language teaching in context

In recent years, foreign language (FL) teaching and learning in schools have gone through a somewhat turbulent period of change at the level of policy that has led to a reassessment of their place in the school curriculum. It could be argued that, although at a rhetorical level FL learning has rarely enjoyed such levels of support, in practice the effect of recent policy initiatives seems to have undermined the subject area.

During the post-Second World War period, when FLs became seen as a desirable pursuit for the most able learners, they were not generally regarded as an essential part of every child's educational experience. Indeed, until the introduction of comprehensive education in the early 1970s, FL learning was very much the preserve of the educational elites who either went to a selective or independent school. Even within the comprehensive system, some pupils were often 'selected out' on the basis that it was considered that they were better off improving their English. Nevertheless, there has always been a fairly strong 'languages for all' lobby that has promoted the wider benefits of FL learning for *all* pupils. The introduction of the National Curriculum in 1988 bestowed on FLs an apparently secure place within the school curriculum to the extent that the subject area enjoyed compulsory status at Key Stages Three and Four for a relatively short period in the late 1990s. For a brief period, knowing a FL was seen as part of what it means to be educated, and an experience that every secondary school child should have. This elevated status of the subject area was short-lived, however, and it was soon to be relegated to optional status at Key Stage Four (KS4) following the publication of the National Framework for Languages in 2002, which provided for the gradual introduction of FL learning in the primary school.

Responses to this policy have ranged from a warm welcome by advocates of early FL learning, to treating those who considered that more was being lost than gained by abandoning compulsory status at Key Stage Four as 'Cassandras'. In fact, within a year, 70 per cent of state schools made FL learning optional after Year 9, exam entries plummeted, and it has become clear that something has to be done to revive what has quickly become a beleaguered area of the school curriculum. Policymakers have begun to realise that, although the longer-term strategy of offering an *entitlement* to learn a FL to every primary school child by the end of the decade may begin to have an impact, it cannot compensate for the loss of status of FLs in the secondary school curriculum. Indeed, the Department for Education and Skills (DfES) as was (now the Department for Children, Schools and Families), in apparent recognition of some misjudgement of the effect of allowing for optionality post-14 years, have expressed the wish for at least 50 per cent of schools to offer FLs as part of the KS4 curriculum.

In 2006 the DfES carried out a review of the 2002 Languages Strategy (see Dearing and King, 2006, 2007) in which a number of important recommendations are made, not least that of a more diverse range of languages to be made available by schools including Mandarin and Arabic, the reaffirmation of FLs becoming a part of the statutory KS2 curriculum and the suggestion that the GCSE be reformed.

How well-equipped are FL teachers to meet the new challenge of winning the argument for their subject area? How susceptible are twenty-first century learners to the arguments made to them for the value of FL learning? Could it be that, over recent years, the focus on the development of excellent practical classroom skills on the part of the teacher and the acquisition of functional language 'skills' on the part of the learner has resulted in a neglect of the intellectual and cultural value of both the teaching and the learning of FLs? The future of FLs is ultimately in the hands of the teachers, and it is an exciting and worthwhile challenge that lies ahead.

What is needed now is a confident reaffirmation by FL teachers and other professionals that FLs *matter*, and that given the dominance of English as the global language of communication, functional and instrumental arguments for FL learning are unlikely to be effective with young people in England. Although personal vocational aims and economic benefits have become the traditional argument for justifying FLs to learners, they are but one argument, and certainly not the essential justification for

FLs in the school curriculum. They provide a limited view of what knowledge of a FL could give young people. Moreover, arguments that seek to make an economic justification for FL learning actually miss the real point about why languages are important. Knowledge of other languages will always be of importance as a cultural achievement whether, or not it is economically important as English becomes the global language of business. The study of FLs has the potential of favouring the universal over the particular in a unique way, of providing a window on the world by enriching people's lives and opening them up to other cultures and literatures.

A confident reaffirmation of the value of FL learning *for its own sake,* as part of every child's educational experience, rather than for instrumental economic reasons, requires teachers who are able to mount both a professional and intellectual defence of their subject area and who believe passionately in the value of FL learning. Such teachers need to be skilled classroom practitioners, but they need to be much more than that. They need to have an excellent knowledge of their subject and of the under-pinning theoretical principles of how FLs are learned, and an understanding of themselves as professionals and their professional role, set in the broader context of education. They need above all to believe in the intellectual and cultural value of FL teaching and learning. A sound intellectual purchase on all these matters is achieved through reading, questioning, discussion, debate and critical reflection. This book sets out to provide a basis for such questioning, discussion, debate and critical reflection, which we believe to be vital both to teachers and to the future of FLs as a subject area.

Part I

The subject

In the first part of this book, we consider the foreign language (FL) subject field both in terms of knowledge *of* the language, where we discuss contesting views of what it means to know a FL, and also knowledge *about* FLs and how they are learned. These two aspects of the subject field raise important issues about the transition from linguist to FL teacher that are explored in more depth later in the book.

We begin, in Chapter 1, by setting FL education in its political context by discussing some of the changes in educational policy characterised by a growth in government intervention into what is taught and how it is taught. We consider briefly some of the possible negative consequences of recent initiatives and thinking about FL education. In so doing, we aim to prompt our readers to reflect critically on the effects of policy initiatives on the role of the FL teacher, and the changing place of FLs in the school curriculum. We consider FLs as a discrete field and compare differing and contested views of subject knowledge. We argue that FLs as a subject discipline are undermined by an instrumental, functional view of knowledge, that expert subject knowledge is a prerequisite for effective teaching, and that this is the essential foundation of FL teacher professionalism upon which sound pedagogical and other professional and theoretical knowledge is predicated.

In Chapter 2 we take the discussion further by attempting to categorise the subject knowledge field and begin to look at ways in which the academic knowledge of the linguist is re-orientated towards teaching and learning. The term 'subject knowledge' comprises a highly differentiated field that extends much beyond the narrow conceptualisation of the generic standards for qualified teacher status (QTS). This chapter explores the dimensions of the teacher's subject knowledge and draws on the three examples of the target language, grammar and cultural awareness to illustrate the relationship between subject knowledge and teacher behaviour. We consider also some of the particular issues relating to the native speaker teacher of FLs, and some of the problems relating to the teaching of a second foreign language (FL2).

Chapter 1

The politics of foreign language learning and the subject knowledge field

INTRODUCTION

Why should a book on teaching and learning foreign languages begin by identifying the field as being in any way political? How is the teaching and learning of FLs political and why? How is this issue important to teachers? These questions have both current and historical aspects to them. The value placed on FLs within the education system at any given time, both in schools and higher education (HE) is a reflection of how we understand what education means. In recent times, attitudes to knowledge have become more functional, and the aims and purposes of education have become closely linked to the perceived needs of society and the economy. What is more, the social aspects of schooling seem to some policymakers to be more important than traditional subject disciplines, and the school curriculum has become infused with 'cross-curricular themes' that have influenced our understanding of the subject knowledge field. In this shifting climate, the place of FLs in the school curriculum, and their value in relation to other subjects, have become more vulnerable to intervention by government. We discuss this issue in more detail in Chapters 4 and 7. Moreover, the decline in interest over a number of years, in England at least, in FLs as an area of academic study at under-graduate level, during a period when FLs were compulsory in the school curriculum up to the age of 16, has increased this vulnerability. The National Languages Strategy (DfES, 2002) has introduced quite sweeping changes regarding when and how FLs are taught in schools, which are also impacting on what FLs feature on the school curriculum. Such changes should not be seen by teachers as simply the latest initiative to be handed down and 'delivered', but should be considered in an objective, critical light. This chapter will consider some of the features of present-day policy on FLs and their implications. We will discuss differing views of what it means to know a FL, and consider its importance in a world where English has become the dominant world language.

WHY POLITICAL?

When the UK became a member of the European Economic Community (EEC) in 1973, many teachers of FLs imagined the dawn of a new era for their subject discipline in schools. Although by that time the majority of 11-year-olds were learning a FL, usually French, in secondary school, the subject area was still seen by many as academic and elitist. Membership of the EEC raised awareness and concerns outside the education community about the UK's poor overall FL capability and fears were expressed that opportunities to reap full benefit of EEC membership would be missed. In 1976, the Prime Minister, James Callaghan, launched 'The Great Debate' on education in a landmark speech at Ruskin College, Oxford, in which he identified 'the need to improve relations between industry and education' (Maclure, 1988, p. 169). The idea that FL learning might have a practical use for more than a very tiny portion of the population was a challenge that raised issues of what should be learned and how. Importantly, the Ruskin College speech indicated for the first time that education should be linked to the needs of the economy and that educational decisions should not be left only to educators: government and other interested parties had a role to play in educational decision-making.

The combination of membership of the EEC and the shift in the relationship between education and society had an impact on the teaching and learning of FLs. First, for FL teachers, membership of the EEC signalled a possible change in attitudes towards FL learning. Greater numbers and a wider range of learner ability, together with the new opportunities for job mobility in the EEC that many people envisaged, led many teachers to believe that learners might see FLs as more attractive and relevant if they had a vocational purpose. The perceived value and purpose of FL began to change quite rapidly. These changes were accompanied by developments in second language research (see Mitchell and Myles, 1998) and FL teaching methodology (see Jones, 1994, and Hawkins, 1996).

However, until the late 1980s and beyond, the majority of developments in teaching and learning FLs at all levels were teacher-led, although,
of course, influenced by outside pressures. For example, developments
in methodology throughout that period towards a focus on FLs for communication, 'authenticity' of task and materials, and the use of native
speakers modelling everyday language were based, in part, on the development of the so-called 'Graded Objectives Movement' that sought to change
how and when achievement in FLs was assessed. There was a distinction
during that period between government, who made policies based on a
political outlook, and educational professionals who were mostly in the
universities, but also in Local Authorities (LAs) and certainly in schools,
who had the freedom to interpret those policies within the educational
system based on their professional knowledge, beliefs and expertise.
Developments in FL pedagogy and curriculum development at that time,
therefore, were seen as a professional responsibility.

Although it is not possible here to go into great historical detail of
the last 25 years (see Hawkins, 1996, and Rowlinson, 1994 for a critical
account of the period), nevertheless, it is possible to point to the Education
Reform Act of 1988 and the subsequent introduction of the National
Curriculum for Schools as a watershed in education in England and Wales.
Increased intervention by government in education continued throughout
the 1990s up to the present time, to the point where all aspects of schooling and school life, from school meals to classroom discipline, are now
the subject of policy initiatives that prescribe practice. Other examples of
prescriptive policies and their effects that relate to the area of FLs are discussed throughout this book; the point here is to emphasise the extent to
which education generally, and FLs specifically, are now seen as important
objects of political interest and public policy, in which the government is
involved to a far greater extent than at any time in the past.

FL teaching has been dogged by the perception that a lot of FL learning is unsuccessful. Some commentators, recognising that FLs are difficult, observe that perhaps too much is expected of learners. The National
Framework for Languages, and in particular, the Key Stage Three (KS3)
Framework are discussed in more detail in Chapter 4. However, this quite
radical shift in government policy at the present time is hailed as an attempt
to indicate a firm political commitment to FL learning and a recognition
of the importance of increasing Britain's FL capacity in both economic
and educational terms, while at the same time acknowledging the difficulty

of the subject area. Perhaps somewhat cynically, it might be seen as a misguided attempt to demonstrate a commitment to boost a somewhat beleaguered curriculum area that will have long-term deleterious effects on FLs in this country. Emerging responses to these recent changes in FL curriculum provision range from applause, tinged with a certain nervousness about how realistic the proposals are (Wicksteed, 2005), to dismay from those who fear for the future of FLs at all levels now that they have been made optional on the school curriculum from the age of 14. Whether seen as a further watershed or a crisis, it is clear that the changes have fuelled both concern and debate over what the FL subject area should constitute, who it should be for and why it is important. It is now more difficult to justify FLs as a subject discipline in its own terms, at a time when what should be taught in schools is increasingly called into question (see White, 2004). Whether, for example, the focus on cross-curricular themes such as information and communications technology (ICT) and citizenship education, as well as the requirement for all teachers to be concerned with literacy and numeracy skills, represents an erosion of our understanding of the subject discipline of FLs or whether it is enhancing, and reflects a change in how we understand subject knowledge, is a matter of some debate. These matters are discussed further in Chapter 7. They do have a significant bearing, however, on FL curriculum content and its knowledge base.

Amidst all the discussion and debate on the perceived intrusiveness of some aspects of government educational policy, FL teachers and teacher educators alike are heard to complain now that they have become 'deliverers' rather than innovators. But this somewhat negative view should be challenged.

However, whatever new structures or curriculum initiatives may be introduced by policymakers, it is still FL teachers who have the expert subject knowledge and it is their belief in, and passion for their subject that enables them to inspire learners, and in this sense knowledge is power! Expert subject knowledge is the basis of a teacher's professional expertise. Belief in the value of FLs as a subject discipline is, therefore, paramount and of overriding importance to whatever structures might be imposed from without. But what do we mean by 'expert' subject knowledge? Indeed, what *is* subject knowledge? What should be the aspirations we have for learners of FLs? These are the questions that we shall turn to in the next section.

WHAT DOES IT MEAN TO KNOW A FL?

'Mastery' and the near-native speaker

In recent times, the ground has shifted quite considerably as to what constitutes 'knowing' a FL. The traditional model of 'near-native speaker' fluency as the ultimate aspiration of the FL learner has been called into question because it is unachievable for most learners and is, therefore, supposedly demotivating. Furthermore, cultural relativists would argue about what the term 'native speaker' actually means. Do we refer to the French spoken in France, the Spanish in Spain, or the variations that exist around the world? Perceptions of what it means to know a FL have changed, and over the past 30 years the trend in both post-16 (A level) and university programmes has been away from the development of FL knowledge through translation, essays, the study of grammar and a heavy emphasis on the study of literature and other cultural knowledge (often called 'civilisation'), to the development of operational language skills, the teaching of cultural 'awareness', which suggests a more ethnographic orientation, and, most importantly, a focus on the target language as the medium through which communication is developed. The study of a large number of texts from the literary canon has been replaced on most degree programmes by more recent works and courses in film and media studies. Indeed, on some modularised degree programmes, it is possible to avoid the study of literature entirely in favour of more 'relevant', often vocationally orientated, modules, such as business languages.

It is neither possible nor necessary here to consider in detail the content and changing nature of HE degree programmes (see Coleman, 1995, pp. 1–15 and 1999, pp. 321–41, for a full discussion of trends in HE). Readers will have their own experiences as students to refer to, but it would seem that there is now a far greater degree of variation in FL learning experience on degree programmes, and, therefore, the subject expertise that might traditionally be seen as the corpus of subject knowledge that was the assumed prerequisite for the linguist seeking to become a FL teacher has changed. Nevertheless, we might assume that there is still likely to be some sort of consensus as to what constitutes the body of FL knowledge that can be seen as constituting 'mastery' that is deemed a desirable, even necessary, basis for admission to the teaching profession.

As a minimum, a high degree of written and oral fluency in the target language, a firm grasp of the grammar of the language and some experience, knowledge and awareness of the culture or cultures in the ethnographic sense where the language is spoken would seem essential. But if these areas of subject knowledge are necessary, are they sufficient? What is it that inspires passion in FL teachers for their subject? It is an important question, particularly as FL beginner teachers most frequently cite their love of and for their subject and the wish to share their knowledge with young people as being their primary motivation for wanting to teach (Lawes, 2004b). But what do they mean? If all that is meant is that they enjoy speaking the language and want to teach others to do the same, it could be that their ability to inspire future generations of FL learners will be limited and their enthusiasm short-lived. A high level of linguistic ability is, of course, a prerequisite of 'mastery', but the heart of FL 'mastery' is the opening up to other cultures, indeed to human culture in all its forms, that is, to *the best* that is thought and known. However, at the present time when much emphasis is placed on the functional and instrumental role of knowledge, and a relativistic view of knowledge prevails, it is not easy to argue for an in-depth knowledge of culture, that is, the literature, arts and history of the country or countries where the FL is spoken, or so-called 'high culture', without being accused of being out-of-date or elitist. But what is elitist about aspiring to the best that is thought and known? In fact, access to *this* body of knowledge is what linguists often cite as being what inspired them most (along with spending periods of time in the country) in their FL learning (see Coleman, 1995). Moreover, it is precisely this cultural knowledge that enables a better understanding of the ethnological forms of culture, that is the traditions, customs, folklore and aspects of daily life. Literature is, after all, the cultural base of the language.

Communicative competence

The term 'communicative competence' has been used for some time to describe what FL knowledge entails and the types of skill that learners might be expected to develop. The term has been used for some time, although the way it is used is often divorced from its original meaning. Mitchell (1994, p. 34), in a thoughtful investigation into communicative language teaching (CLT), points out that the term 'communicative competence' was first popularised by Dell Hymes in the early 1970s and was used to describe 'the competent language user (who) not only commands accurately the grammar and vocabulary of the chosen target language, but also knows how to use that linguistic knowledge appropriately in a range of social situations'. Canale (1983) identified four areas of communicative competence:

- grammatical competence
- discourse competence
- sociolinguistic competence and
- strategic competence.

Communicative competence thus defined suggests a relatively high level of knowledge and practical capability that learners might aspire to. But more recent interpretations, not least in the National Curriculum (NC) and GCSE examination specifications are much weaker. CLT, as the vehicle for developing communicative competence, while remaining what Pachler calls the 'methodological imperative', has, over the last 20 years remained contentious and, some would argue, flawed. There has been a growing perception that CLT needs 'revisiting'. Critics suggest that the particular form of CLT developed in the UK, characterised by topic-based syllabuses, performance objectives and much pupil interaction, trivialises FL teaching by placing too much emphasis on the use of 'fun' activities and games with little attention paid to the formal language system and that this militates against pupils taking their learning seriously. Criticisms of the NC are necessarily criticisms of CLT, as, in England, the NC is the embodiment of CLT. Pachler (2000) argues that 'we are overburdening learners with situation-specific language and idealised dialogues and stock written passages to be memorised and reproduced under examination condition rather than develop in them a real understanding of how language works'. He further suggests that there is a 'need for the inclusion of thought-provoking texts and contexts which allow pupils to perform tasks that make appropriate cognitive demands and emphasise (linguistic) creativity, moving learners on from single-word and short-phrase transactions and interactions' (p. 31). There is a strong current of research-based evidence to suggest that CLT, as it is currently practised in the UK, fails effectively to develop communicative competence in the majority of learners.

FLs in schools

Attitudes to FL learning have changed considerably over recent years, partly as a result of the establishment of FLs as a compulsory subject in the NC up to KS4. The aims, form, content and assessment of FLs have evolved in particular ways, notably, as we have suggested above, through CLT, to take account of the wide range of ability of learners. But the principle of 'languages for all' has failed to take hold. It is now generally understood that most learners neither aspire to nor need a high level of knowledge and that many are poorly motivated towards FLs. Williams (2000) maintains that any compulsory status of FLs in the secondary school curriculum is misguided, arguing his case at a time when a 'languages for all' throughout the secondary curriculum applied. First, he maintains, correctly in our view, that there are 'serious defects in the argument for teaching modern foreign languages on grounds of their vocational usefulness or their role in the generation of wealth' (p. 1). Second he considers that cultural and 'civic' arguments are equally ineffective. However, he confirms that all young people should be 'entitled to the opportunity' of learning at least one FL, but that this should be for only one year, after which they should be allowed to give up on the grounds that they should not be made to learn something that they are not interested in or have no aptitude for. There are many counter-arguments to this, some of which are made later in this chapter, but Williams is used here as an example of the thinking in some quarters: that many young people are not capable of learning FLs beyond a very basic level. Although the sentiment is often not expressed in such overt terms, or even argued as cogently as Williams does, it is present in current policy. The justification for removing the compulsion to learn FLs up to GCSE level is that many young people do not *like* FLs and that they should be given the opportunity to give them up at the end of KS3 in order to learn something more useful and relevant to them. The underlying message here is that most young people in England are not intellectually capable of FL learning, and that FLs are not really that important. At an institutional level, we could be forgiven for thinking that many senior school managers agree with this view. Shortly after the introduction of the National Languages Strategy in September 2004, 70 per cent of secondary schools made FLs an optional subject at KS4. The subsequent attempt by government to set a benchmark of 50 per cent of pupils to take a FL qualification proved difficult to achieve, with less than 25 per cent of schools reaching this goal by 2006 (see CILT/ALL Language Trends Surveys, 2004 and 2006). Paradoxically, policymakers would stress their commitment to FL learning and would point to the massive investment currently being made in the introduction of FLs in the primary school as being the foundation for ensuring the success of FL education in the future. The success or failure of FLs in this country is a complex issue that is considered in various ways throughout this book. It is raised here to draw attention to the urgent need for FL teachers who believe passionately in their subject and can inspire young people to learn it.

But what is it that we might want young people to aspire to? If the ultimate goal and perhaps abilities of most FL learners fall far short of 'mastery' or even 'communicative competence' in its real sense, should more realistic 'benchmarks' be applied? Or could it be that by rejecting the possibility of the highest possible level of achievement, learners restrict their aspirations and have lower horizons, that teachers lower their expectations of their pupils and that potential is lost or not achieved? At what point does FL become an operational skill? These are questions that we might ask in relation to how the life-long occupation of learning a FL is marked out in stages and how decisions are made about who should learn what.

New perspectives on FL knowledge – a European example

There has been an increasing concern for some time to break down, describe and circumscribe areas of FL knowledge, mostly for assessment purposes. It is common now, for example to think of FL learning in terms of 'outcomes'. There are many aspects of this discussed in this book. Indeed, it has become a defining feature of the English education system. However, FLs are a unique case in the sense that they are a political concern within the European Union in a way that no other school subject is. 'Harmonisation' may appear to be merely another EU buzzword, but, since the creation of the EEC, there has been a substantial commitment to influencing FL policy and practice throughout the community (see for example Van Ek, 1976). Notably, in 2001, the Council of Europe published its Common European Framework of Reference for Languages in which it detailed a European-wide 'basis for the elaboration of language syllabuses, curriculum guidelines, examinations, textbooks etc.' (p. 1). The Framework defines, among other things, levels of proficiency that learners might achieve at different stages of their learning and, perhaps more importantly, has promoted 'plurilingualism' as an alternative to multilingualism, presumably in an attempt to combat monolingualism in the spirit of European Union. The notion of plurilingualism is interesting to consider here, because it represents a quite different view of what it means to know a FL. According to the Common European Framework, plurilingualism

> is the knowledge of a number of languages, or the co-existence of different languages in a given society. Multilingualism may be attained by simply diversifying the languages on offer in a particular school or education system . . . Beyond this, the plurilingual approach emphasises the fact that as an individual person's experience of language in its cultural contexts expands, from the language of the home to that of society at large and then to the language of other peoples . . . (he/she) builds up a communicative competence to which all knowledge and experience of language contributes.
>
> (Council of Europe, 2001, p. 4)

The writers describe this view of FL learning as a 'paradigm shift' that teaching professionals should be promoting. Plurilingualism does indeed have different aims to those of 'mastery' or even 'communicative competence' or 'proficiency'. It aims to develop a 'linguistic repertory in which all linguistic abilities have a place' and that rejects the notion of progressive attainment in a particular language or languages. The document gives examples of what such an approach means in practice, for example:

> Those with some knowledge, even slight, may use it to help those with none to communicate by mediating between individuals with no common language. In the absence of a mediator, such individuals may nevertheless achieve some degree of communication by bringing the whole of their linguistic equipment into play, experimenting with alternative forms of expression in different languages or dialects, even exploiting paralinguistics (mime, gesture, facial expression, etc) and radically simplifying their use of language.

What is described here is what all FL learners do to a greater or lesser extent as a matter of course when they are in a foreign country, or among a group of speakers of other languages and they are trying to communicate with others. It is difficult to see it as a paradigm shift, but it is, perhaps, a shift in expectations of what learners might achieve. Although 'plurilingualism' might describe the reality of many learners' experience, what model precisely does it suggest for language teaching and learning? Is it more than legitimising the failure to engage and inspire learners to want to achieve more? If we put ourselves in the place of the learner described above, how might she react to such a situation? Although perhaps being pleased to have been able to communicate with others, the experience might serve as a motivator to improve her FL knowledge and ability to communicate. What is also ignored is that, at least from an English perspective but it is probably true in other European countries, the reality is that the majority of learners will not find themselves in that situation. Sceptical as one might be of the pedagogical implications of plurilingualism, the view it takes of FL learning has gained currency and influence. Indeed, the National Languages Strategy in England, although not using the term, seems to have been influenced by exponents of plurilingualism. What we are arguing for here is a detailed consideration of the pedagogical implications of plurilingualism to avoid it being viewed negatively. For a more detailed discussion, see e.g. Pachler, 2007.

The Common European Framework also defines communicative language competence referred to above. In a similar way to Canale (1983), it identifies three components: linguistic, sociolinguistic and pragmatic. 'Linguistic competence' comprises lexical, phonological and syntactical knowledge and skills and 'other dimensions of the language system' including cognitive organisation and the way language is stored. 'Sociolinguistic competence' comprises an understanding of the sociocultural conditions of language use and sensitivity to social conventions. 'Pragmatic competence' comprises the functional use of language, mastery of discourse, 'coherence and cohesion' and the identification of text types and forms (Council of Europe, 2001, p. 13). These elements describe the knowledge of language and language skills regarded as necessary for communication, as well as an understanding of the cultural context of the language. The Framework also identifies levels by which FL learner progress can be measured, which is intended as a model for FL teaching and learning in Europe. As such, it is an influential document that we cannot afford to ignore.

Assessing FL 'competence', an English example

Indeed, it is interesting to see how the Common European Framework is being used by national government policymakers in the formulation of policy. In England, the levels have been taken up in the recently introduced National Recognition Scheme (2004), which is intended as a complement to existing qualifications. Levels are presented as a 'Languages Ladder' (DfES, 2004a) that identifies six stages of linguistic competence: breakthrough, preliminary, intermediate, advanced, proficiency and mastery (see also Chapter 5). The assessment framework is essentially competence-based, and assessment outcomes are expressed by 'can do' statements, reminiscent of earlier schemes developed from the 1970s (Graded Objectives) to vocational FL assessment schemes of the early 1990s. This goes further than the Common European Framework in terms of specifying particular competences within each level and appears to be a departure from the 'European view' of FL knowledge and 'competence'.

This competence approach as it is applied to the assessment of FL learning in England is of a very particular nature, identifying as it does specific learning outcomes (the 'can do' statements). It reflects a skills-orientated view of FL learning and a particular view of knowledge that has become popular in recent years throughout education and training, despite its somewhat discredited origins in behaviourist learning theories.

Although the idea of 'can do' statements may seem attractive to both learners and teachers, Hyland (1993) reminds us of the objections to a competence-based view of knowledge and assessment. He makes three general criticisms that may be applied specifically to FLs. The first concerns its origins in behaviourist theories of learning that take no account of human understanding and consider knowledge as being something that is always demonstrable. Second, he argues that the notion of 'competence' is conceptually confused, that we do not know what a competence is and that the development of knowledge and understanding cannot be described in behaviourist terms. Hyland reviews the literature on National Vocational Qualifications (NVQs), which is where the 'competence movement' in England began, and he concludes that 'definitions range from the simplistic and specific to the complex and all-embracing' and demonstrate a crude understanding of the complexities involved in defining competence. The third criticism that Hyland raises regarding a competence-based approach, is its embodiment of a restricted, instrumental view of knowledge. There is no suggestion that competent performance is totally independent of knowledge and understanding, but performance is elevated above knowledge, and competence is judged on what an individual *does* rather than what they know (Hyland, 1993, p. 60). The conception of knowledge in the assessment of competence, or the achievement of a particular standard, is reduced to what is relevant and functional. The broader intellectual endeavour that might be seen as fundamental to learning a FL is thus either left unexamined or excluded.

This criticism would seem particularly pertinent to the advanced, proficiency and mastery levels of the Languages Ladder (DfES, 2004a). It is at these more advanced levels that the instrumental view of knowledge embodied in a competence view of FL learning becomes an acute problem. Even if earlier FL learning has been functional, skills-focused and measured by 'outcomes' and 'can do' statements (and these, in themselves, are contestable), advanced study must surely take on a different dimension and purpose. It is difficult to see how, particularly at an advanced level, FL learning can be categorised by 'can do' statements that would have any meaning, except in the most technical sense of FL knowledge. Furthermore, the intellectual dimensions of linguistic knowledge, cultural knowledge and ideas would necessarily be ignored. The problem with seeking to describe and categorise knowledge in a reductionist way, is that not only is the creative potential of the learner stifled, but ultimately the value of independent and critical thought is marginalised. More importantly, the subject discipline is diminished.

DEFENDING FLS AS A SUBJECT DISCIPLINE

Defences of FL as a field of knowledge in its own right are few and far between at present. Even those who recognise the contribution of FLs to the all-round education and personal development of individuals and the subject's potential for broadening the horizons of young people, often still feel the need to justify their arguments in instrumental and functional terms. Perhaps what such arguments miss is the recognition of what is unique about FLs. FL study has a unique transformational capacity that differentiates it from other subject disciplines in the potential that knowledge of FLs has of opening individuals up to human culture and to 'emancipate the learner from parochialism' (Hawkins, 1987, p. 32). FLs have the unique potential of breaking down barriers between people and countries and of promoting a sense of universalism in an individualised world. This is at the heart of what makes the study of FLs unique.

Many teachers and academics writing on FLs adopt a broad theoretical position that is known as 'relativistic' or 'culturally relative'. The idea is that there are many cultures and that they are all different and unique. This is quite different from recognising that, although there are different languages and histories, they exist within one human culture. It is commonly asserted that there are no 'absolute' truths (whatever this may mean) but 'many truths' that are known to particular groups. This widespread relativism is incoherent, and quick and easy, as well as detailed, refutations of relativism have been available for two thousand years (see Plato, Siegel, 1987, or Nozick, 2001, for philosophical criticism; for more political criticism and explanation see Hayes, 2003 and Bailey 2004). The intrusion of philosophical relativism into thinking about FL is not a deep expression of epistemological unease about the nature of truth, but rather a lack of confidence in the subject discipline of FL for which reasons are sought in philosophy. This lack of confidence is part of the mood of the times and affects all subject areas. The solution is to have more confidence in defending FL as a subject and not to become amateur philosophers.

There are at least two myths about FLs that are popularly held views today. First, that the British are 'no good at learning languages', and, second, that FLs are not popular because English is the dominant world language. Perhaps these are not entirely myths, but their importance is inflated, and they are used as excuses for failure both in terms of the individual and of FLs as a subject discipline. Although one would not deny that many people *think* they are not good at FLs, there is no evidence to suggest that this is an inherent feature of the British character or that there is some genetic peculiarity about the British, or indeed that everyone is not capable of learning a FL.

Two examples of recent research point to some of the more plausible explanations for the negativity that surrounds FL at the present time. A study by Milton and Meara (1998) compared FL learning experience and performance of 14-year-old British, Greek and German pupils. Their findings did indeed identify significantly poorer FL performance among the British students compared with their European counterparts, but this was largely attributed to the fact they spent significantly less time in FL study. The study showed that English students were set lower goals, and it suggested that learning needs were not being met in terms of offering either sufficient challenge for the most able or the necessary support for the less able in comparison with those abroad. It also raised issues of methodology as a possible contributing factor. Graham (2003), in a study of pupils' learning strategies in Years 11, 12 and 13, found that learners themselves attributed their lack of success to their own lack of ability, despite the fact that they were 'successful' learners. Graham's research found that success or failure was related to how students went about tasks and that students can be helped to adopt a more positive approach to success and failure by training them to attribute their success to the learning strategies they use. Equally, they can be helped to improve their learning strategies in a systematic way by the teacher. Interest in learning strategies is gaining ground and there is a growing body of research and evidence from practice to suggest that it is an area that can contribute significantly to improving learners' performance in FLs, thereby dispelling the myth that the British are poor at languages.

There is some substance to the argument that the dominant role of English as a world language has had a detrimental effect on FL learning. Indeed, the Milton and Meara study referred to above confirmed that learners of English in Greece and Germany have a high instrumental motivation to learn that contributed to their higher achievement in FLs. They concluded that this is not the same for English pupils learning a FL. However, instrumental arguments for learning are problematic in and of themselves, because they are restrictive and reductive. But instrumental and functional arguments for FLs are prevalent and difficult to challenge in the present climate where FLs are valued largely for their functional use. On the other hand, if we take the view that FLs have a broader cultural and intellectual role to play both in education and society, as well as contributing to the personal enrichment of the individual, then the position of the English language takes on a relative rather than dominant position.

Where do you as a teacher of FLs stand in all this? As an expert in your field with a passion for your subject which you want to share with young people. What that subject field is, as we have seen, is a contentious issue. But if we ask ourselves the question, what is most likely to *inspire* young people, awaken their curiosity for FL learning, develop their cognitive abilities and creativity, is the answer 'functional communication' or could it be something more intrinsically motivating? It is easier, perhaps, to challenge instrumental attitudes to knowledge in young people, than in policymakers and professionals and in society at large.

CONCLUSION

This chapter has attempted to raise some of the debates around FL subject knowledge and has pointed to a shift in understanding about what constitutes FL knowledge. Many of the issues raised here are taken up throughout this book in order to provide you with differing arguments and viewpoints that may be useful to you in the course of your professional career. Examples have been drawn from current policy, research and practice to illustrate this shift and to point to some of the difficulties that an instrumental, functional view of knowledge creates for FLs as a subject discipline. A belief in the value of FLs as a subject discipline, a passion for our subject, and a belief in our ability to inspire young people to share our passion are prerequisites for successful teaching and indispensable to the future of FL learning at all levels.

QUESTIONS FOR DISCUSSION

1   This chapter suggests that we should challenge the idea that FL teachers have become mere 'deliverers' of a prescribed curriculum. What arguments can be put forward to do so?
2   How can FL teachers maintain and develop their own knowledge and enthusiasm for their subject throughout their careers?
3   What might 'revisiting CLT' mean to the FL teacher?
4   What would be *your* defence of FLs as a subject discipline in the school curriculum?
5   Is a 'competence view' of FL learning entirely inappropriate? If not, why not?

Chapter 2

Different categories of foreign language knowledge

INTRODUCTION

It is often argued that a direct relationship exists between a teacher's subject knowledge and her effectiveness as a teacher. In fact, you may believe that as a FL teacher this axiom applies to you more than to most other subject specialists as, in the context of optimum target language (TL) use, you are expected to use your specialist skill as the medium of communication in your lessons. Also, it can be argued that a teacher with good subject knowledge is more likely to have the confidence to exude 'infectious enthusiasm' for her subject and to use this to awaken and sustain pupil motivation in learning.

However, defining more precisely what that subject knowledge is that we aim to foster is not simple. Looking at the source of that knowledge for FL teachers is a case in point. The diversity and variability of undergraduate FL degrees in the UK are known facts. As graduates in French, German, Spanish or other FLs, many readers of this book will, collectively, have experienced a wide and disparate background in language learning. For instance, the amount of FL used in lectures or for coursework purposes will have differed greatly, as will the actual percentage of target language studied as part of your overall course of study. Similarly, the amount of explicit knowledge about their mother tongue (L1) of native-speaker teachers can vary considerably according to the nature and amount of L1 study at school and/or university. Therefore, it seems important to us that we examine the question of what constitutes subject knowledge for FL teachers carefully here.

Another important aspect of this matter is that, as Widdowson (2002, p. 68) rightly points out, FLs in the curriculum are pedagogic constructs, 'versions of reality that have been devised for learning', and 'knowing a language as a subject is not the same as knowing it as it naturally occurs'. Similarly, there is often a considerable divergence in the nature of the FL studied at university with that to be learnt in school, and very rarely, if ever, is the transactional target language needed by the teacher, i.e. the language in which to give instructions and interact with pupils, explicitly taught as part of an undergraduate degree.

Native speakers, by virtue of possessing native linguistic competence, are not necessarily better at using the target language in the FL classroom compared with non-native speakers, nor do they necessarily make the better FL teachers. Compared with non-native speakers, for example, they face a greater challenge when trying to pitch the target language at the appropriate level. This is, of course, not to question the value of native speaker teachers teaching their own language to speakers of other languages in their own countries. Neither does it take away anything from the unique contribution the increasing number of native speakers teaching their own language as a foreign language is able to make to the work of FL departments in the UK and elsewhere, for example, by providing excellent role models or enriching the broader cultural ethos of schools.

Particularly in urban UK settings, FL teachers increasingly work in multilingual contexts that make it difficult for them to build on the range of linguistic expertise in evidence in FL classrooms. It is not unheard of in East London, and elsewhere, for over seventy languages to be spoken by pupils in a single secondary school. In such contexts, the main challenge for both native and non-native speakers would seem to be that of reorientating one's own as well as academic knowledge towards linguistically and culturally sensitive FL teaching. This reorientation is what constitutes the process of professionalisation: learning to be a FL teacher and not 'just' a subject specialist or expert. What this means in terms of process may differ between native and non-native speakers, but how it is achieved is through a combination of the acquisition of a body of professional and theoretical knowledge about how FLs are most effectively taught and learned, with practical experience in the classroom.

Subject knowledge, therefore, is of importance to all FL teachers. It is not confined to knowledge of the FL, knowledge about language, cultural knowledge, knowledge of literature, politics and society, knowledge of

the L1 but, crucially, comprises what might be called 'comparative linguistic knowledge' and 'knowledge of the target language as a FL'.

DIMENSIONS OF SUBJECT KNOWLEDGE

In their work, Grossman *et al.* (1989), summarised in Bourdillon and
Storey (2002, pp. 54–5), identify four general dimensions of subject knowledge that influence the teaching and learning of teachers. They are:

- content knowledge
- substantive knowledge
- syntactic knowledge and
- personal beliefs.

In Chapter 4 we discuss in detail the first of these dimensions (FL teachers'
content knowledge), looking in particular at the way FLs are constructed
by national frameworks such as the NC, so-called national strategies and
examination specifications. For current purposes suffice it to note that a
lack of content knowledge, as Grossman *et al.* (1989) found, can lead to
an over-reliance on textbooks and a conceptualisation of subject knowledge without due critical appraisal of the adequacy, accuracy and salience
of textbooks. Bourdillon and Storey (2002, p. 54) point out that teachers'
lack of content knowledge can lead to an over-reliance on transmission
rather than engaging in discussion and exploration, as this might lead to
pupil questions that teachers are unable to answer.

In relation to substantive knowledge, i.e. 'the framework, or model of
explanation, which guides the inquiry in a discipline' (Bourdillon and
Storey, 2002, p. 54), Grossman *et al.* (1989) indicate that teachers' subject
knowledge has implications for how and what teachers teach. In recent
decades, three main paradigms or perspectives of how language is viewed
can be distinguished: structural, cognitive, and sociocognitive/social-inter-
actionist approaches (see e.g. Kern and Warschauer, 2000).

From a structural perspective, language is seen as an autonomous
system that develops through the transmission from competent users
and the internalisation and emulation of structures and habits through
repetition and corrective feedback, as well as the mastery of a prescriptive norm, imitation of modelled discourse, with minimal errors with the
main unit of analysis being at sentence level. From a cognitive perspective,

language is seen as a mentally constructed system and phenomenon, with learners developing their interlanguage through cognitive processes, problem solving and hypothesis testing, as well as the development and application of learning strategies.

From a sociocognitive or social-interactionist perspective, language is seen as a cognitive and social phenomenon, with language being thought to develop through social interaction and assimilation of speech. Learners are encouraged to attend to form as well as genre, register and style in contexts of real language use, i.e. through processes of negotiation of meaning and collaborative interaction. (For a more detailed discussion see Williams and Burden, 1997.)

Lack of syntactic knowledge, which 'provides the procedures and processes in a subject area' (Bourdillon and Storey, 2002, p. 55), can lead to teachers not teaching their pupils the processes of subject enquiry. In the context of FL teaching and learning, the processes of subject enquiry include not just general learning strategies but also strategies concerning vocabulary learning, dictionary use and use of reference material such as grammar books, strategies for text comprehension and independent reading as well as requisite ethnographic skills. Importantly also, lack of syntactic knowledge by teachers often means that they themselves are less likely to acquire new knowledge or question new theories in their discipline. (For a detailed discussion of learner strategies see the 2007 double Special Issue of the *Language Learning Journal*, 35(1) and (35(2).)

Finally, personal beliefs about subject knowledge can influence the extent to which FL teachers are willing and able to question assumptions about their own subject knowledge and about approaches to teaching and learning. For example, a FL teacher who has learnt the FL through a grammar–translation approach is likely to conceive of language learning as memorising verb paradigms, applying prescriptive rules, parsing sentences and translating texts. And, she is likely to conceive of language teaching syllabuses as entities to be organised around linguistic categories and will view sentences as the primary unit of analysis and practice. Our experience of teaching on various PGCE modern foreign language (MFL) courses strongly suggests that very often personal FL learning histories strongly influence the perceptions and beliefs of beginner teachers about how FLs should be taught.

SUBJECT KNOWLEDGE AND FL TEACHER EFFECTIVENESS

A fundamental question of interest to us in this chapter is whether subject knowledge influences the pedagogic decisions teachers make and the strategies they adopt and whether this, in turn, affects the effectiveness of pupil learning.

Evidence presented by Ralph Tabberer (1996, pp. 3–4), then a researcher at the National Foundation for Educational Research (NFER)[1], would suggest that higher-order subject knowledge does indeed represent a central ingredient of effective teaching.

For FL teachers, subject knowledge can, among other things, be seen to comprise:

- a high level of knowledge of, and proficiency in, the TL;
- good structural knowledge of, as well as the ability to make effective use of, the TL;
- wide-ranging awareness of the culture(s) of the countries where the TL is spoken;
- knowledge of the linguistic theories underpinning the FL learning process; as well as
- a familiarity with the respective statutory framework and related requirements.

More recently it can also be seen to comprise knowledge of and the ability to make appropriate and effective, subject-specific use in ICT.

Anyone involved in interviewing applicants for a place on a PGCE course in MFL will know how enthusiastic many prospective beginner teachers are when talking about their subject, how they view teaching as the most likely way of being able to use their FL(s) on a daily basis and how eager they are to share their FL and culture knowledge with young people, to convince them of the importance of FLs in their lives – however remote the need for FL competence may seem – and not just from a utilitarian perspective but also from the point of view of personal growth. Given the research evidence, which suggests that above all pupils are motivated by a good relationship with their teacher and their teacher's enthusiasm for the subject, the importance of subject knowledge in FL teaching can clearly not be overestimated. Chambers (1999), who studied the motivation of KS3 FL learners and compared it with their counterparts learning English in Germany, for example, found that the most influential motivational factor was the teacher and her relationship with pupils. Enthusiasm for their subject can, therefore, be seen as a central characteristic of an effective teacher. (See also Dörnyei, 2001, pp. 175–80 on the interactive relationship between learners and the teacher.)

An analysis of evidence from OFSTED inspections of initial teacher education courses of history leads Baker *et al.* (2000) to suggest that the level of subject knowledge has an impact on teacher development (quoted here from Bourdillon and Storey, 2002, p. 49):

- It helps beginner teachers to feel confident in the classroom. This confidence underpins their planning and teaching. They are able to focus on developing their subject knowledge pedagogy, to structure individual lessons and sequences of lessons and to select appropriate teaching methods.
- Feeling confident about subject knowledge facilitates the production of classroom resources and learning materials.
- Their teaching reflects their depth of subject knowledge. They rarely make errors and are able to include in their teaching relevant analogies and anecdote.
- They are able to cope with unexpected questions and are able to respond to complex enquiries. Lack of subject knowledge produces incorrect or generalised answers.
- They are adept at helping pupils understand the language and organising concepts of their subject. Where beginner teachers themselves have a clear conceptual framework, they are able to recognise potential difficulties of understanding, and develop their teaching accordingly.
- They understand how the subject teaching links to basic skills.

Although caution in relation to inspection evidence is advisable, as inspection evidence – unlike empirical research evidence – is not based on investigation, description or experimentation but on more or less subjective judgements against statutory requirements and preconceived notions of good practice, which are not necessarily reliable and valid (see McPake, 2002, p. 249), many of these points would seem to hold true and apply equally to FLs. In FLs, where the teacher is required by the NC to make 'maximum' use of the TL for instruction and interaction purposes, additional dimensions such as motivation come into play as well.

Can a teacher with secure subject knowledge better diagnose pupils' learning needs and plan more appropriately? Bourdillon and Storey (2002, pp. 53–4) point to some other research evidence that suggests that there is a potential link between subject knowledge and better teaching, namely that:

- deeper subject knowledge can lead to more conceptual explanations (see Ball 1991); and
- teachers with a larger mental map of their subject are more able to understand the interrelationship between individual topics and skills and the bigger picture (see Leinhart and Smith, 1985).

But what of teachers who are required to teach their FL2, in which they may be less fluent? This issue may be of particular concern for beginner teachers and those in the early stages of their careers because they are still in the process of developing basic teaching skills. A piece of small-scale empirical research, carried out with a group of beginner teachers and their more experienced school-based mentors, provides an illustration of the particular concerns of teachers when their subject knowledge is less secure (see Lawes, 1996). Beginner teachers were asked what strategies they used to compensate for a 'shortfall' in subject knowledge in the FL2, and the effect this had on their approaches to teaching and planning. Both groups said that they planned more carefully and spent much more time in lesson preparation. Beginner teachers were more concerned with improving their fluency and grammatical knowledge, whereas mentors, because of their greater professional knowledge and experience, were more able to adopt a set of specific teaching strategies to compensate for their deficiencies in the FL2. Beginner teachers said they did less oral work and more textbook work, used videos and tapes more as models, made pupils do more speaking to avoid lessons being teacher-led, used more visual aids and checked grammar and vocabulary carefully before lessons. Mentors claimed also to be more reliant on textbook materials, having more narrowly focused lessons, being more pupil-centred and doing more pair and group oral work. Both groups felt that they used less TL in their lessons. But the interesting paradox that emerged from both beginner teachers and mentors was that many of the strategies they used to compensate for their lack of subject knowledge are those considered to be essential to effective FL teaching. This case study highlights the importance of pedagogical knowledge in FL teaching and shows how an understanding of the theoretical underpinnings of effective language learning can compensate to some extent for deficiencies in linguistic fluency, although not for cultural knowledge.

The following three key areas are used here to illustrate, in the FL context, the relationship between subject knowledge and teacher behaviour:

- use of the TL;
- approach to grammar; and
- engagement with the cultural dimension of FL learning.

The target language

Knowing the TL and target culture(s) well allows teachers to anticipate, pre-empt and deal with potential conceptions and misconceptions pupils might have. Also, it will allow them to cope well with pupils' questions and enquiries. Those FL teachers who have themselves learnt the TL as a FL will be able to empathise with pupils, many of whom invariably find learning a FL very difficult because FL learning in a school context is by nature 'acquisition-poor', with only limited opportunity for exposure to input, intake, processing, integration into the existing interlanguage and for output. Hawkins (1987) memorably likened the experience to that of 'gardening in a gale of English'. In addition, unlike most – if not all – other subjects on the secondary curriculum in the UK, FL learning is predicated upon the memorising of a large number of lexical items and phrases and requires an implicit and explicit understanding of grammar rules, which in turn involves a challenging level of abstraction.

Teachers who possess a secure grasp of the TL are likely to be more confident in the classroom when using the TL for purposes of instruction and interaction. They will make fewer errors and provide a better TL model to pupils in terms of pronunciation. Although they too might experience difficulties such as pitching their use of the TL at the correct level, they will be more likely to judge accurately when the use of the TL might be inappropriate or even a hindrance to learning and might feel less paranoid about adhering rigidly to the debatable 'methodological imperative' of maximum TL use required by the MFL NC Order.

FL teachers have been reported as saying that teaching in the TL is tiring; and an exhausted teacher is arguably less effective. However, when questioned FL teachers also report that using the TL has a positive effect on the amount of language acquired subconsciously by pupils, pupils' listening skills and the perceived importance of the FL as a medium of interaction. It is possible to find, within current practice, successful examples of exclusive TL use in which the majority of pupils are well motivated and engaged and have developed confidence in speaking from very early on, but this approach requires, particularly in the early stages of FL learning, complete commitment and consistency on the part of the teacher. A greater focus on the use of the TL for classroom routines such as calling the register and for general classroom language can have the effect of making it more authentic as a means of communication. In classrooms where this approach has been adopted, the use of the TL is naturalised: pupils use it as a matter of course, and are confident enough to take risks and experiment with language. Teachers also have to take risks by resisting the pressure to 'get through' the prescribed syllabus content and to have confidence in themselves and their pupils' abilities. The development of the TL as the only medium of communication in the FL classroom requires a 'long-term view' of language learning that might seem to militate against the present focus on lesson 'outcomes' and short-term goals in the NC Orders.

Grammar

The level of explicit/implicit knowledge of grammar can also be seen to have a bearing on the way FL teachers teach and on the effectiveness of their teaching. For example, a secure explicit knowledge of the grammar of the TL, i.e. a secure conceptual framework of an important part of their subject, will allow the FL teacher to explain abstract concepts in an appropriate manner, inter alia using a well judged level of metalanguage while allowing learners to build and test hypotheses using terminology congruent with their stage of language development. It will ensure FL teachers don't avoid certain aspects of the TL owing to their own insecurity (see e.g. Grossman *et al.*, 1989), such as for example subjunctives, and enable them to provide an accurate TL model to pupils. It also allows FL teachers to break language down into appropriately sized chunks. Importantly, a secure knowledge of the grammar of the TL, and of the processing governing its learning and acquisition, will allow teachers to structure and sequence content appropriately to provide the best possible context for FL learning. For example, it will enable teachers to ensure that the cyclical nature of FL learning is taken into account and due regard is given to revision and repetition, that new forms are made artificially salient etc. Importantly, therefore, grammar knowledge can be seen to have a bearing on the teaching methods used. Teachers without a secure knowledge base are likely to avoid more form-focused approaches, despite there increasingly being evidence to suggest that they can be beneficial. Teachers with secure grammar knowledge will be more likely to employ both inductive and deductive methods of grammar teaching without having to be afraid of losing face in front of pupils or of making undue generalisations about grammar rules.

The trend over a number of years in the UK education system, however, was to shun explicit grammar teaching in the English curriculum, and this was mirrored within FLs through interpretations of CLT that gave precedence to the functional use of the FL and less priority to knowledge and understanding of its grammatical underpinning. Grauberg (1997, p. 34) provides an interesting discussion of what he calls 'the grammar controversy', in which he notes that, '(since) the 1960s different movements have in various ways put in doubt the appropriateness of traditional terms, the usefulness of an analytical and explanatory approach and the importance of grammatical accuracy'. Macaro (2003a) surveys research into grammar teaching and learning and concludes that it is a misconception that grammar is taught in order to improve accuracy, arguing that accuracy and competence should not be equated; rather, it is through focus on form that learners internalise the rules of language and engage with language. He goes on to suggest, controversially, that focus on form should be used to generate more error and more inaccuracy, because this is what ultimately leads to effective internalisation and understanding.

As a result of the decline in formal grammar teaching in both English and FLs in UK schools, a lower level of grammatical knowledge and proficiency has been, and still is, achieved by undergraduates of FLs, and a possible negative view of the importance of grammar has ensued. This claim is confirmed by research projects conducted with FL students engaged in periods of study abroad (see for example Coleman, 1996), which reported particular difficulties experienced by undergraduates. The situation with regard to the teaching of grammar both within the NC Orders for English and for MFL is changing, although, as discussed in Chapter 1, approaches to the teaching of grammar are still a subject of much debate. The recent revival of emphasis on more explicit grammar teaching does not necessarily imply more effective approaches to its teaching, however. The tendency seems to be to revert to more traditional grammar teaching rather than to draw on research and developments in FL pedagogy to inform classroom practice.

Culture

Another area where subject knowledge can be seen to play an important part in FL teaching, particularly in relation to motivation and, therefore, at least indirectly to achievement, is that of culture knowledge. A report commissioned by the Scottish Office Education and Industry Department and conducted by a team of researchers from the Scottish Centre for Information on Language Teaching and Research (McPake *et al.*, 1999), the so-called FLUSS study, found that 16- and 17-year-old students:

> did not agree with the view that there was no need to learn other languages because of the dominance of English as an international medium of communication. Many expressed an active interest in learning more about the cultures of the countries whose languages they were studying, in travelling and in meeting and getting to know native speakers of these languages. . . . However, it also emerged from the students' responses that, in their view, the content of language lessons in Scottish schools [*and, sadly, the situation seems no better at 11–16 in schools in England and Wales*] rarely explored the cultural issues in which they professed an interest. In fact, students were critical of an approach which seemed to foreground the students themselves as the principal source of content; many students objected to such staple topics of conversation in the modern languages classroom as their own families, their pets, their hobbies, their school day, etc.
>
> (McPake, 2002, p. 247)

The seeming reluctance of FL teachers in England and Wales to engage with cultural awareness is partly due to the straightjacket imposed upon them by the examination system at age 16, the General Certificate in Secondary Education (GCSE), which affords little importance to the cultural dimension, partly owing to difficulty in assessing it through a standardised, national exam. Also, it has to be acknowledged that the methodological framework underpinning culture teaching is still in its infancy despite cultural awareness seemingly playing an important part of the Programme of Study of the MFL NC Order. (For a more detailed discussion, see Chapter 4.)

33

Nevertheless, one possible reason for the lack of engagement with cultural awareness, intercultural competence and intercultural communicative competence[2] might be to do with FL teachers' limited expertise and experience in relation to the target culture(s).

In this context the question arises as to what culture actually is. And, what flows from the answer to this question in terms of subject knowledge requirement? Usually, two definitions of culture are distinguished, one coming from the humanities, the other from social sciences. The one 'focuses on the way a social group represents itself and others through its material productions, be they works of art, literature, social institutions, or artefacts of everyday life, and the mechanisms for their reproduction and preservation through history' (Kramsch, 1996, p. 2). The other refers to 'the attitudes and beliefs, ways of thinking, behaving and remembering shared by members of that community' (Kramsch, 1996, p. 2).

Depending on which view of culture is accepted – and it is worth noting here that they are by no means mutually exclusive but rather inclusive – the FL teacher will require a different content and process base of subject knowledge. The traditional definition of culture requires of the teacher – depending on the age of learners and syllabus followed – a more or less detailed knowledge of the target cultures, their works of art and literatures, their histories and architectures, their political and social institutions etc., whereas the other, more recent, definition requires a knowledge of ethnographic methods of data collection and knowledge about how to facilitate and enable first-hand experiences for learners with speakers of the TL, including the use of new technologies in order to gain access to the attitudes, beliefs, ways of thinking, behaving and remembering etc. Arguably, such a knowledge base can only be built up during a sustained period of residence in a country where the TL is spoken. Equally, it might be argued that an anthropological interpretation of cultural knowledge, which tends to focus on traditions, customs, folklore and aspects of daily life, prevails over the teaching of 'culture' in its classical form (see Broady (2004) for a survey of current perspectives). When the emphasis on culture becomes a celebration of 'otherness', 'difference' and 'identity', rather than the best humanity can aspire to, that is, the greatest, most creative works that individuals or a society can produce, there is a danger that the potential of FLs to explore *common humanity*, is lost.

It is also questionable whether modular (as opposed to linear) undergraduate courses allow a sufficiently sustained period of 'acculturation' with the target cultures. In FLs, there can be considerable difference between undergraduate qualifications from different higher education institutions (HEIs) in terms of scope, breadth and depth (see e.g. Coleman, 1996). And, what role – if any – does cultural knowledge play in initial teacher education? This variation might well have an impact on how ready beginner teachers are, for example, to engage with culture in their teaching despite the seeming importance for the levels of pupil motivation. But, if language and culture are seen as inextricably bound, it is surely incumbent upon the FL teacher to ensure that learners are initiated as far as possible into the culture as well as the language of a country.

THE BENCHMARK STATEMENTS FOR LANGUAGES AND RELATED STUDIES

In order to ensure some standardisation across provision offered by higher education institutions, the Quality Assurance Agency (QAA), a quasi non-governmental organisation, has developed of so-called subject benchmark statements (see QAA, 2002). These benchmarks attempt to describe the nature and characteristics of bachelor degrees with honours and they represent general expectations about the standards for the award of such qualifications. In addition, they articulate the attributes and capabilities that those holding such qualifications should be able to demonstrate. Importantly, they are not a specification of a detailed curriculum.

In the field of languages the situation is more complex than in other subject disciplines, not least in so far as there exists no unique pattern for undergraduate degrees. Some are still offered as single honours programmes, but this is no longer the prevailing model. Increasingly, languages are studied on a joint or combined honours basis, in conjunction with other languages or with other disciplines, in particular in the humanities and the social sciences. In addition, a growing number of degree programmes offer a FL component as an integral part in order to enhance the career and employment prospects of graduates. FL units are often available to these students as a minor subject or on an elective basis.

The benchmark document stresses that, in undertaking its work, the benchmark group was keen to emphasise the breadth and diversity of the subject area, which covers classical, medieval and modern languages, and that it took cognisance of other standards-related initiatives in languages, in particular, the National Language Standards, the Common European Framework (CEF) and the European Languages Portfolio.

The benchmark document posits that the study of languages and related studies encompass four complementary dimensions. Languages are seen as:

- a medium of understanding, expression and communication, described here as the **use of the target language;**
- an object of study in their own right, described here as the **explicit knowledge of language;**
- a gateway to related thematic studies comprising various bodies of knowledge and methodological approaches, described here as **knowledge of the cultures, communities and societies where the language is used;** and
- a means of access to other societies and cultures, described here as **intercultural awareness and understanding.**

(QAA, 2002, p. 2)

Therefore, by the end of their undergraduate degree, beginner teachers of FLs should have reached the standards shown in the box on pp. 38–9.

THE COMMON EUROPEAN FRAMEWORK OF REFERENCE FOR LANGUAGES

At a pan-European level, one very significant recent attempt at engaging with subject knowledge in the field of FLs is the development of the Common European Framework of Reference for Languages (Council of Europe, 2001; for a detailed discussion see Little, 2006). It is already discernible that the CEF is beginning to have a significant impact in the UK. One example is the development of Asset Languages by Cambridge Assessment to implement the Languages Ladder (DfES, 2004a), a new framework for accrediting language proficiency modelled on the CEF that aims to accredit clearly defined functional language skills and attempts to provide motivation and support for learning (see e.g. Jones, 2006). The development of a national Language Portfolio by the National Centre for Languages (CILT), particularly for use in the context of the teaching of FLs in primary schools, is another.

The Common European Framework provides a common basis for the elaboration of language syllabuses, curriculum guidelines, examinations, textbooks, etc. across Europe. It describes in a comprehensive way what language learners have to learn to do in order to use a language for communication and what knowledge and skills they have to develop so as to be able to act effectively. The description also covers the cultural context in which language is set. The Framework also defines levels of proficiency which allow learners' progress to be measured at each stage of learning and on a life-long basis.

(Council of Europe, 2001, p. 1)

Schmenk (2004) offers a very interesting discussion of the CEF, with particular reference to drama pedagogy, in which she argues that its

predominant focus on pragmatic and strategic components of language learning and (its) 'output-orientedness' may pose a problem for language educators who conceive of language learning as a personal experience which cannot adequately be conceptualised in terms of scaled competences and strategic behaviours.

(Schmenk, 2004, p. 8)

In the words of the CEF, the approach adopted is an 'action-oriented' one

in so far as it views users and learners of a language primarily as 'social agents', i.e. members of society who have tasks (not exclusively language-related) to accomplish in a given set of circumstances, in a specific environment and within a particular field of action.

(Council of Europe, 2001, p. 9)

The CEF (p. 24) distinguishes six levels of proficiency, grouped into three bands as shown in Table 2.1. These descriptors are subsequently broken down into an array of scales, each featuring numerous 'can do' statements, in an attempt to describe different language competences in as much detail as possible. The fifty-five scales in total comprise inter alia oral production, written production, production strategies, listening comprehension, reading comprehension, watching TV and film, reception strategies, spoken interaction, written interaction, interaction strategies, note-taking and processing text.

One advantage of such an approach is the inherent possibility to differentiate between specific language domains, identify attendant teaching and learning aims and describe learners' proficiency profile. Schmenk (2004, p. 12) sounds a word of caution in that she stresses that any

LEVELS OF ACHIEVEMENT AND GENERIC SKILLS

Minimum standards	Typical standards

6.2 LEVELS OF ACHIEVEMENT

6.2.1 Use of the target language

As determined in the individual programme specification, graduates in the discipline of LRS at honours level will be expected to:

Minimum standards	Typical standards
• achieve effective communication in the target language(s) with native or other competent speakers of the target language(s)	• communicate fluently and appropriately, maintaining a high degree of grammatical accuracy; in the target language(s) with native or other competent speakers of the target language(s)
• be able to exploit for a variety of purposes a range of materials written or spoken in the target language(s)	• be able to exploit for a variety of purposes and, as appropriate, to contextualise a broad range of materials written or spoken in the target language(s)
• be able to make use of their language skills in a professional context	• be able to apply effectively and appropriately their language skills in a professional context

6.2.2 Explicit knowledge of language

As determined in the individual programme specification, graduates in the discipline of LRS at honours level will be expected to:

Minimum standards	Typical standards
• demonstrate a knowledge and understanding of the structures, registers and, as appropriate, varieties of the target language(s)	• demonstrate a detailed knowledge and effective understanding of the structures, registers and, as appropriate, varieties of the target language(s)
• demonstrate a knowledge and understanding of the linguistic principles required to analyse the target language	• demonstrate a detailed knowledge and effective understanding of the linguistic principles required to analyse the target language

6.2.3 Knowledge of related studies

As determined in the individual programme specification, graduates in the discipline of LRS at honours level will be expected to:

Minimum standards	Typical standards
• demonstrate a knowledge and understanding of one or more aspects of the literatures, cultures, linguistic context, history, politics, geography, social and economic structures of the societies of the country or countries of the target language(s)	• demonstrate an ability critically to evaluate through appropriate methodologies, one or more aspects of the literatures, cultures, linguistic context, history, politics, geography, social and economic structures of the societies of the country or countries of the target language(s)

- demonstrate a knowledge and understanding of the cultures and societies of the country of the target language(s) gained through the study of the literatures and/or other cultural products of the target language(s)

6.2.4 Intercultural awareness and understanding

As determined in the individual programme specification, graduates in the discipline of LRS at honours level will be expected to:

- demonstrate an awareness and understanding of one or more cultures and societies, other than their own, that will normally have been significantly enhanced by a period of residence in the country, or countries, of the target language(s)
- demonstrate an awareness and understanding of the similarities and dissimilarities of those cultures or societies in comparison with their own

6.3 GENERIC SKILLS

Graduates in the discipline of LRS at honours level will be expected to:

- be able to identify and describe problems and to work towards their resolution
- be able to communicate information, ideas and arguments both orally and in writing
- be able to gather and process information from a variety of paper, audio-visual and electronic sources
- be able to use IT effectively both as a means of communication and as an aid to learning
- be able to work with others as part of a team
- be able to demonstrate some ability as an independent learner

- demonstrate a broad knowledge and, using appropriate methodologies, one or more aspects of the literatures, cultures, linguistic context, history, politics, geography, social and economic structures of the societies of the country or countries of the target language(s)

As determined in the individual programme specification, graduates in the discipline of LRS at honours level will be expected to:

- demonstrate a reasoned awareness and critical understanding of one or more cultures and societies, other than their own, that will normally have been significantly enhanced by a period of residence in the country, or countries, of the target language(s)
- demonstrate an ability to describe, analyse and evaluate the similarities and dissimilarities of those cultures or societies in comparison with their own

- be able to identify, describe and analyse problems and to devise appropriate strategies for their resolution
- be able to communicate information, ideas and arguments cogently and coherently both orally and in writing with due regard to the target audience
- be able to gather, process and evaluate critically information from a variety of paper, audio-visual and electronic sources
- be able to use IT effectively both as a means of communication and as an aid to learning
- be responsive to the disciplines of working with others and to work effectively as part of a team
- be an effective and self-aware independent learner

(adapted from QAA, 2002, pp. 12–13)

Table 2.1 *Common reference levels: global scale*

Proficient user

C2   Can understand with ease virtually everything heard or read. Can summarise information from different spoken and written sources, reconstructing arguments and accounts in a coherent presentation. Can express him/herself spontaneously, very fluently and precisely, differentiating finer shades of meaning even in more complex situations.

C1   Can understand a wide range of demanding, longer texts, and recognise implicit meaning. Can express him/herself fluently and spontaneously without much obvious searching for expressions. Can use language flexibly and effectively for social, academic and professional purposes. Can produce clear, well-structured, detailed text on complex subjects, showing controlled use of organizational patterns, connectors and cohesive devices.

Independent user

B2   Can understand the main ideas of complex text on both concrete and abstract topics, including technical discussions in his/her field of specialisation. Can interact with a degree of fluency and spontaneity that makes regular interaction with native speakers quite possible without strain for either party. Can produce clear, detailed text on a wide range of subjects and explain a viewpoint on a topical issue giving the advantages and disadvantages of various options.

B1   Can understand the main points of clear standard input on familiar matters regularly encountered in work, school, leisure, etc. Can deal with most situations likely to arise whilst travelling in an area where the language is spoken. Can produce simple connected text on topics which are familiar or of personal interest. Can describe experiences and events, dreams, hopes and ambitions and briefly give reasons and explanations for opinions and plans.

Basic user

A2   Can understand sentences and frequently used expressions related to areas of most immediate relevance (e.g. very basic personal and family information, shopping, local geography, employment). Can communicate in simple and routine tasks requiring a simple and direct exchange of information on familiar and routine matters. Can describe in simple terms aspects of his/her background, immediate environment and matters in areas of immediate need.

A1   Can understand and use familiar everyday expressions and very basic phrases aimed at the satisfaction of needs of a concrete type. Can introduce him/herself and others and can ask and answer questions about personal details such as where he/she lives, people he/she knows and things he/she has. Can interact in a simple way provided the other person talks slowly and clearly and is prepared to help.

proficiency profiles derived from the CEF will invariably reflect learners' proficiency only in relation to competences included in the scales. In her view, as a drama pedagogue, they are too narrow and take insufficient account, for example, of intercultural competence, and she posits (p. 15) that 'affective, aesthetic, intentional, intercultural, etc. dimensions of language, communication and language learning are largely ignored'. The view of language learning underpinning the CEF can be seen to be social-communicative and pragmatic in orientation:

> Language use, embracing language learning, comprises the actions performed by persons who as individuals and as social agents develop a range of **competences**, both **general** and in particular **communicative language competences**. They draw on the competences at their disposal in various contexts under various **conditions** and under various **constraints** to engage in **language activities** involving language processes to produce and/or receive **texts** in relation to **themes** in specific **domains**, activating those **strategies** which seem most appropriate for carrying out the **tasks** to be accomplished. The monitoring of these actions by the participants leads to the reinforcement or modification of their competences.
>
> (Council of Europe, 2001, p. 9)

Finally, Schmenk notes the problem of normativity (pp. 15–16), by which she means the potentially considerable reduction of language curricula orientated in their objectives and learning outcomes towards the CEF:

> the can-do descriptors seem to have triggered the belief that the Framework sets standards for language learning that have to be achieved within a language course. As a result, the descriptors serve as norms against which language performance can be measured rather than as helpful descriptions of what a learner can already do in a second or foreign language.
>
> (Schmenk, 2004, p. 16)

In short, there is an inherent danger in strongly output-orientated, instrumental views of communication, language and language learning through interaction, such as the ones promulgated by the CEF, in that important dimensions of communicative events, such as the emotive and affective dimensions, are easily omitted.

41

HOW SUBJECT KNOWLEDGE IS CONCEIVED OF IN THE UK GOVERNMENT STANDARDS

In England and Wales, the so-called 'standards' for the award of qualified teacher status (QTS), which were first introduced in the early 1990s, have seemingly placed strong emphasis on subject knowledge since their first inception. A number of revisions have taken place since then, but they still remain fairly narrowly conceived around the NC Order and examination specifications as well as the national accreditation system and policy framework. A key term used in the standards for the award of qualified teacher status (see DfES/TTA, 2002, DfES/TDA, 2007) is the need for 'secure knowledge' in a range of areas. However, at no point are there any indication and exemplification as to what 'secure knowledge' of FLs might be taken to mean, and, as has already been noted, the diversity and variability of undergraduate degree programmes make it very difficult to quantify 'a standard equivalent to degree level'. This fuzziness, although not uncharacteristic of government documents of this nature, inter alia to ensure transparency of the documentation among a non-specialist readership and to give sufficient scope for interpretation by OFSTED inspectors, is not at all helpful from the FL teacher's point of view. Although diversity and variability are not dismissed per se, our experience of interviewing prospective beginner teachers for PGCE courses suggests that they mean that depth of study has been sacrificed for breadth of exposure to the FL and its culture, particularly in modular courses. An increasingly vocational orientation of undergraduate programmes and the growth of joint honours degrees (for example, French and European Law) do not necessarily ensure the prerequisite knowledge of the FL that both policymakers and the teaching profession deem essential.

The need to reflect the changes in the distribution of roles and responsibilities of education professionals in the context of workforce remodelling since the introduction of the original standards has been recognised to some extent. There have been some attempts to streamline them and to introduce some positive revisions in relation to a reconceptualisation of teacher professionalism by seeking to ameliorate to some extent the prevailing atomisation of concepts of teaching into a list of skills; as far as assumptions of, and approaches to, subject knowledge, little if any change is discernible.

In England, teacher educators have to work to detailed prescriptions from central government and its agencies, not all based on sound empirical evidence (see for example, Pachler, 2003) but which specify in minute detail not just the required outcomes but, by implication, the contents and process of initial teacher education. Therefore, cynics might interject here, a lack of specific government guidance in this area might not be such a bad thing – and they are probably right. The comprehensive nature of the standards can be argued to lead only to a superficial level of engagement by FL teachers with subject knowledge and to their learning of how to manage certain activities and procedures rather than develop subject expertise and associated pedagogies (see Calderhead and Shorrock, 1997).

When reading the various sets of standards governing the work of teacher educators, which apply to all routes into teaching, that have been introduced over the years it is hard to argue with the rectitude of any particular statement. Indeed, as a collection, such statements have a certain coherence. Sadly, however, the overall framework contains a number of serious flaws that, owing to lack of space, can only be touched upon here rather than be discussed in the amount of detail they warrant. (For a fuller discussion, see Lambert and Pachler, 2002.) For example:

- they are prescriptive and seek to impose a particular, normative view of core professional values, knowledge and skills;
- they make a simplistic equation of the amount of time spent in school with quality of learning about teaching;
- the terms of reference are narrowly constrained by current government policy;
- the standards themselves are too extensive in scope to be covered satisfactorily in the time available (less than one calendar year for the PGCE); and
- one particular weakness of the standards for us is the lack of importance they afford to an evidence-based conceptualisation of what characterises 'good teaching'.

In order to render them useful, therefore, for the FL teaching and learning context, it seems desirable to 'translate' the standards into more subject-specific descriptors that, in line with current OFSTED inspection practice, might be conceived of at levels of adequate, good and very good match. Table 2.2 below attempts to take the centrally prescribed conceptualisations and, on the basis of professional experience, identify and exemplify what they might mean in terms of FL skills and cultural

Table 2.2 FL-specific interpretations of the QTS standards framework

Issue	Subject knowledge and understanding		
	Very good	Good	Adequate
Language skills	Possesses near-native proficiency	Fluent, accurate and confident written and spoken FL1 (and FL2 where applicable) Able to cope with unpredictable demands	Sufficiently accurate and fluent spoken and written FL for the age and stage of learners taught
Cultural knowledge	Uses knowledge to inform classroom planning and practice	Demonstrates a sustained interest in the target culture(s) e.g. keeping up to date with current developments, use of foreign language assistant (FLA), use of the internet, visits to cultural institutions, reading of periodicals, media	Sufficiently knowledgeable about target culture(s) for the age and stage of learners taught

knowledge. Although no causal relationship between characteristics and competences delineated and effective teaching is claimed, it is suggested there is at least a reciprocal relationship. Importantly, the columns have to be read cumulatively from right to left, i.e. a 'good' beginner teacher is one who is able to satisfy the requirements of the right and the middle column, and a 'very good' beginner teacher is able to satisfy all three columns.

Although the category of 'adequate' meets the requirements for beginner teachers to achieve QTS in terms of subject knowledge, it might best be seen as the minimum standard that future FL teachers should possess. When asked about 'teacher knowledge', most beginner teachers identify expertise in the FL as being the most important part of what a teacher should know (Lawes, 2004b), stressing that this is what gives them confidence in the classroom. In this respect, native speakers of the FL have a distinct advantage, although they face other problems when training to teach their own language in a foreign country, some of which we will now consider.

SUBJECT KNOWLEDGE AND THE NATIVE SPEAKER

Many PGCE courses in England recruit a significant number of native speakers, in particular native speakers of French, German, Spanish and Italian. Learning to teach and to work in a foreign country presents particular challenges for them, not only in terms of professional and social acculturation, but in learning to see their own language from a different perspective and to become conscious of the difficulties it presents to learners in England. Research into the attitudes of French beginner teachers on PGCE courses confirms that adapting their use of language to a level appropriate to their learners is a key concern in the early stages of their training (Lawes, 2004). One beginner teacher, Catherine, summarised her difficulties in the following way:

> When I first started my teaching practice, there was so much that was different. In France, when I was in school, most of my teachers didn't use English very much in the classroom, except when working from the textbook, and yet I have a feeling that the standard was higher. In my school here the teachers used both languages, but more French than English. I found it very difficult to express myself at such a low level in French and the pupils couldn't understand me, and that led to

discipline problems. But also at first, I wasn't very confident with my English, even though I've always been told it is very good, but being in school is different – using the right words and even understanding what some of the pupils were saying to me was quite a problem. So I felt unsure in both languages. I realised that this was something I had to work on, so I made a big effort to speak a bit more slowly and to use set phrases with the pupils. Also I observed other teachers, teaching other subjects, and listened carefully to how they talked to pupils and what pupils said to them. I learned a lot from that. Also, teaching grammar was difficult, trying to make it part of the lesson and not just a set of rules.

When asked about what she thought about teaching aspects of French culture in her lessons, she admitted that she probably didn't do very much. Despite her enthusiasm for her language, she realised that she was missing an important area of authentic knowledge and experience that she, as a French national, could share with her pupils. Catherine's experience is a very common one among French native speakers, and most likely also for speakers of other languages.

Vasseur (2000, p. 54), also drawing on interviews and questionnaires with French beginner teachers during their period of initial teacher training in England, reports that they found certain aspects of FL teaching methodology difficult to adjust to, notably: the absence of formal grammar teaching, a methodological approach that focused on pupil motivation; and the importance given to participation over 'the acceptability of spoken utterances and their analysis. Our students found this new "national" orientation a striking contrast with the French language teaching tradition, which is much more metalinguistic in character.' Equally, somewhat negative attitudes to FL learning, in English society in general and among English school pupils in particular, are often an unexpected challenge for beginner teachers from other countries that requires them to review their own attitudes to language learning and begin to think more consciously and objectively about the considerable body of knowledge that they have and that they need to put to professional use in the classroom.

Widdowson (2002, p. 69) argues that the fact that native speakers didn't have to learn the TL as a FL makes it more difficult for them to teach it. Authenticity, therefore, is no guarantee of representativeness, learnability, learning and meaning potential. According to Widdowson, in addition to TL knowledge, FL teachers need to have knowledge of the

TL as a FL. However, as has been noted above, a significant proportion of FL teachers and beginner teachers in England are native speakers of the language they teach. How might we turn what Widdowson sees as a disadvantage, others as an additional challenge, into a distinctive professional asset? The answer to this question is often seen as being a matter of gaining more classroom experience, which in and of itself enables the native-speaker FL teacher to acquire better insights into the difficulties of FL learners. There is no doubt some truth in this, although what that experience might comprise needs careful consideration. Native-speaker teachers of FLs may also need to learn more about their own language in order to understand how others see it as a FL. Equally, both English speakers of FLs and native speakers should have knowledge of the theoretical underpinning of second and foreign language learning, and it is to this we turn in the next section.

KNOWLEDGE ABOUT FLS AND HOW THEY ARE LEARNED

Whether FL teachers are native speakers of that language or have learned it as a second or even third language, in the process of becoming teachers, both groups have necessarily to take their personal body of knowledge, that is, their expertise in the language as a subject discipline, and transform it into a field of knowledge for other learners to acquire. In order to do this effectively they need to begin to explore the unique and vast area of theoretical knowledge about language and language learning upon which, at least in principle, classroom practice is based. It is not enough to know *what* to do to teach a 'good' lesson or, indeed, *how* to do it in practice, although these are big enough challenges for teachers in the early stages of their careers. To understand *why* is what gives the *what* and the *how* meaning and is the life-blood of teachers' professional and intellectual development. Teaching, in our view, is as much about knowing and thinking as about doing. Applied linguistics, sociolinguistics, language learning theories, SLA are each vast areas of specialist enquiry in themselves in which FL teachers may not be required to be an expert, but they should at least be acquainted with some of the key theories and debates from the outset of their careers in order to develop as effective teachers of FLs. As Mitchell and Myles (1998), asserting the need better to understand second language learning, point out: for FL teachers, theories of language learning should be interesting in their own right, as well as contributing to other fields of human learning.

Issues such as those discussed briefly above – the use of the TL, the teaching of grammar and cultural awareness – are not simply questions of technical skill or personal preference but require a deeper understanding through theoretical knowledge. Macaro (2003a) provides an excellent introduction to theoretical perspectives through an engaging exploration of research and theorising in language learning over recent years and is successful not only in appealing to the interests of language teachers, but also in contributing to the mediation of theory in practice. He suggests (2003, p. 21) that the two most fundamental questions in second language learning are:

1 Through what processes do learners learn a second language?
2 How can teachers best enable and support those processes?

These questions, he suggests, can only be answered properly through theoretical knowledge. Macaro relates research-based theory to classroom-based learning through a succinct overview of the major SLA theories and their impact on FL teaching methodology. Calling for a strengthening of the partnership between teachers and researchers, he argues that FL teachers should not only be well informed about the nature of language and language learning, but that they also should be actively involved in shaping the direction of research.

CONCLUSION

This attempt to categorise FL knowledge is by no means exhaustive, but what we have tried to do is to emphasise the importance to the FL teacher of knowledge *about* as well as knowledge *of* the language and culture. The examples of TL, grammar and culture were used to illustrate how categories of FL knowledge are the subject of competing ideas and theories about language learning with which teachers need to be familiar in order to make their own professional judgements in the classroom, as well as have an intellectual purchase on the nature of FL teaching and learning. The importance of high-level knowledge of the FL as being a secure base from which to learn how to teach has been explored, both from the point of view of the native and non-native speaker. Expert knowledge *of* language is the source of inspiration for the aspiring FL teacher to learn more *about* language, and this is partly what transforms you from subject specialist to teacher. Without both these fields of knowledge, the initial skills of FL teaching may be acquired, but future professional development is likely to be limited to a superficial understanding of teaching and learning that is unlikely to provide professional sustenance even in the short term. The standards required for the achievement of QTS may be seen as a baseline of competence for the beginner teacher, but, as has been suggested here, there is danger in prescribing teacher knowledge and expertise in such a framework, in that teaching may be seen as an almost entirely practical matter, the business of learning quite straight-forward, and education as being simply a matter of 'delivering' a national curriculum. The chapters that follow seek to challenge such notions by considering further areas of professional knowledge with which teachers must necessarily engage if they are to aspire to being principled professionals and even educational thinkers and not just competent practitioners.

NOTES

1 See www.nfer.ac.uk
2 Although the term 'intercultural competence' encompasses the disposition, skills, knowledge and understanding required to be empathetic towards, interested in and find out about people from other cultures and how they live, the term 'intercultural communicative competence' in our estimation entails a notion of the ability to use the target language in the process in engaging with other cultures.

QUESTIONS FOR DISCUSSION

1 What are the main features of the different dimensions of FL subject knowledge?
2 What, in your view, is the relationship between a FL teacher's subject knowledge and his/her effectiveness as a FL teacher?
3 What view of subject knowledge is implicit in the standards for QTS?
4 Of what relevance is knowledge of how FLs are learnt?
5 Does the CEF represent a useful tool for FL learning, teaching and assessment?

6 How relevant are the benchmark standards in terms of preparing FL learners for a career in teaching and what, if any, links are there to the subject knowledge components of the standards for QTS?

7 How do the 'benchmark' standards of FL knowledge compare or contrast with the idea of 'mastery' and 'subject expert' discussed in Chapter 1?

Part II

Using the subject in the classroom

The second part of our book focuses on various aspects of FL use in the classroom. The discussion starts from the premise that FL learning, for a host of reasons such as the interference between L1 and FL, is more complex and difficult than that of other curriculum subjects. It is, therefore, important for us as FL teachers to ask questions not only about what to teach and how to teach it but also about how languages are learnt.

In particular, in Chapter 3 we examine the relationship between being proficient at listening to, speaking, reading and writing the target language as a teacher and being able to teach the language effectively as a foreign language, and we look in detail at grammar teaching, task-based learning and ICT. In addition, we look at what other types of knowledge FL teachers need in addition to linguistic proficiency and how they relate to each other. This discussion, we hope, will allow readers to contextualise the experiences of FL teaching you had as pupils and reflect on and re-examine your personal views on FL teaching, as these experiences and views tend to have a considerable influence on approaches taken by beginner teachers. And, we explore whether native speakers face particular challenges in making their mother tongue accessible and learnable for pupils. Among other things, we raise the question of how the complex interplay between language and identity affects the process of FL teaching and learning.

In Chapter 4 we discuss what FL knowledge, skills and understanding we should teach to, and develop in, pupils of compulsory school age by examining the NC Order for FLs as well as the Key Stage Three Framework by asking whether it is a curriculum of the past or one of the future. In addition, we look at how the statutory requirements came into being. We discuss how curricular content can be organised, and who should make decisions about what to teach:

what is the role of government, of the school and of individual teachers as well as, of course, of the pupils themselves? As one possible alternative to the prevailing model, we examine content-based language learning. As well as offering a framework for curricular analysis we also offer some advice on how to approach coursebook analysis. Inextricably bound up in discussions about the curriculum are questions about the purposes of FL study, which we explore. Finally, we briefly explore curricular guidelines and organisational models at the Primary level.

In Chapter 5 we look in detail at how pupils learn and what the implications are for FL teaching. We argue that pupil cognition forms an integral part of an interrelationship between teacher knowledge, curricular knowledge and pupil knowledge. What do and should pupils know, not only in relation to the target language but also in terms of the curriculum, as well as metacognition, i.e. learning about learning. And, how important are pupil beliefs and attitudes?

Chapter 3

Pedagogical knowledge and pedagogical content knowledge

INTRODUCTION

Traditionally it has been understood that, in order to become and remain an effective FL teacher, you need to possess at least a good level of subject knowledge. What has been less clear, however, is what other types of knowledge in addition to linguistic proficiency you require. In fact, until not too long ago it was possible to enter the teaching profession without a bespoke teaching qualification. Although up until the early 1970s subject knowledge was considered to be a sufficient prerequisite to enter the teaching profession – graduates could traditionally become teachers without any pedagogical and methodological training – teaching as a profession of certificated members has evolved in England and Wales since 1973, when it became a requirement that all those wishing to teach in maintained schools should complete an identified course of teacher education before they could obtain a teaching post. At the time of writing this is still not a requirement in the independent sector. In the post-compulsory sector, changes towards professionalisation are being introduced, and a teaching qualification is becoming a requirement. Arguably, certification of the teaching profession has a causal link to the introduction of comprehensive schools from the mid 1960s and the resultant diversification in pupil population, which seemingly rendered a mere grounding in subject knowledge through academic study in itself an inadequate prerequisite for subject teaching. In this chapter, we argue that, in view of the increasing diversification of the pupil population, particularly in urban contexts, pedagogical and methodological training are essential, and we discuss in detail other knowledge bases for FL teachers, with a particular emphasis on pedagogical knowledge as well as the knowledge required to make FLs learnable; this we call pedagogical content knowledge (PCK) here.

The curricula of secondary schools throughout the UK – and many other countries for that matter – are characterised by organisation into subject disciplines, and, as far as possible, subjects are taught by specialists. Although it is not within the purview of this chapter, or indeed this book, to examine the relative merits or the historical, organisational and intellectual reasons and rationale for this approach to curriculum organisation, it is, nevertheless, of importance for the topic examined here, in so far at least as this organisational principle foregrounds subject-specialist teacher knowledge over general knowledge but also of subject-specialist over general pedagogical and methodological approaches. Chapter 4 critically examines the curricular/content knowledge required by FL teachers in England. In this chapter we discuss the complex interplay between FL teachers' subject knowledge and pedagogical knowledge and examine, at least in part, the knowledge base for FL teachers beyond proficiency in the FL and knowledge of the FL culture.

There is growing evidence (see e.g. Bourdillon and Storey, 2002, p. 44; Hayes, 2002; BBC, 2002) that in the UK – at least in certain so-called 'shortage' subjects including FLs – a very significant number of classes are in fact taught by non-specialist teachers, i.e. teachers who are not trained in the subject they teach. For example, in the year from January 2001 to January 2002, an increase from 2,300 to 7,600 was recorded. In addition to a number of untrained native speakers, the comparatively high number of non-specialist teachers can be explained by the fact that the education system allows for any teacher who has obtained QTS through one of the many routes available to teach any subject in any phase, provided the head teacher deems her knowledge, skills, understanding and prior experience commensurate with what is required. In cases where subject-specialist teachers have been in short supply, such as FLs, head teachers often have to resort to allocating teachers who have QTS but who are not trained in teaching the subject in order to ensure coverage of certain curriculum areas. In the case of FLs, non-specialist teachers often possess at least some requisite subject knowledge by virtue, for example, of being native speakers, but – often due to a lack or limited amount of formal teacher education – they do not always possess the necessary curricular, pedagogical and methodological knowledge. In FLs it has also been common for trained

FL teachers to teach languages in which they possess little or limited proficiency rather than see these languages being taken off the curriculum owing to a shortage of qualified teaching staff.

We argue here that, in order to improve the standing of FL teachers as professionals, and the part you play in that as an individual practitioner, it is important to raise awareness of the importance of pedagogical knowledge and PCK in relation to FL teaching. We are also arguing that FL teachers benefit from a good grounding in how the knowledge bases of the so-called foundation disciplines, such as the history of education, educational psychology, philosophy and sociology, impact on teaching and learning, as subject-specific pedagogical knowledge is inextricably linked to a network of educationally relevant knowledge frameworks.

In part at least in order to reduce the number of non-specialist teachers given, for example, the concerns expressed in various annual reports by Her Majesty's Chief Inspector of Schools[1] about the implications for the quality of teaching and for pupil learning, the government has introduced a range of new routes into teaching[2] for candidates with the requisite subject knowledge who do not wish to/cannot complete a full course of Initial Teacher Education (ITE) at a university or college, notably the Graduate Teacher Programme (GTP), an employment-based route that allows candidates to 'train on the job'. Although such programmes can be seen to present viable alternatives for some people, they arguably do not represent the best option for the majority of candidates, as these programmes require a high amount of autonomy as well as initiative and as they are characterised by a lack of tutor mediation and a supportive peer group, as well as ample opportunity to compare professional experiences with those of colleagues working in different contexts and settings. Furthermore, it is questionable to what extent all aspects of pedagogical knowledge (learning to teach) and pedagogical content knowledge (learning of subject-specific methodology) discussed below can be adequately addressed through an employment-based route into teaching. The development of such a foundation is crucial to the professional formation of teachers as otherwise they are in danger of accepting all too readily what is asked of and imposed on them by policymakers.

In view of the recent changes in curricular requirements following the publication of a national languages strategy for England (DfES, 2002), i.e. the fact that FL study is no longer compulsory beyond the age of 14, the problem of non-specialist FL teaching may soon cease to exist at secondary level in England. Emerging evidence (see e.g. Pachler, 2005b) suggests that these changes are leading to a considerable reduction in FL provision in maintained schools. Also, the introduction of the afore-mentioned new routes into teaching is likely to alleviate the problem at secondary level and might make the lack of subject-specialist teachers a defining issue of the emerging primary provision instead. However, the challenge of developing adequate pedagogical and PCK remains a reality for all FL teachers. How are these forms of knowledge visible in the FL teaching context and how do they affect you as teacher?

PROFESSIONAL KNOWLEDGE BASES OF FL TEACHERS

Macaro (2003a, p. 17) rightly reminds us of the three fundamental differ-ences in FL learning compared with the learning of other subjects that in his – and our – view make FL-related pedagogical (content) knowledge that much more complex than that of other subjects:

1 unlike in other subjects, the subject matter to be taught in FL lessons is also the medium through which pupils learn the subject, i.e. the TL, and rather than there being a compartmentalised body of knowledge to be learnt, there exists an interrelationship between language acquisition and language use;

2 FL learning is bound up in the learner's identity: by acquiring a new language and engaging in a different culture, learners invariably become different people; and

3 there is a constant interference from another subject, namely the first language.

Consequently, we would argue, there exist considerably more literature and a much wider knowledge and skills base to engage with for FL teachers than for any other subject, and the pedagogical dimension of a FL teacher's job is arguably much more complicated than for any other group of subject teachers, certainly in the secondary phase.

In addition, as we discuss in some detail in Chapter 4, in recent years there has been a growing interest in FL pedagogy of policymakers – perceived by a number of scholars in the field as well as by FL teachers as interference – in the form of numerous 'frameworks', e.g. the NC, Schemes of Work, a KS3 strategy etc. They all attempt to 'guide' and prescribe FL teachers' pedagogical actions, to a considerable level of detail but often with little or no reference to what is known from research into

SLA and FL learning. All of this obviously doesn't make the complex task of FL teaching easier or, indeed, more attractive for dedicated and well-educated professionals.

In her book on expert teaching, Turner-Bisset rightly posits that there coexist a multiplicity of paradigms or metaphors of teaching, each claiming to be good ways of conceptualising the practice of teaching. Drawing on the work of Squires she lists the following:

- teaching as a common-sense activity;
- teaching as an art;
- teaching as a craft;
- teaching as an applied science;
- teaching as a system;
- teaching as reflective practice; and
- teaching as competence.

She points out that each paradigm acts like a lens through which our perceptions of teaching are filtered (see Turner-Bisset, 2001, p. 2). She comes to the conclusion that all of these paradigms and conceptualisations of teaching are inadequate in some way and that they only offer a partial model of teaching. In her view, with which we concur, a wide range of knowledge bases, and not a narrow set of assumptions, must be employed and underpin professional practice.

Turner-Bisset (2001, pp. 10–11) also rightly points out that beliefs about a subject are important and constitutive of teachers' thinking, discourse and actions. For example, a teacher's conceptualisation of teaching as knowledge transmission as opposed to shared knowledge construction will shape her professional practice. The importance of values, emotions and concerns is also noted by Golombek (1998, p. 460) who stresses that teachers' knowledge 'is bound up in how they place themselves in relation to others and how their actions affect themselves as well as others'. From this she concludes that empirically grounded knowledge and theory should be filtered through experiential knowledge (see Golombek, 1998, p. 461).

We adopt a cognitive–interpretivist view of FL teaching here (see e.g. Freeman, 1994 and 1996, or Ellis, 1997), which emphasises the importance of the knowledge bases on which FL teachers draw when they teach. Consequently, we view FL teaching as a highly complex process of decision making in which FL teachers act in accordance with their implicit or explicit theories of teaching and learning as well as their professional experiences. Specialist literature and research have an obvious contribution to make in this view, as pedagogical, methodological and disciplinary knowledge obtained from background reading, be it empirical, theoretical/conceptual or professional, can help FL teachers construct, articulate, test out and modify personal theories of teaching. At the same time, we see professional teacher knowledge as constructed and reconstructed in and through experiences and professional engagement with colleagues (see Golombek, 1998). The interpretivist dimension is premised on the recognition that FL teachers' behaviours and thinking as well as their decision making are contingent upon the specific contexts within which they work, i.e. teachers have to be able to combine technical proficiency with analytical skill to analyse classroom situations and the ability to identify appropriate and context-sensitive options.

In the specialist literature (see e.g. Eraut, 1994) there is considerable debate about how to codify professional knowledge. Differences in opinion abound, for example, about the extent to which theoretical and practical knowledge are important and to what extent teachers should be able to articulate and provide rationales and a coherent reasoning for their many professional actions and decisions. Eraut (1994), for example, distinguishes:

- propositional knowledge: theories and concepts, pedagogical principles, situation-specific propositions;
- practical knowledge: routines, procedures, processes;
- tacit knowledge: what we know but can't tell/remains untold; and
- 'know-how': any combination of the above working in action.

In this book we take the view that conceptual/theoretical and practical knowledge, as well as empirical and professional knowledge, are important.

The 1980s saw the publication of Shulman's seminal work on PCK (1986, 1987), which attempted to bridge the gap between traditional distinctions of teachers' subject matter knowledge and teachers' knowledge of pedagogy. According to Rowan *et al.*:

Shulman argued that a distinctive form of teachers' professional knowledge that he called pedagogical content knowledge exists, and that this form of knowledge builds upon, but is different from, teachers' subject matter knowledge or knowledge of general principles of pedagogy.

In Shulman's view, pedagogical content knowledge is a form of *practical* knowledge that is used by teachers to guide their actions in highly contextualized classroom settings. In Shulman's view, this form of practical knowledge entails, among other things: (a) knowledge of how to structure and represent academic content for direct teaching to students; (b) knowledge of common conceptions, misconceptions, and difficulties that students encounter when learning particular content; and (c) knowledge of the specific teaching strategies that can be used to address students' learning needs in particular classroom circumstances. In the view of Shulman (and others), pedagogical content knowledge builds on other forms of professional knowledge, and is therefore a critical – and perhaps even the paramount – constitutive element in the knowledge base of teaching.

(Rowan *et al.*, 2001, pp. 2–3)

By delineating the following seven categories of teacher knowledge, Shulman (1987) clearly underlines the complexity of the teaching process (see Pachler and Field, 2001a, based on Bennet, 1993):

1 **Content knowledge**: referring to the amount and organisation of knowledge in the mind of the teacher; this includes both substantive and syntactic structure of a subject, i.e. the variety of ways in which the basic concepts and principles of the discipline are organised, and the ways in which truth or falsehood, validity or invalidity, are established; that is, the substantive structures refer to the facts and concepts of a discipline and how they are organised; the syntactic knowledge refers to how, i.e. through which skills and processes they are generated.
2 **General pedagogical knowledge**: with special reference to both broad principles and strategies of classroom management and organisation that appear to transcend subject matter.
3 **Curriculum knowledge**: with particular grasp of the materials and programmes that serve as 'tools of the trade' for teachers.
4 **Pedagogical content knowledge**: that form of content knowledge that embodies the aspect of content most germane to its teachability; it includes, for any given subject area, the most useful forms of the presentation of those ideas, the most powerful analogies, illustrations, examples, explanations and demonstrations; in other words, the ways of representing and

59

formulating the subject that make it comprehensible to others.

5 **Knowledge of learners and their characteristics.**

6 **Knowledge of educational contexts:** ranging from the workings of the group or classroom, the governance and financing of schools, to the character of communities and cultures.

7 **Knowledge of educational ends, purposes and values, and philosophical and historical background.**

By separating out the different key categories from the complex mesh of knowledge bases of teaching, Shulman's taxonomy allows us to focus more clearly on each area and, hence, to work more effectively towards the goals related to each one. However, as Shulman himself admitted, the list does not clarify how the various knowledge bases interact with each other beyond suggesting a 'blending of content and pedagogy into an understanding of how particular topics are transformed, organised, represented and adapted to the varying interests and abilities of learners' (Turner-Bisset 2001, p. 12). How can Shulman's categories fit with your understanding of what is involved in the process of language teaching?

We adopt Shulman's concept of PCK here, albeit in a form that foregrounds knowledge of SLA and FL learning theory. We do so, among other things, as in our view this goes some way towards breaking down traditional notions of fixed content knowledge that is to be learned and mastered by would-be teachers, with teaching methods and approaches being viewed as 'packaging for content' (see Freeman, 2002, p. 4). In such a model, Freeman argues that:

> 'good' teaching conveys the same content to diverse learners such that, should the learners not learn, the shortcoming is generally seen as lying in the teaching process and, by extension, in the teacher's competence. There is thus an on-going tension between the fixed value of the content knowledge and the local, contextual adjustment of teaching practices that the teacher must learn to navigate.
>
> (Freeman, 2002, pp. 4–5)

The concept of PCK, in our view, offers ample scope for attention to be paid to contextual information in the professional knowledge formation process of teachers. Rather than viewing PCK as static, we want to stress here the importance of situational variables and context features pertaining to learner and teacher characteristics as well as external factors such as the technological aids and tools available etc.

In support of the importance of professional content and other knowledge bases, research studies by Brown and McIntyre (1993), Cooper and McIntyre (1996) and Rudduck *et al.* (1996) suggest that, at secondary school level, 'good' teachers are perceived by pupils to be ones who:

- present work in a way that they find interesting and motivating;
- ensure pupils understand the work;
- make clear what pupils have to do and how;
- help pupils who experience difficulties;
- treat pupils as individuals;
- are fair to all pupils;
- provide autonomy;
- provide intellectual challenge and engaging learning activities;
- display a willingness to make use of pupils ideas about how to make new knowledge accessible; and
- provide ample opportunities for pupils to construct and share their own understandings (see McCallum *et al.*, 2000, p. 277).

This taxonomy of characteristics strongly supports the view that subject knowledge is by far not the only important knowledge base of 'good' teachers, however 'good' best be defined, and that pedagogical considerations are key.

Similarly, Freeman and Freeman's list of factors influencing FL teaching (1994) is worth noting here:

(a) how teachers were taught themselves;
(b) how teachers were trained and the content of that training;
(c) teachers' colleagues and the administration;
(d) exposure to new ideas;
(e) materials available;
(f) the type of students; and
(g) personal views of learners and learning.

This list also supports the view that subject knowledge is but one important factor in determining teacher effectiveness.

61

The considerable emphasis in recent years on a strong evidence base for decision making in education and teaching has led to a move away from implicit, tacit knowledge towards explicit and declarative knowledge. Nutley *et al.* (2002) identify five types of knowledge that they think are necessary in order to implement an evidence-based/evidence-informed/evidence-aware[3] approach (to subject teaching):

- know *about* problems: for example, the current policy efforts directed at social inclusion reflect a considerable knowledge base on health, wealth and social inequalities;
- know *what* works: i.e. what policies, strategies or specific interventions will bring about desired outcomes;
- know *how* to put into practice: knowing what should be done is not the same thing as being able to do it effectively;
- know *who* to involve: such knowledge covers estimates of client needs as well as information on key stakeholders necessary for potential solutions;
- know *why*: knowledge about why action is required, e.g. relationship to values.

Not only is it, therefore, important for FL teachers to know about 'what works' but, also, they need to be able to identify problems before they can even start to try to address them, have the disposition, skills, knowledge and understanding, i.e. the know-how, to implement the strategies and interventions they have identified and to do so in conjunction with the relevant people and with due consideration of everybody involved. To achieve this, pedagogical knowledge and PCK seem central.

Most importantly from our point of view, FL teachers also require knowledge about why to implement specific interventions and try out certain strategies in the first place and how they relate to their professional and personal values and beliefs. The ability and willingness to query decisions and to ask for the reasons governing them have sadly been marginalised in recent years; years that were characterised by what might be called 'restricted professionalism', a commodification of education and a strongly utilitarian and market-oriented model of educational provision.

Cochran-Smith and Lytle (2001, pp. 46–9) distinguish three conceptions of teacher learning that seem highly relevant in the context of the current discussion:

- knowledge for practice
- knowledge in practice and
- knowledge of practice.

'Knowledge for practice' for them is formal knowledge and theories generated by university researchers for teachers. 'Knowledge in practice' emphasises practical knowledge and teachers are thought to deepen their knowledge by probing the knowledge and expertise embedded in their work. 'Knowledge of practice' assumes the breaking down of barriers between formal knowledge and practical knowledge, and it is thought that:

> the knowledge teachers need to teach well is generated when teachers treat their own classrooms and schools as sites for intentional investigation at the same time that they treat the knowledge and theory produced by others as generative material for interrogation and interpretation.
>
> (Cochran-Smith and Lytle, 2001, p. 48)

For Cochran-Smith and Lytle, the concept of 'inquiry as a stance' is central to teacher learning. According to them, through enquiry teachers problematise their own knowledge and practice as well as that of others.

It is only fair to note here that in the research literature some studies exist that examine the effect of teachers' pedagogical knowledge on students' academic achievement, but the effect sizes reported are quite small. This, in our view, does not invalidate the emphasis on pedagogical knowledge and PCK in this chapter, as the same phenomenon applies to studies covering subject matter knowledge. The limit in effect size shown in studies might well be due to the fact that proxy measures of key constructs of interest, such as for example the number of classes in professional or subject matter studies taken, were being used (see Rowan *et al.*, 2001).

In our view, more recent work by Lee and Judith Shulman (2004) offers a useful addition to more traditional conceptualisations of PCK; owing to a lack of space we can only introduce them here briefly. By his own admission, Shulman's earlier constructs of teacher learning were strictly cognitive and individual and were mainly orientated towards a notion of centrality of subject knowledge and subject-specific differences in teaching and learning (Shulman and Shulman, 2004, p. 258). Schulman's thinking has moved away from a mainly cognitive paradigm towards one that is bound up in a notion of learning communities:

> *An accomplished teacher* [i.e. a pedagogically versed teacher; our explication] *is a member of a professional community who is ready, willing, and able to teach and to learn from his or her teaching experiences.* Thus, the elements of the theory are: Ready (*possessing vision*), Willing (*having motivation*), Able (*both knowing and being able 'to do'*), Reflective (*learning from experience*), and Communal (*acting as a member of a professional community*).
>
> (Shulman and Shulman, 2004)

In such a model the social interactionist dimension of (professional teacher) knowledge is much more foregrounded, and personal pedagogical practice is embedded on the one hand in collective understandings and on the other in values and dispositions. By implication, PCK can only be achieved at the personal level through critical reflection on, and learning from, individual experiences as well as those of others. In short, Shulman's extended model of PCK adds an additional layer by reflecting the inter-action of the individual with the professional community within which (s)he practises.

If the concept of PCK provides a key structuring framework for the development of teaching competence, how well does it fit within teacher education courses where such development formally begins? The prevailing structure of ITE in England and Wales, where all 'traditional' routes into teaching, e.g. the PGCE, BEd and BA (QTS), have the following common elements (see Pachler and Watson, 1996):

- Beginner teachers study subject-specific courses of applied methodology that equip them to guide learners to acquire and understand relevant subject-related knowledge, skills and understanding.
- They follow a so-called professional studies component that provides them with knowledge of the education system within which they will work and introduces them to a range of 'theories'[4] and concepts/frameworks on which their practice as teachers will be based.
- And they carry out extensive teaching experience. Beginner teachers are placed in schools willing to accept them on the basis

of a contractual agreement setting out the respective roles and responsibilities and in return for an agreed fee. There are no schools identified specifically to train beginner teachers other than the so-called 'training schools',[5] which receive special government funding for proactive engagement in ITE.

In principle the structures outlined above appear to allow for adequate coverage of Shulman's categories of teacher knowledge. However, in practice – partly because of systemic constraints – it is questionable whether adequate coverage can be achieved. For one thing, as we already discussed in Chapter 2, it is not always clear that FL undergraduate degrees necessarily provide adequate coverage of content knowledge, not just in terms of the levels of general linguistic proficiency achieved by graduates but also in terms of their level of preparedness for curricular knowledge requirements. Second, it is questionable whether the balance between practical teaching experience (two thirds) and subject and professional studies (one third) is appropriate to ensuring sufficiently detailed engagement with relevant concepts across a wide range of topics with sufficient reference to subject-specific background literature and conceptual/theoretical considerations. In view of the limited embedding of specific professional experiences in broader contexts in school-based work, we deem a more integrated approach to ITE desirable, i.e. one that makes the role of the school mentor, in particular in relation to theory and how it relates to beginner teachers' classroom practice and their development as reflective practitioners, more central (see e.g. Pachler and Field, 2001b).

Moreover, for logistical and organisational reasons, professional studies work is often conceptualised and taught in interdisciplinary groups and frequently focuses on issues of general educational and pedagogical principles and government policy that apply across academic subjects and phases rather than on enquiries into specific forms of pedagogical and content knowledge required for the teaching of specific content to particular groups of pupils. Professional studies work also rarely enables students to engage in a systematic knowledge construction process in relation to issues pertaining to the foundation disciplines of psychology, sociology, history of education and comparative education (see e.g. Lawes, 2003).

Returning to the subject of pedagogical thinking as the context in which PCK will have the most immediate and tangible impact on your practice as a FL teacher, we will focus for the remainder of this chapter on five key areas of FL teaching in order to show how in each case appropriate PCK forms the basis of your understanding and practice.

Teaching grammar

One central challenge for all FL teachers has traditionally been the teaching of grammar. Grammar teaching is a hotly contested field and requires – apart from the requisite subject knowledge, i.e. grammatical competence and knowledge of relevant metalinguistic terminology – strongly developed and differentiated PCK, e.g. knowledge about grammatical progression; knowledge of available methodological choices such as inductive or deductive approaches; knowledge of pupils' conceptions and their possible misconceptions; knowledge of when and when not to use metalinguistic description or when and when not to use intra- or interlingual comparison etc.

In the context of CLT, the prevalent paradigm of FL teaching and learning in the UK (see e.g. Pachler, 2000), Krashen's input hypothesis (1985) has been very influential. According to this hypothesis, language acquisition depends on the amount of exposure to context-embedded TL input to be adjusted by the FL teacher to the linguistic competence of learners. Krashen calls this 'comprehensible input'. Given that FL teachers tend to work with classes of in excess of twenty or even thirty students and given the fact that each of these students invariably has a different level of interlanguage, the targeting of input at a level just beyond that at which learners are currently operating is near to impossible for even the most experienced teacher, try as they may. Without requisite PCK, in this instance knowledge about SLA and FL learning processes, FL teachers might not easily be able to question the appropriateness of such widely promulgated views and assess their feasibility or devise alternative teaching approaches that are more effective in bringing about pupil learning.

In a similar vein, PCK is important in order to assess assertions made by highly influential researchers, such as Krashen, for example in relation to the lack of usefulness, or even detrimental influence, of recourse to grammatical knowledge. Although relevant empirical studies are not (yet) able to offer conclusive evidence (see e.g. Ellis, 1997), there is a growing realisation that explicit and implicit reference to grammatical forms and features, and frequent exposure to the TL, as well as ample opportunities to produce and reproduce TL forms, are all essential ingredients in the FL learning process, provided teacher expectations concerning the short- and medium-term effectiveness of form-focused approaches to FL teaching are realistic in view of the lack of linearity and immediacy of the FL learning process.

Teachers with requisite PCK will appreciate that the specialist literature distinguishes between two main methodological options, 'focus on form' and 'focus on forms', with the former being deemed to be superior to the latter. Among other things, form-focused FL teaching aims to sensitise learners to linguistic forms in order for them to notice the gap between their own linguistic expressions and proficiency and the ideal of the native-speaker input. Focus on form differs from focus on forms in so far as, in the former the noticing of formal linguistic features occurs as a by-product of meaning-oriented FL teaching. Focus on forms on the other hand is best described as formal grammar teaching where grammatical structures feature as discrete aims and learning objectives. So-called 'pedagogical intrusions' (Doughty, 2001), i.e. teacher recasts that focus directly on specific learner errors during acts of communication, are increasingly thought to be more effective pedagogical interventions.

FL teachers who are not able or willing to question the methodological orthodoxies of the day, in this example the avoidance of a systematic engagement with grammar, be it explicit or implicit, in the prevailing version of CLT, are in danger of adopting pedagogical practices that run counter to the cognitive nature of FL acquisition and learning processes, whereby language is not a series of products that are acquired sequentially but a series of interlanguage stages that gradually develop into grammatically correct forms. In other words, just because a particular grammatical form, for example the past participle, has been the focus of a few lessons does not necessarily mean it has been assimilated, internalised and learnt by pupils in a way that allows them to use it error-free in their own language production as:

(a) it normally takes much longer for grammatical forms to be accommodated in a pupil's interlanguage and
(b) the pupils might not be at the required developmental stage to accommodate this new grammatical form.

Consequently, frequent recycling of grammatical features is imperative, as is a recognition that linguistic forms are not acquired in a linear fashion and not fully at once, i.e. there will be lapses and incorrect usage by pupils that are not necessarily to be seen as a reflection of 'bad' or 'ineffective' teaching but at least equally likely as a reflection of the cyclical nature of FL learning.

Macaro (2003a, p. 60) posits that research points to a paradox whereby 'grammatical competence must be an integral part of communicative competence but learning grammar does not seem to help either with communication nor with grammatical competence'. He draws the conclusion that one must not equate accuracy with competence and that grammar teaching can only lead to an increase in accuracy over a very long term. In the short and medium term, a focus on form enables the learner to make progress with internalising the rules of a language, to formulate new hypotheses about language and to move on to a new stage in their interlanguage. Macaro (2003a, p. 61) also asserts that ready-made language chunks are as important as productive rules.

Task-based language teaching

In order to be able to develop and use appropriate pedagogical approaches to FL teaching, you need to engage with developments in the research, pedagogical and professional literature, both during ITE as well as throughout your teaching career. Our understanding of how FLs are learnt and best taught develops continuously, and as FL teachers we need to keep abreast of new insights as well as current issues and debates if we want to be able to do well by our pupils.

Recent years have seen a growing interest in task-based language teaching (TBLT), which is viewed by many as a logical next developmental step in FL teaching methodology. For a detailed discussion see, for example, Ellis (2003) and Klapper (2003).

According to Macaro (2003a, p. 40), TBLT starts with the notion that the problem-solving properties in a task are the driving force behind the learning of new language instead of tasks being used for exemplifying or assessing language learnt. The literature distinguishes task-supported and task-based FL teaching. Task-supported language teaching uses tasks for practice or testing purposes. In TBLT, tasks are viewed as vehicles for FL learning through communication. Tasks are considered to be essential as well as, by some, in themselves sufficient for FL learning, and it is argued that they should form the basis of curriculum planning. TBLT works on the premise that tasks enable learners to experience, inside the classroom, how language is used as a means of communication in preparation for real-life use.

Proponents of TBLT argue that linguistically orientated syllabuses, i.e. syllabuses that are constructed around isolated grammatical forms, are insufficient and ineffective in so far as they represent futile attempts to interrupt the cognitive processes of FL acquisition and development, which are based on the gradual linking and restructuring of grammatical and semantic forms and functions with existing knowledge. FL learning is characterised by a lack of immediacy and it takes place via transitional constructs and developmental stages called interlanguages (see e.g. Selinker, 1972). Linguistically orientated syllabuses and teaching based around notions of focus on forms cannot change those processes.

A further distinction relevant here is that between tasks and exercises, with the former seen as fostering predominantly meaning-focused language use, and the latter seen as fostering predominantly form-focused language use. TBLT views learners as participants and language users who engage in communicative processes and in so doing develop language skills. According to Ellis a task:

> is a workplan that requires learners to process language pragmatically in order to achieve an outcome that can be evaluated in terms of whether the correct or appropriate propositional content has been conveyed. To this end, it requires them to give primary attention to meaning and to make use of their own linguistic resources, although the design of the task may predispose them to choose particular forms. A task is intended to result in language use that bears a resemblance, direct or indirect, to the way language is used in the real world. Like other language activities, a task can engage productive or receptive, and oral or written skills, and also various cognitive processes.
>
> (Ellis, 2003, p. 16)

In the specialist literature three phases of TBLT tend to be delineated:

1 a preparation and planning phase;
2 an implementation or task phase; and
3 a post-task phase.

During the preparation and planning phase, learners can be involved in designing the task parameters or they can be engaged in carrying out a similar task. The implementation or task phase can be controlled by allowing for more or less time or by the number of people involved in carrying out a task. The post-task phase can involve the learners in writing a reflective account of their participation in, and their learning from, the task or it can consist of a repeat run of the task.

Ellis (2003) notes the following key pedagogical questions in relation to making sustained use of TBLT:

- How are tasks best classified? According to pedagogical, rhetorical, cognitive or psycholinguistic criteria?
- What content is most appropriate for TBLT?
- What criteria are best used to classify tasks: input, context/variables, procedures or outcomes?

Only once these questions have been considered can tasks be used in a systematic matter in FL teaching and learning and syllabuses be built around them.

In terms of a framework for describing tasks so as to make them shareable (and, thereby, contestable), Ellis (2003, pp. 21 and 217) suggests the following headings:

- aims
- input
- variables
- processes
- outcomes (products and processes).

Doughty and Long (2003) outline ten methodological principles of TBLT that aim at functional language proficiency without jettisoning grammatical accuracy and that, according to them, are based on the findings of SLA and FL learning research (see Table 3.1). In addition to these methodological principles, they deem certain pedagogical principles, such as teacher preferences, the ages, previous knowledge and ability of learners, learning objectives or the learning environment etc., as warranting consideration.

Studies such as these (as well as, for example, Ellis, 2003, or Macaro, 2003a) not only provide helpful guidance for FL teachers but also food for thought in terms of questioning prevailing methodological orthodoxies such as the 'presentation–practice–production' (PPP) model.

Table 3.1 *Methodological principles*

Activities	MP1	Use tasks, not texts, as the unit of analysis
	MP2	Promote learning by doing
Input	MP3	Elaborate input (do not simplify; do not solely rely on 'authentic' texts)
	MP4	Provide rich (not impoverished) input
Learning processes	MP5	Encourage inductive (chunk) learning
	MP6	Focus on form
	MP7	Provide negative feedback
	MP8	Respect 'learner syllabuses'/developmental processes
	MP9	Promote co-operative/collaborative learning
Learners	MP10	Individualise instruction (according to communicative needs, and psycholinguistically)

Source: Doughty and Long, 2003

The presentation–practice–production model

In view of the above, the widely prevailing PPP model, which features tasks only in the third or 'production' phase of teaching, must be viewed as problematic in so far at least as there is a tendency for it to focus on grammatical forms and isolated linguistic features rather than on meaning. The PPP model assumes linear linguistic progression that is premised on the isolated learning of language forms and features as well as a process of understanding, internalising and activating, whereas research evidence strongly suggests a cyclical model with troughs and peaks around recycling. The PPP model builds on Littlewood's (1981) methodological construct, which asserts a developmental trajectory from pre-communicative to quasi-communicative and communicative activities, i.e. from structural to functional and interactive activities.

Nunan and Lamb (1996) note that learners and teachers assume different roles in the different stages of the PPP model, e.g. model speaker, facilitator, listener, interlocutor, that different tasks, exercises and working modalities find application, e.g. presentation, information gap, role play;

and that different interaction modes are used, e.g. whole class, group, partner and individual work. From this they conclude that the PPP model is useful and can be effective for achieving discrete FL goals. However, they acknowledge that it is not suitable for achieving contextualised and integrated goals, for which a more differentiated model is required.

Skehan (1996) expresses the view that the popularity of the PPP model is due to the fact that it affords a high level of control over classroom proceedings as well as that it is easily teachable. Broady (2002) concurs with the view that the PPP model offers novice teachers a ready means of achieving some control in the highly complex undertaking that is FL teaching. As such she welcomes it, at least for the very initial stages of a teacher's professional practice, provided they are not afraid of straying from it as soon as they feel ready to do so. She posits that isolated lesson aims and learning objectives are a 'useful fiction, tools to help us think, act and reflect, rather than as representations of "the truth"'. Therefore, the PPP model seems to fit into Littlewood's pre-communicative phase because in most FL classrooms so-called 'free' communication is little more than public renditions of memorised language (chunks) or so-called 'display language'.

Klapper (2003) proposes a reversal of order in the PPP model: an initial, TBLT-orientated production phase followed by a presentation and practice phase. That way the findings of SLA and FL learning would be adhered to more closely than in the traditional PPP model as, in this modified version, the primacy of FL learning through exposure to the FL is retained, and learners are offered the opportunity to engage, in real time, in meaning-focused interaction in accordance with their respective stage of inter-language development. Interaction is followed by a systematic skill focus supported by some focus on form, through practice and reinforcement, leading to proceduralisation and, eventually, automatic language production.

Teaching aims and learning objectives of FL teaching

Another important aspect of PCK is an ongoing debate about FL teaching aims and learning objectives. Curricular prescriptions in England favour a very specific set of learning outcomes around the acquisition of knowledge, an understanding of the TL and FL learning skills, with some lip-service being paid to the development of cultural awareness with the ultimate, yet – in view of the unfavourable contextual factors such as lack of curriculum time and opportunities to use the FL in real life – quite unrealistic, aim of near-native linguistic proficiency. In view of an ever-changing socio-political landscape in the context, for example, of an ever-growing European Union, the question arises whether a more inter-culturally orientated set of aims would not be more appropriate and desirable rather than the prevailing focus on specific languages. In addition, an increased emphasis on language awareness or a broader conceptual-isation of literacy encompassing new technologies (electronic literacy, critical media literacy etc) seems worth considering.

Intercultural communicative competence takes into account the way of living in which others speak and write. It also acknowledges that language and culture are interrelated and that, for language to be properly under-stood and used, learners require socio-cultural and world knowledge. This applies not only at the semantic and idiomatic levels but also at syntactic and morphological levels. For example, cultural knowledge is very import-ant for learners in order to avoid socio-pragmatic failure: learners need the requisite cultural knowledge to know how to initiate and finish con-versations, what conventions exist in relation to turn-taking, turn-keeping and turn-giving, and in relation to topic nomination or topic change.

As stimulus for meaning-focused, culture-orientated FL teaching, Neuner and Huhnfeld (1993, p. 113) suggest what they call 'universal experiences of life', in particular:

- fundamental experiences, e.g. birth, death, living;
- personal identity, e.g. personal characteristics;
- social identity, e.g. private self, family; neighbourhood, local community, nation;
- partnership, e.g. friendship, love;
- environment, e.g. house and home; local area, nature, civilisation;
- work, e.g. making a living;
- education;
- subsistence, e.g. food, clothing;
- mobility, e.g. traffic;
- leisure and art;
- communication, e.g. media;
- health care, e.g. health, illness, hygiene;
- ethics, e.g. morals, values, religion;
- events, e.g. past, present, future;
- spirituality, creativity, imagination, emotions, memory; etc.

A comparative methodology around the direct engagement with authentic material and also direct interactions with TL speakers can be used. This can lead to the recognition of similarities and differences with others and, in turn, to an acceptance of alternative perspectives as well as an understanding of how others experience the world. At the same time it is a starting point for relativising one's own life experiences.

Using information and communication technologies

The use of ICT offers exciting new possibilities in pedagogical terms, in particular in relation to intercultural aims. Policymakers in England acknowledged this potential by introducing ICT-related standards that have to be met if one wants to become a qualified teacher:

1 Planning, e.g.:
   - understanding and considering the advantages and disadvantages of using ICT;
   - planning to use ICT so as to provide access to the curriculum for those pupils who might otherwise have difficulties because of their special educational needs;
   - preparing for lessons using ICT by selecting and preparing appropriate sources of information, relevant software and the appropriate technology, and deciding on the most effective organisation of the classroom and pupils.
2 Teaching, e.g.:
   - extending pupils' MFL learning through the use of ICT;
   - intervening and posing questions to stimulate, direct, monitor and assess the learning of pupils who are using ICT;
   - employing the most appropriate technologies for working with whole classes;
   - combining the use of ICT with other resources and methods to achieve teaching objectives.
3 Assessing and evaluating, e.g.:
   - enabling pupils to demonstrate their knowledge, understanding and skills in MFL while using ICT;
   - ensuring pupils' MFL learning is not masked by the technology being used;

- judging how the use of ICT can alter expectations of pupils' attainment;
- judging the effectiveness of using ICT in achieving teaching objectives.

4 Personal and professional ICT use, e.g.:
- using generic and/or subject-specific hardware and software, e.g. databases, internet, presentation tools, scanners, printers etc.;
- using ICT to aid record-keeping, analysis of data, target-setting, reporting, transfer of information etc.;
- accessing and using relevant resources;
- accessing research and inspection evidence.

(TTA, 1999)

The above list also raises a more general point: it shows that the conceptualisation of ICT use implicit in government thinking is by and large restricted to the domain of how to teach and learn and to a view of new technologies as an opportunity for faster and easier access to information. FL teachers well versed in PCK and relevant literature will be aware that this view restricts the potential of new technologies in terms of educational change. In order to fulfil the real potential of new technologies in FL teaching and learning, the focus needs to be placed on what kinds of new knowledge they make accessible rather than simply on how to do old things in new ways (see e.g. Noss and Pachler, 1999).

In the FL context ICT can be seen to be of particular interest, not only in terms of the scope it affords learners to become members of learning communities and to generate knowledge through social interaction via computer-mediated communication (CMC) but also the ability to access multimodal (combining text, image and sound), up-to-the-minute, interactive, authentic material to supplement (not replace!) traditional print and audio material. One FL example for effective CMC use is the Tandem network[6] which enables FL learning by way of email exchanges with peers abroad. The use of ICT, far from making it redundant, makes the role of the teacher more important in terms of identifying, selecting and sequencing material etc., but ICT use requires new pedagogical skills from teachers, such as the ability to evaluate multimodal resources and to know when best (not) to use them as well as how to ensure smooth classroom management and TL use in computer rooms etc. In addition, of course, it requires of them requisite technical skills and knowledge.

When evaluating ICT resources, the tendency prevails to focus narrowly on technology-related criteria such as ease of installation etc., rather than how the resources support the FL learning process. On the basis of what is known about how FLs are learnt, Chapelle (1998) lists the following seven hypotheses about beneficial characteristics of ICT resources, which seem a useful starting point and framework for engagement with ICT in FL contexts:

1 The linguistic characteristics of TL input need to be made salient.
2 Learners should receive help in comprehending semantic and syntactic aspects of linguistic input.
3 Learners need to have opportunities to produce TL output.
4 Learners need to notice errors in their own output.
5 Learners need to correct their linguistic output.
6 Learners need to engage in TL interaction the structure of which can be modified for negotiation of meaning.
7 Learners should engage in L2 tasks designed to maximise opportunities for good interaction.

Again without requisite PCK, FL teachers would not be able to improve their effectiveness through the use of ICT.

In order to be successful, web-based projects need to have very clear aims and objectives and a clearly defined thematic structure (see e.g. Neuner and Huhnfeld, 1993) and time-frame. It is often best if classes are divided into smaller groups which in turn communicate with small groups in a partner school. Project work might comprise the following phases (Pachler and Field, 2001a; see also Pachler, 2005a):

- Preparation: co-ordination between teachers in both schools.
- Phase 1: pupils introduce themselves, their schools, their environment in writing and pictures.
- Phase 2: questions and answers, exchange of information.
- Phase 3: exchange of detailed answers based on research; follow-up questions.
- Phase 4: analysis and comparison of results.
- Phase 5: (joint) presentation of results (e.g. compilation of a display, brochure, newspaper, video/audio recording or webpages), summary of learning outcomes, project evaluation, goodbye letters.

Group work supported by learner logs and diaries for recording reflections on their work as well as new linguistic features (semantic and syntactic) should be supplemented by plenaries during which the teacher provides necessary input. Projects can meaningfully be linked to controversial topics, about which pupils have an opinion that they are keen to communicate, as well as to real-life experiences of pupils.

This brief discussion of ICT also demonstrates, in addition to the centrality of the role of the FL teacher, the complexity brought about by the introduction of a new variable into FL teaching, which requires new subject and pedagogical (content) knowledge in order to ensure pupil learning. In the literature the term 'technological pedagogical content knowledge (TPCK)' is being used (see Mishra and Koehler, 2006).

The recent emphasis in government policy as well as in relevant professional and scholarly writing on the application of ICT is a good example of how the field of PCK keeps developing and changing. It would seem that the key pedagogical skills of planning, teaching and assessment can no longer be considered without at least some reference to ICT. The recent popularity of interactive whiteboards (IWBs) is a case in point.

Moss *et al.* (2005) identify the following features of IWBs: drag and drop; cover and reveal; colour and highlight; the facility to prepare and then preload a given sequence of 'pages'; the facility to annotate and then save texts produced during the course of the lesson; the facility to incorporate moving and still images into teacher-created texts; the facility to use a variety of dedicated software and courseware; the facility to visit and use subject-specific websites during lesson time; the facility to devise activities that require pupil interaction with IWB texts. It is hardly surprising, therefore, that IWBs are widely seen as having considerable potential for bringing about fundamental changes in pedagogical practices in FL teaching. The important question, however, is this: are these changes necessarily for the better? Moss *et al.* found that the use of the IWB predominantly happens during whole class teaching time, sometimes in an attempt to reinforce teacher control and achieve attention in whole-class activities. They also note that their use in much the same way as worksheets or textbooks to focus learners' attention on tasks is not uncommon. IWBs can be seen to be used more productively when the intention is to engage learners in active problem solving by affording opportunities for individuals to manipulate materials that form part of the display. The report also notes that IWBs can be used effectively to influence pace in lessons. Interestingly for the context of the current discussion, Moss *et al.* note that the use of particular features of IWBs seems to depend upon the teachers' pedagogic intent and the many factors which influence this – including subject knowledge; confidence in classroom management; commitment to a particular pedagogic style; understanding of the learning needs of the pupils; time available to plan for the IWB; demands of the subject itself – rather than the teachers' confidence in the technology per se.

In a recent piece, Cogill (2006) examines what elements within her proposed model of teacher knowledge, based on Banks *et al.* (1999), are affected by the use of IWBs. Key to Cogill's model of teacher knowledge is knowledge contribution to observable practice, which she considers affected not only by teachers' pedagogical knowledge, content knowledge and curriculum knowledge but also by beliefs, values, educational context and teaching experiences. In relation to PCK, for example, she lists the following points elicited from the eleven teachers in her study:

- The whiteboard focuses essential information, so discussion may be shorter but it is also better for reaching the learning points, as less time is spent by me explaining and writing on an ordinary board.
- It is very good for modelling with the whole class, for example if I want to show them how to (construct) a piece of writing.
- The facility to change pages easily avoids restriction to just one board and allows backwards and forwards movement if a point is not understood.
- My preparation has changed completely since using the whiteboard and I still planned the same way last week when the projector bulb went and I had a couple of days without the board. I think more carefully about what to teach and how to teach it.
- I think I'm more prepared for what may happen next when I'm teaching as all the information is there and it's possible to return to the previous page if necessary – 'the teaching is all at your fingertips'.
- I feel the whiteboard inspires my teaching as it gives another dimension to how I can explain the learning. It must be used professionally though: 'Is the material appropriate and will it enhance teaching and learning?'

- I now find with plenaries that I can use children's learning much more easily with the whiteboard so that we can all analyse their work together. 'We can all learn from their learning.'

(Cogill, 2006, p. 12)

Despite the focus of this study being on secondary mathematics teachers and despite the fact that by Cogill's own admission the points made by teachers are quite subtle, these findings seem pertinent here.

In the twenty-first century, a good FL teacher is invariably only one who is able to make effective use of ICT. Although ICT is, in our view, unlikely to replace FL teachers, those teachers who are unable to use ICT effectively are likely to be replaced by those who can use it!

CONCLUSION

Klapper (2003) rightly points out that debates about methodology can be unsettling for FL teachers and result in a reluctance to engage in them, as they require us to question instinctive and often long-established pedagogical approaches and practices and the received knowledge bases that underpin them. We would argue that this is no bad thing and very much in line with the prevailing notion of reflective practice, the hallmark of teacher education and professional development.

Engagement with PCK will more likely than not lead you to the realisation that there is – and can be – no one best pedagogical approach to FL teaching that is universally applicable, and that, therefore, our professionalism demands of us always to engage critically with available professional, theoretical and conceptual writing and thinking in order to develop new perspectives on FLs teaching practices and insights into how FL are learnt.

QUESTIONS FOR DISCUSSION

1 What do you consider to be the key considerations of being a native speaker/non-native speaker in terms of pedagogical content knowledge? Do native speakers require different knowledge bases to non-native speaker FL teachers?

2 Macaro (2003a) distinguishes three main differences between FL learning and that of other subjects: the medium of instruction, the link of language to identity, and interference from L1. Do you agree? Are there any others you consider to be of significance?

3 We argued that FL teachers act in accordance with their implicit or explicit theories of teaching and learning as well as their professional experiences. What theories of teaching and learning do you subscribe to and what aspects of your professional experience do you consider to be most influential?

4 Do you agree that there are conceptual, theoretical, practical as well as empirical dimensions to professional knowledge?

5 Cochran-Smith and Lytle (2001) distinguish three conceptions of teacher learning: knowledge for practice, knowledge in practice and knowledge of practice. Which do you consider most important and why?

6 In this chapter we introduced the notion of PCK, the specialist subject and pedagogical knowledge to enhance the learnability of FLs for students. What do you consider to be the key components of PCK for FL teachers?

NOTES

1 For details see www.ofsted.gov.uk.

2 For details of possible routes into teaching see the websites of the Training and Development Agency for Schools (TDA) at www.tda.gov.uk or of the Centre for Information on Language Teaching and Research (CILT) at www.cilt.org.uk.

3 Given the apparent lack of explicit links of educational policy and educational practice to a clearly discernible (empirical) evidence base as well as the problems with validity of research evidence – due partly to the difficulty of controlling variables in educational contexts – it might be better to think of educational policies and practices that make explicit reference to research evidence as evidence-informed or evidence-aware rather than evidence-based.

4 For a critical appraisal of the term 'theory' see e.g. Thomas, 2002.

5 See www.teachernet.gov.uk/management/atoz/t/trainingschools.

6 See www.slf.ruhr-uni-bochum.de/etandem/etindex-en.html.

Chapter 4

Curricular knowledge

INTRODUCTION

In this chapter we shift our attention from subject- and teacher-orientated forms of knowledge to the curricular 'packaging' that official policymakers produce and require teachers to 'implement' and 'transmit'. If you are a beginner or experienced languages teacher in England you are doubtless already very familiar with at least some of the detail of the NC for FL. However, what you may not yet have done is to reflect on the value systems and knowledge perspectives that underpin the official framework of the FL curriculum in which you are asked to operate. In our view critical reflection on the value systems and approaches adopted in the curriculum provides teachers with a clearer view of the direction in which they are working and to which their day-to-day pedagogical decisions contribute. From the point of view of broader professional understanding, engagement with curricular knowledge is justified because it is important for teachers to recognise that curricula inherently reflect particular views of society and the distribution of life chances; also, societies tend to rely on the school curriculum to give their next generation access to existing knowledge (see Young, 1999, p. 469). It seems essential, therefore, to examine closely what values and assumptions are inherent in the curriculum, in our case the FL curriculum.

The decision by policymakers in England to confine the compulsory study of a FL to a period of three years from ages 11 to 14 must be seen as one such value, or rather, it is not only indicative of how undervalued FLs are in England, but also, in an age of globalisation and a steadily expanding European Union, it speaks volumes about a lack of aspirations for young people in terms of their ability to contribute fully to, and gain most from, the increasingly multilingual and multicultural world they live in. In our professional view, the rhetoric in the national languages strategy (DfES, 2002) about an entitlement by 2010 to an early start, as well in the international strategy for education to transform our capability to speak and use other languages (DfES, 2004b), does not really stand up to close scrutiny (see e.g. Pachler, 2002).

Although separate FL curricula exist in Wales, Scotland and Northern Ireland, this chapter will use the MFL NC Order for England as in force at the time of writing as its key point of reference in order to be able to advance a coherent and focused line of argument. In a view of a modified NC Order coming into effect in England from September 2008 as well as in view of differences in curricular requirements elsewhere, we deliberately structure our discussion around a set of generic principles and questions that, we hope, allow easy transfer of the issues raised and observations made to other contexts.

Having discussed different categories of FL knowledge as well as pedagogical knowledge and PCK in previous chapters, we now turn to an in-depth examination of curricular knowledge.

On the one hand, curricular knowledge has to be understood as the requirements set out in documents published by government and its agencies, such as the NC (see www.nc.uk.net/nc/contents/MFL-home.htm and curriculum.qca.org.uk/subjects/modern-foreign-languages/index.aspx) and examination specifications (formerly known as syllabuses) published by Awarding Bodies (see www.aqa.org.uk/, www.edexcel.org.uk, www.ocr.org.uk). Curricular knowledge does, however, also refer to the content presented in coursebooks and the schemes of work in use in different schools.

THE NATIONAL CURRICULUM AND THE FL ORDER FOR ENGLAND

In England the decision to have a unified curriculum, the so-called NC, was taken by the then Secretary of State for Education, Kenneth Baker, as recently as the late 1980s, for a number of reasons, including the perceived need for an increase in accountability of schools and teachers, for standardisation of provision across the country, for a clearer definition of standards as well as for a common assessment framework. The NC for England, therefore, can be seen to possess at least the twin function of curriculum plan and assessment tool. Beginner teachers often do not realise that, until as recently as some 15 years ago, bar some minor prescriptions, in particular in relation to the coverage of religious and physical education, it was up to individual schools and their teachers to decide what subjects to teach and how to teach them. Examples such as these inter alia emphasise the need for teachers to engage with aspects of the history of education, as otherwise they might take the existence and necessity of something as fundamental as the NC for granted.

The remit letter from the Secretary of State to the various chairs of the subject-based panels of 'experts' set out a unified structure requiring the inclusion of programmes of study (PoSs) – in the original, 1992 MFL Order these included prescribed areas of experience, i.e. specific topics for study such as the world of work or the world around us – as well as attainment targets featuring a prescribed number of levels. The carefully chosen subject panels were also told to base the respective subject curriculum on notions of knowledge, skills and understanding. Again as a beginner teacher, you might take the heavy focus of the current MFL Order on skills for granted, whereas they are a rather recent addition to what teachers are expected to cover and students are expected to acquire and learn. The remit letter makes clear that the parameters within which subject panels could set out their definition of what subject knowledge entails were heavily circumscribed. And it shows that 'concepts of knowledge are sanctioned in the curriculum through a process of social stratification that reflects the power of some groups to assert their view of knowledge as beyond dispute' (Young, 1999, p. 468).

KEY ISSUES IN CURRICULUM PLANNING

At a generic level, the discussion of the inception of the NC for England raises two fundamental questions: who determines the curriculum? And, who are the so-called stakeholders? In answer to the first question, it is worth pointing out that a noticeable trend in the UK – as opposed to many other European countries – is the exclusion, by and large, of the subject-specialist community in higher education, in particular in education departments, from the decision- and policymaking processes. This can be seen to be the case partly owing to a certain latent anti-intellectual climate and partly, of course, also because of the inherent difficulties and problems for government of subjecting policy proposal to critical scrutiny at the point of inception. Invariably, decision-making in the area of policy-making is a 'diffuse, haphazard, and somewhat volatile process' (Lomas, 2000, p. 140):

> The values for a decision, especially in public policy, emerge from a process of cognitive dissonance reduction. Individuals, organizations and policy sub-systems try to bring into congruence often competing messages from their interests, ideologies and beliefs. . . . Furthermore, . . . the window of opportunity to make a major change, however compelling the research, opens only rarely and briefly when the constellation of values may happen to coincide with the research's implications.
>
> (Lomas, 2000, p. 143)

(For a detailed discussion of evidence-informed practice see Pachler, 2003.)

Who, then, is to make the decisions as to the legitimacy of curricular content? A sociological point of view would suggest – as Young (1999, p. 467) points out – that, rather than being 'given', 'the objectivity of knowledge' is located 'in the shared understandings of communities of specialists or experts'. Young goes on to remind his readers that sociology 'locates the *givenness* of the curriculum, its subjects and its selection of content, in its professional, institutional and social history. It follows that any particular curriculum cannot avoid expressing certain interests and values.' In this chapter, among other things, we attempt to examine what interests and values the FL 'curriculum' in England expresses, explicitly or otherwise.

One important aspect in the FL context of Young's notion of 'givenness' concerns the sharp disjuncture of curricula at pre- and post-16. (For a detailed discussion see e.g. Pachler and Field, 2001a, and Pachler, 1999.) The tension arises in part owing to unsynchronised reforms to the curriculum and examination prescriptions in both phases of education in recent years. Although, in the wake of the comprehensivisation of secondary schools since the mid-1960s, the examination requirements have seen a fundamental overhaul at pre-16 in the mid 1980s with the introduction of the GCSE, and, as we have seen earlier, there has been a re-conceptualisation of curricular requirements with the introduction of a NC from the late 1980s, at post-16 such a change did not take place until the late 1990s with the restructuring of the two-year vertical into a modular, horizontal A level. In other words, whereas it was possible to take Advanced Supplementary level examinations that required students to study half the content within a period of two years but at the same level of complexity and depth as the full Advanced level (hence, vertical), it did not prove to be popular with students. Reforms in the late 1990s brought in the Advanced Subsidiary level examination, which allows students to exit after one year of study having completed three modules at AS rather than A2 level (hence, horizontal). However, in essence owing to political pressures, fuelled by an annual outcry in the national press about an alleged erosion of standards in view of seemingly ever-increasing pass rates, it is fundamentally still the same examination that was designed in 1951 for 3 per cent of each cohort. With post-16 participation in excess of 70 per cent by the late 1990s and with A/AS level qualifications now taken by some 30 per cent of students, the question about the appropriateness of the A/AS level examination requirements in relation to the make-up and nature of the students studying at that level, as well as in relation to what comes before, is, in our view, legitimate. As Young notes (1999, p. 467), '(to) what extent should their assumptions about the selection and organisation of knowledge continue to dominate a 16–19 curriculum which now aims to include the whole of each cohort?' We anticipate with interest whether the recent curriculum and qualifications reform for the A/AS level curriculum led by Her Majesty's former Chief Inspector, Sir Mike Tomlinson, yielded few tangible outcomes (see Working Group on 14–19 Reform, 2004).

Young's assertions suggest that, given the central prescriptions governing the FL curriculum at a macro level, there exist invariable differences around its interpretation by groups of subject teachers in individual schools according to the professional and educational histories of the teachers and the institutional history of the school. For example, the MFL Order is likely to be interpreted differently by a teacher who has herself learnt the FL with pre-communicative methodology and in pre-GCSE days to a teacher who has taken GCSEs and followed the NC as a pupil herself (see e.g. Block, 2002). Or, in Moore's words:

> (every) schoolteacher operates according to a theory or theories of learning and within the context of a philosophy of what education should be fundamentally about. . . . Sometimes these theories are very consciously held and operated upon by the teacher, perhaps carefully referenced to published theory in the field, while others are held and operated upon rather less consciously, with perhaps little or no reference to published theory.
>
> (Moore, 2000, p. 1)

Moore (2000, p. 2) goes on to point out that 'favoured models of teaching and learning espoused by teachers chime or fail to chime with the models advocated explicitly or implicitly in government policy'. Depending on which is the case, teachers will find it comparatively easy or difficult to adopt curricular prescriptions.

Similarly, there will be differences in interpretation of the curriculum in a specialist language college compared with an 'ordinary' comprehensive school etc.

At the same time, the belief system of learners plays an important role in the interpretation and re-interpretation of content and tasks presented by teachers.

In short, when discussing curricular content, at least two levels of curriculum need to be distinguished: the national and the local. It is worth noting, though, that local interpretations of the curriculum, for example through schemes of work, have been under scrutiny in England by a system of OFSTED inspection that expects adherence to, and implementation of, national prescriptions. As a consequence, many FL teachers and departments have tended to abandon their own schemes of work in favour of the ones prepared by the government through the Qualifications and Curriculum Authority (see QCA, 2002).

At a local level, the following curriculum distinctions can be made: formal, informal and hidden. The formal curriculum normally is the local interpretation of the national policy prescription; the informal curriculum occurs in a more spontaneous manner, is less deliberately planned and links to the mission and ethos of a particular school; the so-called 'hidden' curriculum consists of all those things that are transmitted implicitly through the culture of a particular educational establishment and/or environment and in particular concerns the knowledge, values, attitudes, norms and beliefs implicit in the way education is interpreted.

An example of values that have a bearing on curriculum policy decisions came to the fore in recent debates about revisions to the assessment regime attendant to the NC at KS4 (ages 14–16) as well as at A/AS level (ages 16–19). Endeavours by educationists who argued for the introduction of modular, instead of traditional linear syllabuses were widely viewed by the national press as attempts to dumb down the standard of the GCSE (end of school leaving examination) and A level. Instead of examining the educational benefits of modular syllabuses, such as increased feedback and responsibility for their own learning, an ideological opposition prevailed that made it difficult to demonstrate how the inherent weaknesses of modularisation could be minimised through rules of combination and synoptic assessment (see Young, 1999, p. 469).

Another interesting example of values concerns the continued superiority of knowledge, understanding and skills acquired by individuals over that of groups. It strikes us as curious to note how little value is afforded the ability of working effectively in a team, as well as joint knowledge construction, despite the fact that many job specifications foreground the ability to work collegially and in a team, as well as our understanding of learning as socially grounded and of knowledge as co-constructed. Nevertheless, traditional notions of assessment and testing of individuals tend to prevail, where the emphasis is on the product, the tangible outcome of learning, rather than the process undergone by individuals. A similar point could be made about the priority given to written over oral forms of presenting knowledge.

Third, in terms of values, it is interesting to note, as Moore does in his book (2000, p. 2), that 'the presence of *explicit* theory related to the process of teaching and learning in public policy documents has been generally conspicuous by its absence', an observation that adds support to our earlier assertion about the prevalence of a certain anti-intellectual climate. The same analysis applies to the extent to which aspects of the FL Order are implicitly underpinned by SLA and FL learning research.

A CRITICAL ANALYSIS OF THE MFL ORDER

Young (1999, pp. 469–70) offers a useful tool for curriculum analysis. He distinguishes the 'Curriculum of the Past' and the 'Curriculum of the Future', to which he ascribes the following attributes:

1 The Curriculum of the Past:
   - embodies a concept of knowledge and learning 'for its own sake';
   - is almost exclusively concerned with transmitting existing knowledge;
   - places a higher value on subject knowledge than on knowledge of the relationships between subjects; and
   - assumes a hierarchy and a boundary between school and everyday knowledge, thereby creating the problem of the transferability of school knowledge to non-school contexts.

2 The Curriculum of the Future:
- is a transformative concept of knowledge that emphasises its power to give learners a sense that they can act on the world;
- focuses on the creation of new knowledge as well as the transmission of existing knowledge; and
- emphasises the interdependence of knowledge areas and the relevance of school knowledge to everyday problems.

Before we can endeavour to answer the question as to whether the MFL Order best be described as a curriculum of the past or as a curriculum of the future, it is important to note that, in addition to the overt curriculum set down in the NC Order, there is a covert or hidden curriculum in the shape of examination specifications and, more recently, the so-called KS3 MFL strategy, which increasingly determine how the MFL Order is operationalised in schools. Therefore, no straightforward answer is possible because – as is the case, for example, in relation to the use of dictionaries and reference material – the examination specifications and the NC are in tension with each other. For example, whereas the NC requires pupils to be taught to use dictionaries and other reference materials appropriately and effectively, the examination specifications forbid their use, following public anxiety that allowing them in examinations would either lead to pupils who were unable to use them to waste a lot of time looking up words or make the examination too easy for those who knew how to use them effectively. Similarly, the NC requires pupils to be taught about different countries and cultures; yet the examination specifications hardly feature the cultural awareness dimension as it is notoriously difficult to test through standardised examinations. Also, the examination specifications at GCSE place a heavy emphasis on the memorisation of linguistic items and phrases that are typically quickly forgotten by students after the exam, thereby undermining the emphasis of the NC on the development of language-learning skills, in particular learner independence.

Overall, the MFL Order cannot really be described as promoting learning for learning's sake, as it is not characterised by what might be called 'esoteric' knowledge. Strangely for a curriculum, the current MFL Order makes no attempt really to define content knowledge, for example, in terms of linguistic structures or topics – this is done via the 'hidden' curriculum of the examination specifications. Instead, it foregrounds processes in which learners should be engaged and skills that they should be taught, at the same time as setting out eight plus one exceptional levels of attainment across the four attainment targets of listening, speaking, reading and writing, which are descriptors of what sort of linguistic behaviour pupils should be able to demonstrate at a given level irrespective of the topic and context. From this follows that the NC MFL Order cannot really be charged with adopting a transmission of knowledge mode as it does not really contain much by way of knowledge. However, the examination specifications feature long lists of lexical items (at GCSE level for foundation and higher tiers but not at A/AS level) as well as linguistic structures that students are expected to know and be able to apply.

Unfortunately, in our view, the MFL Order – though not discouraging them as such – makes no tangible provision for cross-curricular approaches. Where specifications existed that, for example, examined aspects of business studies through a FL, they never enjoyed great popularity, for example owing to the inherent danger of pupils gaining a lower grade than they would taking the examination in English, thereby negatively impacting on the examination results of the school and its standing in the league tables, and have largely been withdrawn. This example shows how curriculum debates are often as much ideological as they are educational as, in this instance clearly, a particular, i.e. market-orientated, view of schooling is given priority over the educational benefits to be had by individual pupils from undertaking a certain course of study.

In addition to cross-curricular approaches, content-based instruction offers some interesting perspectives on curriculum planning. As we have already noted, in the UK this approach to curriculum coverage of FLs has found some adopters in recent years, in particular in the context of the teaching of geography, science or business studies through the medium of the FL. In general, language- and content-learning objectives and rationales are distinguished, i.e. content-based instruction (CBI) provides students with an opportunity to continue their subject domain-specific development as well as concurrently work on their language proficiency. In terms of curriculum planning, different models exist according to shifting emphases on content and language.

Stoller (2004) distinguishes the following curricular models:

- cognitive academic language learning approach (CALLA)
- concept-orientated reading instruction (CORI) and
- foreign languages across the curriculum (FLAC or LAC).

CALLA is known for its focus on knowledge of the TL, knowledge of the content area and knowledge of how tasks are to be completed.

CORI, according to Stoller (p. 271) has evolved around four stages:

1 immersion into a main theme through students' personal engagement with the topic;
2 wide reading and information gathering on the theme across multiple information sources;
3 reading strategy instruction to assist with comprehension; and
4 project work leading to a product that demonstrates what students have learned.

In addition, strategy instruction beyond strategy training (e.g. vocabulary development, fluency practice, extensive reading) is of central importance to support textual input. (F)LAC offer students the opportunity to extend their formal language education through the use of the TL outside FL classes, by subject domain teachers using the FL as a medium for instruction and interaction.

In her exploration of the general characteristics of CBI, Stoller (pp. 267–8) identifies the following challenges:

• the identification and development of appropriate content;
• the selection and sequencing of language items dictated by content sources rather than a predetermined language syllabus;
• the alignment of content with structures and functions that emerge from subject matter;
• the choice of appropriate materials and the decision to use (or not to use) textbooks;
• (staff) development that assists language instructors in handling unfamiliar subject matter and content-area instructors in handling language issues;
• language- and content-faculty collaboration;
• the institutionalisation of CBI in light of available resources and the needs of faculty and students;
• systematic assessment to demonstrate
  1 students' language and content learning and
  2 program effectiveness.

Despite a number of challenges, CBI promises to afford some interesting perspectives of curriculum organisation in FLs, which might well lead the way to a cognitively and intellectually more satisfying learning experience for FL learners.

The final one of Young's defining characteristics of a curriculum of the past, namely that of it creating boundaries between school and everyday knowledge and problems around transferability of knowledge learnt in school to the so-called 'real' world is a complex issue in the context of FLs. Suffice it to note here that, although the topics and context within which communicative competence is practised in the FL classroom are supposedly modelled on real-life situations and fundamentally concerned with their simulation and with transfer to them, as we have noted elsewhere (see e.g. Pachler, 2005b), at least some of the topics and contexts can be seen to be of limited relevance and appropriateness as they are modelled on the linguistic needs of migrant workers and tourists rather than on those of 11–16-year-old adolescents. Furthermore, the paucity of the systemic conditions – i.e. the strictly limited amount of curriculum time available and the lack of opportunity to use and practise what has been learnt in the classroom outside school, as well as the overemphasis on memorisation of narrowly contextualised linguistic items and phrases, often with only little consideration of transfer across topics and often also with little recourse to the language system – result in pupils being able to do well in examinations. In other words, the GCSE examination tends to require performance, i.e. the ability to use the FL, rather than understanding and knowledge of the FL, and it tends to require little more than the memorisation of information. Therefore, despite the seeming emphasis on FL use in real-life situations and despite the process orientation of the MFL Order, which can, indeed, be considered to be the very essence of FL study, ironically, the transferability of FL knowledge acquired at school must sadly be deemed to be very low.

In view of the above, it can be argued that, although the MFL Order in itself is not necessarily a curriculum of the past, seen together with the GCSE, the examination typically taken by pupils aged 16 at the end of their compulsory schooling and, therefore, the examination testing the NC, it has to be deemed as such.

Also, the GCSE can be seen on balance to be at best only partially fit for the purpose of testing the NC MFL Order.

Owing to the increasing importance of ICT in everyday life, through the introduction of new technologies, such as the internet and Web 2.0

tools, as well as their becoming embedded in how we go about what we do and how we do it, for example through wireless networking, increasingly doing new things in new ways becomes possible, if not essential, in order to prepare pupils for the social and economic circumstances of the present and the future.

Kress (2000, p. 133), for example, argues that, in an era of social and economic instability, the curriculum should no longer be viewed as a means for cultural reproduction. Instead, he proposes the metaphor of 'design' (p. 134), i.e. curriculum as a design for the future, while pointing out that what needs to remain constant is 'the fundamental aim of all serious education: to provide those skills, knowledges, aptitudes and disposi-tions which would allow the young who are experiencing that curriculum to lead productive lives in the societies of their adult periods'. Kress (2000, p. 134) argues that the perceived needs of the nineteenth-century nation state, which state education for all was intended to serve, no longer pertain, and new configurations, such as globalisation, are starting to emerge. He (2000, pp. 135–6) analyses these changes in relation to eleven frames of education:

a) the frame around the institution of education;
b) the frame around the site of education;
c) the frame around the time of education;
d) the frame around the educational audience;
e) the frame around educational knowledge;
f) the framing between education as work and education as pleasure;
g) the frame between state and market;
h) the frame around locations of authority;
i) the frames of the globalisation of finance capital;
j) the changing frames of transport, whether of physical entities (commodities and people) or of information; and
k) the changing frames of a society being transformed willy-nilly from a conception of a homogeneously monocultural society to a decisively pluricultural one.

For the context of FL education this, for example, means: who is supposed to be providing FL education and who is to receive it? Where, when and how is it to take place? We would argue that this line of argumentation in particular strengthens the need for a reconceptualisation of curricular aims away from problematic notions of emulation of native-speaker ideals (see Chapter 5) and tourist topics towards intercultural (communicative) aims rooted in life in multicultural Britain and Europe.

Kress (2000, p. 138) furthermore stresses the changing landscapes of representation and communication, which he considers to have the most radically transformative effects on knowledge. In particular, he draws attention to the new media of communication, i.e. the shift from the era of mass communication to one of individuated communication, a shift from unidirectional communication to multidirectional communication, as well as the attendant shift from a passive audience to an interactive audience. In the context of FL education, these shifts are particularly pertinent as new technologies make available TL and target culture knowledge and information much more readily and allow for a hitherto unimaginable increase in access and exposure to FL acquisition (as opposed to learning) opportunities, unmediated by school, teachers or coursebooks. Individualised acquisition and learning opportunities embedded in new forms of computer-mediated, online learning networks potentially have a huge implication for what is learnt and how it is learnt.

Recent years have seen an increased focus on the notions of 'pupil participation' and 'pupil perspective'. In curricular terms, they relate to the extent of opportunities pupils have – or should have – to determine what is taught and how it is taught. Although strongly arguing the case for increased pupil participation and having led the research effort in this area for a number of years, Rudduck and Flutter (2000, p. 75) note that there are difficulties in directly eliciting pupils' views on the curriculum, in particular because they have no basis for comparing different versions and usually lack 'any systematic sense of curriculum possibilities'. In their experience, pupils have little to say about the curriculum as such, but they talk about forms of teaching and learning and what they call 'conditions of learning' in schools (see Figure 4.1).

Rudduck and Flutter posit that respect for pupils as individuals, fairness, autonomy and 'intellectual challenge that helps pupils to experience learning as a dynamic, engaging and empowering activity' (McCallum *et al.*, 2000, p. 277) affect pupils' commitment to learning and their identity as learners. In a similar vein, Cooper and McIntyre (1996, p. 89) argue that active involvement of pupils in the learning process is essential – cognitively and physically we would argue; that the teacher needs to possess a willingness to listen to and incorporate pupils' ideas; and that there needs to be an emphasis on pupils' constructing and sharing their own understandings during lessons. Rudduck and Flutter note the concept of

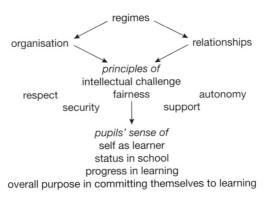

Figure 4.1 *The conditions of learning in school*
Source: Rudduck and Flutter, 2000, p. 85.

'relevance' in relation to curricular content but note that often an adult view of what was meaningful for young people tended to prevail. Incorporating pupil participation and pupil perspectives is, therefore, not (just) about FL teachers constructing choices for pupils, but about actually listening to what they have to say.

Rudduck and Flutter (2000, p. 76) argue, and we agree with them, that education professionals could do more to help pupils 'develop a language for talking about learning and about themselves as learners so that they feel it is legitimate for them actively to contribute to discussions about schoolwork with teachers and with each other'. We see this as one important curricular imperative for FL teachers. A key question is: are there spaces for pupils to have input in the process of curriculum planning?

Meighan (1998, pp. 36–8) distinguishes between a 'consultative curriculum', a 'negotiated curriculum' and a 'democratic curriculum'. According to him, a consultative curriculum is based on a teacher-led programme that features regular consultation opportunities for learners on the basis of which certain modifications are made. The negotiated curriculum is characterised by an increased degree of 'power sharing', akin to the negotiation of a contract about the curriculum. And the democratic curriculum notion sees learners writing, implementing and reviewing their own curriculum.

Kress (2000, p. 140) rightly stresses that his notion of design rests on agency, that 'it takes agency for granted, still as work, but no longer as acquisition but now definitely as "shaping work"'. We see this as the main challenge in relation to FL education. FL learning is notorious for its perceived difficulty, and a real question is whether learners will be able to find the levels of motivation to invest the necessary time and energy in FL learning without the 'systemic coercion' provided by timetabled lessons, watchful teachers and state examinations.

Finally, we want to mention the notion of 'multiliteracies' and 'multimodality' in this context to signal the profound changes to subject knowledge inherent in the increased use of new technologies. Basically, the terms stress the inter-connectedness of different semiotic modes – written and spoken language as well as still and moving images – in digital communication. In terms of the FL curriculum, the implications are that traditional conceptions of text no longer hold true and that learners need to be sensitised to using, and taught to be able to produce, multimodal text. Digital video production and video diaries etc. play a particularly pertinent role here (see e.g. Burn 2005).

An important organising principle used by the MFL Order, which has already been alluded to but is important to note specifically here, is the division into attainment targets. Although attainment targets as such were prescribed to the working group developing the MFL Order, the decision to adopt a distinct skill, e.g. listening, speaking, reading and writing, rather than a mixed skill approach, e.g. so-called receptive and productive skills, was one taken by the group. Unfortunately the group's deliberations are not available for public scrutiny, and it is, therefore, only possible to surmise that it has inter alia been adopted to reflect the traditional organisation of FL examination papers as well as the model adopted by the NC English Order some years earlier. In addition, the separation of the FL curriculum into distinct skill areas fits in neatly with a model of steady, linear and incremental development, which is evident in the level descriptors, and which Moore (2000) points out is regularly prioritised in educational policy documents and practices:

> When OFSTED inspectors visit schools, for example, they appear to expect to be able to perceive – and to report on – development or 'progression in each student's learning *during the course of the lesson itself* . . .' and not to be interested in the possibility that learning may proceed on occasions – or even at the level of generality – according to other possible models.
>
> (Moore, 2000, p. 29)

In conclusion to the above remarks, we would posit, with Young (1999, p. 475), that what is needed is a set of principles, underpinning curriculum planning and organisation, that relate the situated and codified aspects of knowledge, what he calls 'connective specialisation'. By that Young means a curriculum that still emphasises subject learning but not as an end in itself, that stresses the links between subject learning, the experience of learners and the purpose of the curriculum as a whole. In FL terms this means a curriculum that gives due consideration to cross-curricular work, the developmental stage of learners and their needs and interests as well as, by means of an increased focus on language awareness, the macro-political reality of globalisation and pan-Europeanisation.

To complement Young's tool for curricular analysis, we also – albeit only rather briefly – want to introduce a framework for coursebook analysis here, not least in view of the fact that coursebooks often constitute a hidden curriculum. Mamiala and Treagust (2003) stress the fact that coursebooks may be viewed as 'explanatory artefacts' that have a considerable influence on how learners construct phenomena of the subject domain and how to explain them. They further note that it is through coursebooks that learners normally acquire images of the subject domain. These, of course, at times sit ill at ease and/or are incompatible with their own experience of these phenomena. On the basis of previous frameworks, they propose six broad categories:

1 *Nature of explanation* is where the relationship between the phenomenon and the explanation may be one of either structure or function.
2 *Presentational format* determines whether the textbook's style of presentation is text-based or pictorial.
3 *Condition* is the degree of abstraction of an explanation and examines the extent to which a textbook used concrete examples to explain abstract phenomena/concepts.
4 *Level of enrichment* refers to a situation where attributes or limitations of an explanation are highlighted.
5 *Meaning making* refers to a sense-making process that is divided into four parts: creating differences, constructing entities, transforming knowledge and putting meaning to matter.
6 *Style of explanation* focuses on the form of presentation of concepts in the textbooks.

The ability to evaluate coursebooks and associated material, to know how best to use the coursebook and, where necessary, to supplement it with appropriate multimodal resources constitutes an important dimension of a FL teacher's subject knowledge. This becomes all the more important as FL pedagogy continues to move away from foregrounding grammatical knowledge and/or communicative competence towards focusing on intercultural communicative competence. Intercultural communicative competence, i.e. knowledge, skills, understanding and awareness of one's own culture and the ability to interpret and understand other cultures making effective use of the TL, is predicated on direct engagement with TL speakers, through direct interaction or via cultural artefacts. This, as experienced FL teachers will know, is not easily achieved by paper-based coursebooks only but also requires carefully planned first-hand exposure to the ways of thinking and believing that underpin the various ways of speaking and being. Coursebooks can be seen to provide a main vehicle for mediated exposure in FL teaching, and, in order to provide a better understanding of requisite concepts of the subject domain, in this case the TL as well as the associated foreign culture(s), it is essential that any material used focuses carefully on the nature and types of explanation given and the means and mechanisms deployed to bring about meaning making.

THE MFL ORDER FOR ENGLAND AND THE PURPOSES OF EDUCATION

It is interesting to note that since the so-called Harris Report in 1990, named after the chair of the working party convened by the Secretary of State to develop the MFL Order (DES/Welsh Office, 1990), none of the various MFL Orders published subsequently have deemed it necessary to set out an explicit set of purposes for the study of FLs in the secondary school. This can hardly be interpreted as a sign of confidence on the part of policymakers in FL study as an integral part of the secondary school curriculum as, since the recommendations were published, the place of FLs on the curriculum has been all but eroded. The purposes for FLs in the secondary school curriculum can probably best be explained with reference to the wording of the PoS, which implicitly picks up on many of the purposes identified in the 1990 report:

- to develop the ability to use the language effectively for purposes of practical communication;

- to form a sound base of the skills, language and attitudes required for further study, work and leisure;
- to offer insights into the culture and civilisation of the countries where the target language is spoken;
- to develop an awareness of the nature of language and language learning;
- to provide enjoyment and intellectual stimulation;
- to encourage positive attitudes to foreign language learning and to speakers of foreign languages and a sympathetic approach to other cultures and civilisations;
- to promote learning of skills of more general application (e.g. analysis, memorising, drawing of inferences);
- to develop pupils' understanding of themselves and their own culture.

(DES/Welsh Office, 1990, p. 3)

It is only in a recent guidance document for KS4 governing FLs in the part of compulsory schooling during which a FL is optional that the government (QCA, 2004) has set out how FLs can contribute to a broad and balanced curriculum. As these statements are very similar to the ones quoted above we will not list them here in detail. Suffice it to note, though, that it is curious that exactly at the point in time when FLs have been withdrawn from the KS4 curriculum because pupils all too often fail to see the purpose of learning a FL, the government seems to see the need to reiterate the principles and purposes for FLs in the hope, seemingly, to convince at least some schools not altogether to drop FLs at 14. It is less surprising that government once again approaches the subject from a strong vocational perspective, e.g. '(FLs) broaden the range and variety of accessible careers, improving employability and facilitating personal mobility' (QCA, 2004, p. 4), despite the fact that such attempts have at best only been of very limited benefit in the past. Some would argue that in fact the vocational rationale seen as an extension of a utilitarian rationale is mostly counter-productive, not least because there is 'a conspicuous lack of hard evidence that (FL) knowledge will increase productivity and employment' (Williams, 2000, p. 12).

In this chapter we do not offer a summary of the MFL Order as this has been done elsewhere (see Pachler and Field, 2001a). For a discussion of the 2007 NC Order see below as well as Pachler, Barnes and Field, 2008. Instead we home in on some key aspects that seem worth exploring. In particular, it seems of relevance here to question the match between the purposes supposedly underpinning the MFL Order and the extent to which they are actually picked up on in the Order itself.

Before we do so, it seems necessary to comment on the appropriateness and relevance of the objectives delineated above. Although such judgements invariably involve personal preferences and choices, and although there are questions around the comprehensiveness of the objectives listed, particularly in relation to the development of in-depth knowledge of the TL system, and the relative importance of the objectives, we would not argue with the objectives identified by the working group. We would, however, by way of comparison with curricula and the legislative frameworks in other countries, draw to the readers' attention the difficulties in achieving what is expected by the MFL Order in a context where pupils might have on average as few as 300 statutory FL lessons in classes of thirty or more. This compares very unfavourably with the amount of curriculum time available in other countries and with statutory frameworks in some Continental European countries, which stipulate much more favourable staff-student ratios.

It would be hard to argue, even for the fiercest critic, that the MFL Order does not focus on aspects of practical communication given the approach taken by the GCSE examination specifications, which – as we have noted already – are the real driver behind the schemes of work in use in schools, certainly in Years 10 and 11, i.e. at KS4, in which the study of FLs is now no longer compulsory, but also earlier. In many departments the curriculum is based around topic-based notions that map neatly onto the examination specifications either in a way that spreads topics thinly across KS3 and 4 and, thereby, ensures each topic is covered once with a period of intensive revision in Year 11, or a model that sees most topics covered more briefly but twice, namely once in each KS. The topic-based approach is aided, and as we would argue abetted, by another key driver, namely the hidden curriculum stipulated by the coursebook. Unfortunately, teaching by the book still prevails widely. In the defence of those FL teachers who draw heavily on the use of coursebooks, it has to be said that in view of the large number of lessons to be taught in an average week this is easily understandable. Also, of course, coursebooks can provide useful structure and support, not only for less experienced colleagues who are still exploring their pedagogical repertoire, but also for pupils for whom it can provide essential scaffolding. Nevertheless, we would warn of the potentially stifling effects of excessive adherence to any particular coursebook, as none is likely to cover all aspects of the FL curriculum equally well, and as slavish adherence can quell creativity, imagination and variety, which are all essential ingredients of good FL teaching. Also, as Alptekin (1993) rightly points out, coursebook writers invariably operate through culture-specific schemas and consciously or subconsciously transmit the views, values, beliefs, attitudes and feelings of specific societies. By implication, learners are exposed to – and tempted to acquire – as part of their evolving subject knowledge a certain cultural system that might – or might not as the case may be – accord with the realities of the dominant contexts in which the TL is spoken.

Whether or not the approach adopted by the overt and hidden curricula necessarily leads to effective language use we have already questioned.

The second, third and fourth objectives concerning the preparation for lifelong FL learning, cultural awareness and language awareness have to some extent already been discussed above: although in principle the structure of the MFL Order seems very well suited to the development of a sound basis for future learning, with the inclusion of two entire sections on language-learning skills, cultural awareness and language awareness in the PoS, the requirements of the examination specifications run counter to it by not sufficiently foregrounding them in the assessment and testing regime adopted.

The fifth and sixth objectives above, many commentators would argue, are least well catered for by the MFL Order. Indeed, it might be said that the staple diet of the GCSE and its emphasis on simple, transaction-orientated conversations and dialogues across many topics allow for little intellectual stimulation. Texts that are longer than a few sentences are the exception rather than the rule, and the topics prescribed by examination specifications can hardly be described as intellectually stimulating. Although there is nothing in the MFL Order that stops teachers from adopting an approach that is based on an enjoyable learning experience, the pressure brought to bear on them by a narrowly outcome-orientated system that judges their professional standing not by the extent to which pupils have an enjoyable and positive learning experience but by the grades they obtain in public examinations, means that enjoyment is not always top of the agenda. Nevertheless, many FL teachers go to great lengths, particularly in KS3, i.e. with pupils aged 11–14, to use games and playful approaches in order to keep pupils engaged. Sometimes playful approaches can come at the expense of effective learning experiences as they can mask the fundamental need for pupils to memorise a significant number of lexical items and phrases in the initial phases of their FL learning experience in order to build up a critical mass of vocabulary that will allow them to develop a syntactic understanding of the FL as well as furnish them with the ability to generate language and meaning of their own, and thereby make the FL learning experience a meaningful one. At A/AS level there clearly is a much stronger emphasis on intellectual challenge, with there being considerably more opportunity to work with longer texts and some examination specifications retaining the opportunity to study literary texts in the FL. In addition, a stronger emphasis on an engagement with the grammatical aspects of the TL adds intellectual challenge.

We have already alluded to the difficulties FL teachers have in relation to pupils understanding their own, and developing a sympathetic approach to other, cultures and civilisations. Given the context of a society that aligns itself much more strongly to the English-speaking world rather than multilingual Europe, the time allocation afforded the study of a FL on the curriculum has to be considered to be minimal and insufficient. Compared with many other European countries it can be argued to be. The societal context as well as the undisputed difficulty of FL study, particularly in the initial stages, make it very difficult for FL teachers to encourage positive attitudes to FL learning, particularly when pupils receive little to no reinforcement outside the classroom. Once again, at A/AS level there is much more scope – and curriculum time – to develop sympathetic approaches in pupils to other cultures.

It can be noted that of late there has been a welcome emphasis in FL classrooms on the promotion of learning skills more generally. This has been prompted by a considerable interest in this area in the specialist literature and has been mediated effectively in the professional literature (see in particular the two-part Special Issue of the *Language Learning Journal* in 2007 (35(1) and 35(2)) and Harris, 1997). Nevertheless, in relation to vocabulary learning – which for all intents and purposes can be seen as a central aspect of FL learning – comparatively little notice appears to have been taken of findings of SLA and FL learning research.

A number of researchers take the view that language processing is very often, particularly under the pressure of real-time communication, lexical in nature, i.e. frequently whole phrases and language chunks are being copied without internal processing and with little attention to their grammatical dimensions. We conclude from this that memorisation has a very important role to play in FL learning, possibly a more important role even than the understanding of grammatical rules, particularly in the initial phases of FL learning. We also conclude that the selection of input according to lexical criteria is very important.

In a very interesting study, Groot (2000) argues that the selection of relevant vocabulary is problematical in so far as the frequency of words rapidly diminishes after the 1,200 most frequent words and that the frequency of vocabulary depends significantly on the corpus used. This is particularly significant as in the initial phases of FL learning pupils tend not to learn more than approximately 2,000 high-frequency words. However, in order to achieve functional language competence a much larger vocabulary is necessary. Studies suggest that, to ensure reading comprehension of a non-specialist text, a minimal vocabulary of 5,000 words is required. For specialist academic texts the number doubles. Groot also points out that, in order to ensure sufficient comprehension, readers must be acquainted with more than 90 per cent of words in a text. The challenge, therefore, for FL teachers and learners is considerable. Not only do these assertions throw into question the sometimes dogmatic insistence on an emphasis on authentic material, which is strongly promoted by the MFL Order and which – owing to lack of space – cannot be discussed in any detail here, but also they bring to the fore the importance of a systematic approach to vocabulary learning and teaching.

Groot points out, rightly in our view, that although word explanations in the TL can be useful in the memorisation of vocabulary, the isolated presentation of vocabulary in bilingual lists is not effective in the long run. Natural and incidental first-language processes, as well as deduction of meaning through work with authentic texts, also don't offer a viable way forward. They require a much higher frequency of occurrence in order to lead to a staged embedding in the mental lexicon of learners than is possible in the context of classroom-based FL learning. Also, authentic texts are by and large produced with the intention of conveying information and not in order to illustrate meaning and use of specific words. Furthermore, Groot points out that it is often only access to the wider context that affords insights into the meaning and semantic properties of words, which the tendency in FL lessons to work with excerpts militates against. The most important reason for Groot as to why authentic texts are often not effective for emulating naturalistic vocabulary acquisition processes is simply the fact that they contain too many unknown words.

From all this Groot concludes that there is no way around intentional vocabulary learning. Although bilingual word lists might appear a more attractive short cut than presentation of new vocabulary in context and although they can yield quite good results in short-term memorisation, in relation to long-term learning they yield very disappointing results. The main question in the context of this chapter arising from this discussion is: do curricular prescriptions sufficiently draw on research findings such as these? In the case of vocabulary learning and acquisition in the context of the MFL Order the answer has to be: no.

THE NATIONAL CURRICULUM UNDER REVIEW

At the time of writing, the NC Orders for England were under review, with implementation of a new curriculum planned from September 2008. The review can be seen as a logical, and in part necessary, attempt to ensure that the curricular framework keeps up with developments in the educational world and that it evolves over time. Yet, the relative merits of the decision to make the study of a foreign language optional post-14 remains keenly debated among commentators and teachers alike.

The intention is for the revised programme of study to give teachers more flexibility and to reduce prescription, thereby creating more opportunity for teachers to cater for the needs of individual students. It represents an attempt to make the curriculum more interesting for pupils – the importance of enjoyment is stressed, for example – and it is also intended to provide a firmer foundation for education post-14. There is an emphasis on mutual understanding, personal fulfilment and global citizenship. Details can be found at www.qca.org.uk/secondarycurriculumreview.

The key concepts of the PoS are:

- linguistic competence
- knowledge about language
- creativity, and
- intercultural understanding.

In addition, the following key processes are identified:

- developing language-learning strategies; and
- developing language skills.

The expectation is for FL teachers to offer specific opportunities, such as use of ICT and authentic material, and to draw on a range of contexts, such as those afforded by learning about different countries and cultures.

Another significant change from earlier versions of the NC Orders lies in the expansion of the list of languages available for study to include Mandarin, Urdu or Arabic, depending on local needs and circumstances. This means that schools will no longer be required to offer a European language.

It is also important to note that the NC Orders are characterised by a set of underpinning values (self, relationships, society, environment), a personal, learning and thinking skills framework, as well as four curriculum dimensions, which are meant to provide a context and focus for work within and between subjects, namely:

- a global dimension
- enterprise
- creativity, and
- cultural understanding and diversity.

This brings into focus the question of whether the QAA proposals satisfy Young's criteria for a curriculum of the future, i.e. to what extent are they characterised by a knowledge creation orientation, or a transformative concept of knowledge, and how are they relevant to everyday life?

The new curriculum can certainly be seen to be addressing important issues of early twenty-first century life in multi-ethnic and multilingual Britain and Europe, namely the purpose of the curriculum of contributing to community cohesion as well as the development of values, not only in relation to the self but also in relation to others, society and the environment, notably respect and care for others, responsibility as a citizen, respect for religious and cultural diversity and the promotion of participation in the democratic process.

In relation to knowledge creation, the curriculum proposals are forward looking in so far as they afford equal importance to the 'how' of learning as well as the 'what', with their stronger focus on the skills of learning to learn and the personalisation of the curriculum. The question is to what extent these ambitions will be embraced.

THE FRAMEWORK FOR TEACHING MFL AT KS3

In contrast to the rather vague NC MFL Order, the government has introduced a set of detailed – if not to say interventionist – teaching objectives for FLs in Years 7–9, the only Key Stage at which the study of a FL is currently compulsory. Although the framework itself is non-statutory, pressure exerted through OFSTED makes non-compliance a virtual impossibility. In so doing, the government can be seen to be tightening its grip on what is being taught and how and, thereby, limiting the scope for professional judgement of FL teachers further. At the same time, it is extending its definition of curricular knowledge.

In the executive summary, the Framework (DfES, 2003, p. 7) makes some bold claims: 'The Framework is about learning languages and also about creating confident language learners, equipped with the skills and conventions of language learning. With this confidence and understanding, pupils should be well placed to learn other languages later.'

Noble though these assertions might be, the question remains whether they constitute wishful thinking. How secure is the evidence base under-pinning the Framework and what view of FL learning does it champion?

The Framework of objectives is set out under five headings: words; sentences; texts: reading and writing; listening and speaking; and cultural knowledge and contact. How valid is this assumed word-, sentence- and text-level hierarchy? And, how realistic is the assumed progression from 'foundation' in Year 7 via 'acceleration' in Year 8 to 'independence' in Year 9? How productive is the imposed structure of explicit teaching objectives, starters and plenaries?

By way of exemplification, Table 4.1 shows the staggering array of objectives to be covered in Year 7 by way of laying a foundation (see www.standards.dfes.gov.uk/secondary/keystage3/respub/mflframework/).

One wonders how realistic this complex web of requirements is for a period of study extending from at most 80 to 120 FL lessons.

FL EDUCATION AT PRIMARY LEVEL

The publication of the National Languages Strategy in December 2002 (DfES, 2002), saw the introduction of a commitment to an entitlement to FL learning so that every pupil at KS2 (aged 7–11) is offered the opportunity to study at least one FL and to develop their interest in the culture of other nations, at least in part in class time, by 2010, at the cost of making FL study at KS4 (age 14–16) optional. It would go beyond the scope of this chapter to discuss the virtues, or otherwise, of this policy in relation to the research evidence available. Suffice it to note that we

Table 4.1 *Year 7 MFL framework objectives*

Words

Pupils should be taught:

7W1   How to build and re-apply a stock of words relating to everyday contexts and settings

7W2   How to learn, use and appreciate the importance of some basic high-frequency words found in many contexts

7W3   How to accumulate and apply a stock of words for use in language learning and classroom talk

7W4   That gender and plural patterns in nouns may differ from English and how other words can be affected

7W5   Present tense forms of high-frequency verbs, examples of past and other tense forms for set phrases

7W6   The alphabet, common letter strings and syllables, sound patterns, accents and other characters

7W7   How to find and memorise the spelling, sound, meaning and main attributes of words

7W8   How to find or work out and give the meaning of unfamiliar words

Sentences

Pupils should be taught:

7S1   How to recognise and apply typical word order in short phrases and sentences

7S2   How to work out the gist of a sentence by picking out the main words and seeing how the sentence is constructed compared with English

7S3   How to adapt a simple sentence to change its meaning or communicate personal information

7S4   How to formulate a basic question

7S5   How to formulate a basic negative statement

7S6   How to formulate compound sentences by linking two main clauses with a simple connective

7S7   To look for time expressions and verb tense in simple sentences referring to present, past or close future events

7S8   Punctuation and orthographic features specific to phrases and sentences in the target language

7S9   How to understand and produce simple sentences containing familiar language for routine classroom or social communication

Table 4.1 (continued)

Texts

Pupils should be taught:

7T1 How to read and understand simple texts using cues in language, layout and context to aid understanding

7T2 How to read aloud a simple written text, attempting authentic pronunciation and some expression with regard to content

7T3 How to assess simple texts for gist, purpose, intended audience and degree of difficulty as a preliminary to reading

7T4 How to use a dictionary and other resources appropriately when working on text

7T5 How to assemble a short text using familiar sentence structure and known vocabulary

7T6 How to use simple texts as models or prompts for their own writing

7T7 How to evaluate and improve the quality of their written work

Listening and speaking

Pupils should be taught:

7L1 How to engage with the sound patterns and other characteristics of the spoken language

7L2 How to improve their capacity to follow speech of different kinds and in different contexts

7L3 To identify gist and some detail in continuous spoken passages about specific contexts

7L4 How to respond to face-to-face instructions, questions and explanations

7L5 How to contribute to spontaneous talk in the target language

7L6 How to evaluate and improve the quality and fluency of what they say

Cultural knowledge and contact

Pupils should:

7C1 Learn some basic geographical facts about the country and where its language is spoken

7C2 Learn about some aspects of everyday culture and how these compare with their own

7C3 Use authentic materials and experience direct or indirect contact with native speakers and writers

7C4 Meet simple stories, songs or jokes, or texts based on them, in the target language

7C5 Learn the social and linguistic conventions of common situations such as greetings

remain sceptical about the merits of this fundamental shift in approach to FL study at a policy level.

Sharpe delineates the following six main aims associated with early FL teaching:

- to exploit the linguistic and cognitive flexibility of primary-age children (the 'young learners are better learners' argument);
- to exploit the attitudinal and motivational flexibility of primary-age children (the 'young learners are more eager and malleable learners' argument);
- to raise levels of achievement through learning (possibly more) languages for longer (the 'higher standards' argument);
- to exploit the opportunities presented by the particular circumstances of the context of primary schooling for promoting language awareness and second language acquisition (the 'primary context advantages' argument);
- to provide young children with an important and enriching experience that will better equip them to understand the realities of life in the third millennium (the European/global citizenship 'entitlement' argument); and
- to equip the next generation with the requisite knowledge, skills and understanding that will enable them to function effectively in international contexts (the 'social and economic benefits' argument).

(Sharpe, 2001, p. 32)

Once again, a detailed discussion of these aims goes well beyond the scope of this chapter. However, it is worth noting that together they advance a strong rationale in support of an early start for FL learning. Nevertheless, it is important to note that research evidence from work on SLA and FL learning is inconclusive about some of these arguments and assertions. McLaughlin (1992), for example, expresses the view that the beliefs that children learn second languages quickly and easily and that the younger the child, the more skilled in acquiring a second language they become are but myths.

In curricular terms the policy document states categorically that it is within the responsibility of head teachers how to operationalise this entitlement, with a network approach being particularly promoted. CILT provides some guidance on curricular models and approaches based on various projects (see www.nacell.org.uk/profdev/ell_curricular_models. pdf). Its models are grouped in the following three broad categories:

1 individual primary schools using limited resources and introducing some exposure to FLs, perhaps as part of the citizenship or literacy curriculum;
2 clusters of primary schools, working in partnership with a language college and other local secondary schools; and
3 schemes supported by the LEA, involving close liaison between primary and secondary schools and offering broad provision of languages integrated into the curriculum.

Driscoll (1999, pp. 14–16) distinguishes language acquisition and sensitisation programmes, with the former focusing on the development of linguistic competence and the latter foregrounding the cultivation of positive attitudes towards language learning. In addition to approaches to teaching aims, she (1999, pp. 17–19) distinguishes approaches to instruction in terms of what she calls an overt teaching approach and a holistic one. The former sees the FL timetabled as an additional subject in the curriculum, with FL learning being the central focus of lessons and taught systematically; the latter approach integrates the FL in a variety of ways into the existing curriculum. According to Driscoll (1999, p. 18), 'the majority of holistic models include a stand-alone component to introduce, practice, and reinforce the language systems and vocabulary as preparation for activities which take place throughout the day.'

Sharpe (2001, pp. 113–17) argues that the choice of approaches to teaching aims and instruction, at least in part, is related to the adoption of specialist versus generalist teaching, which in turn is sometimes predicated on conviction but often also on the availability or otherwise of specialist FL teaching expertise. He lists the following specific advantages and disadvantages of using specialist teachers:

- Advantages:
  1 excellent expert linguistic role model;
  2 correct pronunciation and intonation are taught;
  3 specialist teachers are able to use the TL spontaneously;

> 4 specialist teachers have knowledge of the linguistic and cultural context;
>
> 5 lessons are planned in the context of full knowledge of the TL.

- Disadvantages:
    1 variability in pedagogic expertise;
    2 outsider status: fragmented teacher–pupil relationships;
    3 inability to integrate the foreign language into the whole curriculum or embed it in pupil experience.

Sharpe (2001, p 117) concludes that the actual difference between most non-native specialists and secondary FL teachers on the one hand and primary generalist FL teachers on the other is a difference of degree, not kind.

In relation to the knowledge of FL teachers working at primary level, a recently published systematic review of the characteristics of effective FL teaching to pupils between ages 7 and 11 (Modern Languages Review Group, 2004, pp. 4–5), found that teachers' knowledge is important and encompasses the following:

- the subject:
    - the foreign language content
    - the skill to use the target language
    - the target culture
- subject-specific teaching methods
- age-specific teaching methods
- resources
- primary curriculum
- children as individuals
- children's learning needs.

Also of importance in terms of FL teacher subject knowledge is, of course, the KS2 framework, published in 2005, which identifies three strands of teaching and learning: oracy, literacy and intercultural understanding. These strands are underpinned by opportunities in the areas of knowledge about language (KAL) and language learning strategies (LLSs). In relation to KAL, the framework is based on the premise that, when children learn a new language, they reinforce and reinterpret knowledge and understanding from their L1. With regard to LLSs, the framework suggests that, in the early years, children should develop an awareness of some of the basic approaches to learning a new language with a view to applying them to use known language in new contexts. Secondary FL teachers need to be cognisant of these requirements and processes in the transition from primary to secondary.

For a detailed discussion of secondary school FL teacher knowledge see Chapter 2.

Of particular importance for FL teachers at secondary level is the issue of transition from the primary school to the secondary classroom, for example in terms of avoiding repetition and building on established foundations in terms of knowledge, skills and understanding, as well as, of course, in terms of approaches to teaching and learning. In view of the disparate patterns of primary provision seemingly emerging across the country, this would seem to be a key concern for years to come.

CONCLUSION

In this chapter we examined the curricular knowledge faced by FL teachers in England in the context of a more general examination of the variables influencing curriculum planning and organisation. In particular, we stressed the influence of dominant societal and cultural values and beliefs. In the context of England, and the United Kingdom more widely, we bemoaned the prevalence of a certain anti-intellectual and anti-European climate, which presents considerable challenges for FL teachers in making their subject palatable to learners. We distinguished curricula at national and local levels as well as formal, informal and hidden curricula. As far as the hidden curriculum is concerned, we stressed the importance of various non-statutory documents as well as the influence of the coursebook on the teaching and learning process. Also, we noted the desirability of cross-curricular approaches to FL teaching and discussed the potential of content-based instruction in bringing about a new type of FL curriculum. Finally, we discussed the recent FL policy emphasis on primary FLs and its implications, in particular in terms of curriculum organisation and planning.

QUESTIONS FOR DISCUSSION

1   Which views of society do you consider the NC MFL Order to imply? What values and assumptions does it contain? What is the rationale for FL study in the NC?

2   We identified different approaches to curriculum organisation: FLs as a separate subject, cross-curricular integration and content-based instruction. What are the relative strengths and weaknesses of these approaches? And, what do you deem to be the merits of an increased focus on pupil participation?

3   Our discussion discerns formal and hidden curriculum. Which types of hidden FL curricula can be distinguished and what is their impact?

4   Is the NC MFL Order a curriculum of the past or a curriculum of the future (Young, 1999)?

5   What, in your view, are the FL-specific skills, knowledges, aptitudes and dispositions pupils need in order to lead productive lives in the societies of their adult life (Kress, 2000)?

6   What do you consider to be the implications of new technologies and new media of communication for the FL curriculum?

7   Consider Meighan's (1988) notions of a 'consultative', 'negotiated' and 'democratic curriculum'. What do you consider their relative merits to be and how realistic are they in the context of the NC FL Order and your school?

8   Are you convinced by any of the arguments listed here in support of primary FL learning?

CURRICULUM, POLICY AND GUIDANCE/EXEMPLIFICATION DOCUMENTS

At a policy level the National Languages Strategy is key reading:

DfES (2002) *Languages for All: languages for life. A strategy for England,* London: DfES. Available www.dfes.gov.uk/languagesstrategy/.

The following documents set out the curricular requirements for FLs at 11–16:

DfES (2003) *Framework for Teaching Modern Foreign Languages: Years 7, 8 and 9,* London: DfES. Available www.standards.dfes.gov.uk/keystage3/respub/mflframework/.

DfES/QCA (1999) *The National Curriculum for England: modern foreign languages.* London: DfES. Available www.nc.uk.net.

QCA (2000) *GCSE Criteria for Modern Foreign Languages.* London: QCA. Available www.qca.org.uk/subjects/downloads/modern_foreign_lang.pdf.

QCA (2000) *Schemes of Work: secondary modern foreign languages.* London: QCA. Available www.standards.dfes.gov.uk/schemes3/subjects/?view=get.

QCA (2004) *Modern Foreign Languages in the Key Stage 4 Curriculum.* London: QCA. Available www.qca.org.uk/ages14-19/downloads/MFL_at_KS4_web.pdf.

QCA (2007) *The Secondary Curriculum Review.* Available www.qca.org.uk/secondarycurriculumreview/.

QCA (2007) *Modern Foreign Languages. Programme of study: Key Stage 3.* Available online at www.qca.org.uk/libraryAssets/media/MFL_KS3_PoS.pdf.

At the time of writing there is only one core document for the 16–19 phase:

QCA, ACCAC, CCEA (1999) *Subject Criteria for Modern Foreign Languages: GCE advanced subsidiary and advanced level specifications.* London: QCA, ACCAC, CCEA. Available www.qca.org.uk/ages14-19/subjects/mfl_1736.html.

For the primary school context the following documents are of importance:

CILT (no date) *Early Language Learning: curricular models.* Available www.nacell.org.uk/profdev/ell_curricular_models.pdf.

CILT (2006) *Primary Languages – the training zone for teaching and learning languages at Key Stage 2.* Available www.primarylanguages.org.uk/.

DfEE (1998) *National Literacy Strategy Framework for Teaching.* London: DfEE. Available www.standards.dfes.gov.uk/literacy/.

DfES (2005) *Key Stage 2 Framework for Languages.* London: DfES. Available www.standards.dfes.gov.uk/primary/publications/languages/framework/.

DfES/QCA (1999) *The National Curriculum for England: modern foreign languages.* London: DfES/QCA. Available www.nc.uk.net.

QCA (2000) *Schemes of Work: primary modern foreign languages.* London: QCA. Available www.standards.dfes.gov.uk/schemes3/subjects/?view=get.

Chapter 5

Understanding pupil knowledge

INTRODUCTION

As pupil learning is the ultimate goal of all FL teaching, the question of pupil knowledge is often taken for granted in theories of FL pedagogy. Affecting how and what pupils think about languages and language learning is in many ways the central purpose of language teaching, underlying almost all aspects of FL education, yet reflection on the issue separately and as an in-depth object of study in its own right has been largely overlooked by both theorists and classroom practitioners. However, if teacher cognition is rightly recognised as an important element in the process of classroom language education then it seems equally legitimate to argue for a theory of pupil cognition in this learning context. In fact, the argument we are making in this book is that the role of pupil cognition forms part of a threefold interrelationship between teacher knowledge (individual teachers' knowledge, beliefs and assumptions related to language teaching and learning), curricular knowledge (in its broadest sense, consisting of different interlinking domains such as subject knowledge, corpus knowledge, professional knowledge) and pupil knowledge.

It should be said at the outset that we are not proposing here a simplistic, symmetrical framework that sees the teacher as a didactic agent of the teaching experience who transmits aspects of the curricular knowledge, seen as a given and incontrovertible body of information, to the pupil who is both the recipient and the outcome of the process. Each of these elements in the equation is complex, diverse and changing. The relationship between them is also complex. Effective teachers learn from their pupils by being alert to their response to the teaching, which in turn is informed and affected by that response. Equally, what we are calling curricular knowledge (the content of language courses, of exam specifications, of the NC and so on) is defined in terms of teacher and pupil knowledge. The language content and skills objectives are selected inter alia, as we have seen in Chapter 3, on the basis of what has been called pedagogical content knowledge (Shulman, 1987). In other words, there is a rationale for selecting and omitting certain elements of grammar and vocabulary on the basis of teaching objectives rather than purely linguistic ones. Similarly, this rationale takes account of the learner context. In the case of secondary school language learning, the content is framed in situations that present themselves as being authentic to adolescent discourse. The vocabulary and phrases taught are ones that claim to be the sort of language a teenager might use in these situations. In other words, the three elements in this equation are each both a source and an effect of influence on each other.

WHAT IS PUPIL COGNITION?

This term is used here as a global construct to refer to the internal, mental processes that pupils employ or can be encouraged to employ in relation to their study and learning of a FL at school. If we took descriptions of 'teacher cognition' as a starting-point, we would identify the following main categories of cognition: knowledge, belief and assumptions. To put it very simply, at the risk of distortion, FL teachers' knowledge consists of their knowledge of the language and the culture(s) of the countries where the TL is spoken; their beliefs could be about how best to teach languages (e.g. that grammar is best taught deductively) or about how pupils learn FLs (e.g. belief that learning a FL at an early, primary school age leads to improved chances of acquisition in the long run); assumptions refer to tacit beliefs that are either subconscious and often invisible to the person themselves but visible to a colleague or researcher, or they can be beliefs that the teacher does not make explicit because he or she assumes they are shared by many other people.

The importance that researchers have given to the study of teacher cognition is most often linked to frameworks for explaining FL teachers' decision making in the classroom.

How far can the term 'pupil cognition' mirror the properties and purposes outlined above? It is worth considering each category separately.

115

Knowledge domains

One way to define the word 'knowledge' in relation to FL teaching and learning is to consider the different types of knowledge goal it refers to in these contexts. These knowledge goals or 'domains' are clearly not fixed permanently but are dependent on decisions taken on the curriculum, by the QCA, Awarding Bodies, policymakers, school inspectors (HMI) and coursebook authors, as well as, potentially, by different teachers and learners individually. However, despite this transience, they are relatively easy to identify because they are usually made public in some way or another.

The following is an adapted version of a set of 'domains of pedagogical knowledge' that a language teacher might be expected to access as part of the function of classroom practice. This list is an adapted version of one produced by Gatbonton (1999) with reference to adult teachers of English as a second language (ESL):

- knowledge about the goals and subject matter of teaching;
- knowledge of how to manage specific language items so that pupils can learn them;
- knowledge about the pupils and what they bring to the classroom;
- knowledge about class management techniques and procedures;
- knowledge about appropriate teacher–pupil relationships;
- knowledge about evaluation of pupil learning and performance.

Pupil knowledge can also be said to have distinctive qualities and to be divisible into separate domains:

- knowledge of the subject matter taught;
- knowledge of the curriculum: course content;
- knowledge of language learning strategies;
- knowledge of own progress: metacognition.

Looking at the first domain in the second list, one might ask oneself the question: what does it mean to know a language?

Declarative and procedural knowledge

Knowledge is commonly divided into two categories: declarative know-ledge, also known as content knowledge (knowing that . . .), and procedural knowledge (knowing how to . . .). In FL learning, the development of proficiency in the four language skills can be described as a form of procedural knowledge. Another way of describing this form of knowledge is to refer to it as 'language use'. Pupils' competence in understanding and formulating grammatical rules could, on the other hand, be described as an example of declarative knowledge. This distinction applies equally to the development of cultural awareness within the FL framework. Learning facts about the target culture(s) (with respect to both high and low culture) is a form of content knowledge learning, whereas developing pragmatic and intercultural competence involves procedural knowledge.

Is knowledge competence or proficiency or mastery?

The richness of the English language can sometimes unfortunately be a source of obfuscation. Often these knowledge-related terms are used interchangeably or in a circular chain of definitions that, if handled loosely, fail to provide us with a clear understanding of the phenomenon in question. The terms, for instance, of 'competence' and 'proficiency' are often used interchangeably. After all, many European languages do not have a separate word for 'proficiency'. *Compétence* in French or *competencia* in Spanish are used to distinguish nuances of meaning and use that in English are often highlighted through the alternative use of the words 'competence' and 'proficiency'. One of the differences is in the use of 'proficiency' as referring to something measurable, as in 'proficiency tests', in contrast to 'competence', which, according to Duranti (1997, p. 14), can refer to 'the capacity for language, that is, the knowledge – mostly unconscious – that a native speaker has of the principles that allow for the interpretation and use of a particular language'. However, consider the use of the word in the UK government's 'Languages Ladder' scheme (DfES, 2004a), which aims at providing endorsement of 'competence in FL learning' from primary to adult language learning (see Table 5.1). It is unfortunate that 'proficiency' and 'mastery' are used as labels to indicate separate levels of 'competence'.

Perhaps the most apt connotation of the word 'proficiency' derives from its etymology: *proficere*, meaning 'to advance' or 'to make progress' in Latin; *pro* (forward) + *facere* (to make). This aptly captures the notion of movement, continuation and progression that is at the heart of the development of FL proficiency.

However, rather than looking for definitional distinctions between these terms, it may prove more fruitful to consider theoretical models of

Table 5.1 Mapping of qualification levels

NQF	NC levels	General qualifications	Language Ladder stages	Common European Framework (approx.)
Entry level	1–3	Entry 1–3	Breakthrough 1–3	A1 (A2)
Level 1	4–6	Foundation GCSE	Preliminary 4–6	A2 (B1)
Level 2	7–EP	Higher GCSE	Intermediate 7–9	B1
Level 3		AS/A/AEA	Advanced 10–12	B2
Level 4			Proficiency 13	C1
Level 5			Mastery 14	C2

Source: www.dfes.gov.uk/languages/DSP_languagesladder.cfm

knowledge in this context. 'Theory' here is seen as a conceptual scheme that presents a relatively small number of propositions that seek to describe, explain or predict human mental processes. One of the first extended attempts to outline a theory of knowledge in the context of FL learning was made by Stern (1983). The following list offers a summary of the key features of L1 he identified as being relevant to second language teaching.

1   The language user knows the rules governing his/her native language and s/he can apply them without paying attention to them.

2   The native speaker has an intuitive grasp of the linguistic, cognitive, affective and sociocultural meanings expressed by language forms.

3   Linguistic competence refers to formal and semantic features of the language.

4   The native speaker spontaneously uses language for the purpose of communication and has an intuitive understanding of the sociolinguistic functions of a language in use.

5   Linguistic and communicative competence manifests itself in language behaviour receptively and productively.

6   The native speaker uses the L1 'creatively'.

7   A child has linguistic and communicative competence. As language development takes place, the child advances from a single competence through stages of increasing differentiation to one in which his/her language use reaches that of the adult environment in which he/she lives.

8   Different L1 users are likely to have competence to different degrees.

9   The native speaker has 'an internal system', 'mechanism', 'structure', 'network' or 'schema', the first language competence or proficiency, which processes language.

10   Each individual has his/her own competence.

11   The concept of competence (or proficiency) is a construct that is accessible only through inference from the language behaviour of the individual, his/her performance in listening, speaking, reading, or writing.

Underlying Stern's model are a number of assumptions that have more recently been both influential and recognised as inadequate with reference to FL learning.

Native-like proficiency

The influence of this idea underlies the communicative competence model of language learning and is a tacit ideal that the learner strives to attain as an ultimate goal. The practical adoption of this notion is perhaps most clearly apparent in the mark scheme for the FLs GCSE exam, normally taken at age 16, which used the criterion of 'comprehensibility to a sympathetic native speaker' as a criterion for judging pupils' work. But which native speaker should the learner emulate? Given the range of dialects, accents, levels of articulacy, shades of register from formal to slang, and the multicultural tapestry of all discourse communities, this construct is of limited use as a definition of pupils' language knowledge. The extent to which reference to the notion of 'native speaker' has become unfashionable can be gauged from the following quote from the preamble to the Common European Framework:

> [The aim of language education] is no longer seen as simply to achieve 'mastery' of one or two, or even three languages, each taken in isolation, with the 'ideal native speaker' as the ultimate model. Instead the aim is to develop a linguistic repertory, in which all linguistic abilities have a place.
>
> (Council of Europe Modern Languages
> Division, 2001, p. 5)

In their study into the decline of uptake in FLs at Higher Grade in Scottish secondary schools, McPake *et al.* (1999) concluded that the unrealistic aspirations set by the native-like fluency ideal behind current courses are a significant contributory factor to pupils' lack of confidence in their ability to communicate with native speakers.

A different framework for defining the language learning context turns on the notion of 'authenticity'. Instead of seeing this in terms of communication between the learner as a non-native speaker and a hypothetical native speaker (NNS → NS), 'authenticity' can be viewed as TL proficiency at the service of meaningful, 'real', communication with other non-native speakers (NNS → NNS). English is not the only 'global language', though it is the most widespread. There will be situations in life where French or German, say, will be the common language between an English native speaker and another national who does not speak English. Of more immediate relevance, however, is the aim of developing pupils' use of the TL in the FL classroom in order to communicate effectively and meaningfully with each other. Authenticity here is established through focus on the message rather than on the linguistic status of the addressee. With younger pupils, such exchanges will emerge within defined pair work tasks, whereas, with older and more advanced pupils, this will also take the form of extended presentations or less controlled whole-class discussion.

'Competence' in Stern's model draws on the Chomskyan distinction between competence and performance, the former referring to an internal, subconscious state of knowledge that influences outward visible performance. For FL teachers, the aim is to infer the level of a pupil's competence in the FL from performance in outward data such as tests, classroom interaction, homework and so on.

The qualities of FL pupil knowledge

Examining the qualities of pupil FL knowledge in the context of FL learning, seven key features need to be recognised at the outset.

First, in contrast to most other holders of knowledge, pupils studying FLs at school are developing what is essentially 'beginner's knowledge'. This is of course literally the case in Year 7, the first year of secondary school, or earlier if studied at primary school, but throughout KS3 (Years 7–9) and KS4 (Years 10–11), with the exception of fluent and exceptionally able pupils, the extent of acquisition will remain limited though growing. There is, therefore and unsurprisingly, a heavy dependence on sources of knowledge, primarily the teacher, but also others such as the coursebook, dictionary, media resources, native speakers, other learners in their class, parents and so on. Consequently, although interesting and valuable work has been done on the importance of developing learner independence, it is widely accepted (by language educationists from Comenius onwards) that this develops in more advanced stages of FL learning. It is equally accepted that the key factor in early stages is 'comprehensible input' (Krashen, 1985, p. 2) from a number of sources, including the teacher, despite the practical difficulties of operationalising this concept with a class of thirty or so pupils.

121

Second, pupil knowledge acquisition in the FL context can be described as an **ongoing process**. Although this is true of virtually all subjects, it is particularly so in the case of FL learning. Pupils do not reach a stage at which they can claim to master, say, the ability to write in French in the way that a pupil learning science can be said to have good knowledge of electricity as a result of focused study of the topic.

Third, unlike many other subjects, the stages of FL teaching do not often begin with knowledge input because it is usually not the initial stimulus in the language acquisition process. What form of knowledge is exhibited in a pupil's being able to say, in appropriate contexts, '*J'aime le dessin*' or '*Nous sommes allés au cinéma*' or '*Quelle heure est-il?*'? In most cases, such phrases are learnt as unanalysed chunks, memorised through repeated whole-class oral practice (see e.g. Mitchell and Martin, 1997, pp. 15–16). Competence in using these phrases does entail a degree of understanding (for instance, here, the correct gender, the correct auxiliary, the inverted form all require the operationalisation of formal knowledge). But existing research (e.g. Green and Hecht, 1992; East, 1995) and common sense tell us that learners can use the language correctly and still be unable to provide correct explanations for the grammar. Pupil knowledge of a FL is therefore largely **dependent on memory processes and language use** and less dependent on factual information.

Fourth, a key feature of all language acquisition, whether of L1 or L2, and at all levels of competence, is the process of **automatization** whereby parts of the language enter the learner's subconscious and s/he is able to make use of it effectively without paying full attention to the fact. Johnson (2001, p. 107) illustrates this phenomenon by comparing it with the condition in driving whereby a learner driver eventually is able to perform gear changes without thinking about it in the course of driving. In the language context, the process of automaticity 'frees up' space in the learner's mind either in order to use more language in an utterance by focusing less on one aspect that has now been acquired, or it can be seen as freeing the learner 'to think about *what* he is saying, not *how* he is saying it'.

Fifth, as many researchers have pointed out (e.g. Macrory and Stone, 2000; McLaughlin, 1990), pupil cognition of a FL does not progress in a linear and incremental way towards 'TL norms' but is characterised by a fluctuating process of loss and gain that forms a complementary **restructuring** of acquired language:

Seen in these terms, an increase in error rate in one area may reflect an increase in complexity or accuracy in another, followed by over-generalization of a newly acquired structure, or simply a sort of overload of complexity which forces a restructuring, or at least a simplification, in another part of the system.

(Lightbown, 1985, p. 177)

Sixth, although the first feature in our list emphasises the fresh start element of school FL learning, there is a sense in which this is not entirely a case of *tabula rasa*. FL teachers can exploit at least two dimensions of prior knowledge with their pupils. First, some individual pupils will have had personal contact with the language and country they are studying. They may have visited the country with parents, may have friends and relatives of that nationality, may have penfriends and so on. This personal contact, however slight, may contribute to the learner's early interest and, therefore, acquisition of the language. Second, and on a more widespread scale, all FL learners already have knowledge of a L1. The precise extent and manner in which L2 learning is influenced by L1 knowledge are debatable, but that there is or could be a link is widely acknowledged. One way in which this is manifest is through the overt teaching of literacy in the FL classroom. This is often carried out in English (with the approval of the NC) and, therefore, pupils' prior understanding of English language and grammar as taught in their primary school will be activated in their learning about, say, the use of adjectives in French. In addition, individual learners are liable mentally to make connections between the new language they are learning and their own mother tongue. Pupils may silently notice for themselves that the written form of '*melon*' in French is the same as in English or that '*azúcar*' in Spanish is like 'sugar'. Pupils may instinctively make comparisons between the languages, and teachers can develop strategies to exploit this form of knowledge base. Even within the communicative classroom, therefore, **comparisons and contrasts between L1 and L2** (the essence of translation) have a place.

Finally, pupils' knowledge of the L2 they are learning is **vulnerable** in the sense of being liable to fade due to insufficient opportunities to practise or reinforce that knowledge outside the classroom. Though the internet and other aspects of the modern global world have increased the opportunities for supporting FLs beyond the classroom, this remains a remote prospect. Although pupils are often able implicitly and incidentally to reinforce their knowledge of English, Maths and Science, for instance,

123

through everyday interaction at home, this is not the case for the majority of pupils learning a FL. Natural, unplanned opportunities for consolidation, practice or extension are, for many, negligible. Hawkins (1981) famously used the metaphor of 'gardening in the gale' to describe the struggle that a pupil's FL has to make in the onslaught of mother tongue exposure outside the classroom. It is not only, however, the storm of the L1 that the budding L2 has to contend with but also, very often, with acute lack of nourishment.

Beliefs

As with the matter of pupil knowledge, beliefs can be treated as factors that pre-exist in the pupils' conscious and subconscious mind or as phenomena that can be developed by the teacher in order to foster greater openness to the TL and cultures and, therefore, more effective learning. In other words, pupil beliefs can either be seen as something that the teacher or researcher can seek to bring into the open in order better to understand the pupils' disposition underlying their performance in the classroom, or, alternatively, the teacher can seek to influence or nurture certain beliefs while dispelling others in the interests of more effective reception of the teaching.

FL teachers are frequently confronted with signals from their pupils during lessons that are intended to indicate hidden views and attitudes. Often these signals are playful and part of the pupil–teacher banter on the classroom stage. For instance, the staple question, usually at Year 7, aimed at practising 'likes and dislikes + school subjects', '*Tu aimes le français?*' invariably elicits the cheeky reply '*Non, je déteste le français!*'

More often than not, this does not express the pupil's real views but is the expected response in front of an expectant audience. In the full flow of the lesson it is natural for a teacher to brush aside these signals as unwelcome distractions that interrupt the teaching of the main objectives. Equally, teachers can legitimately feel that, especially in whole-class situations, taking the lid off pupils' attitudes and beliefs towards the FL and to the process of studying it can quickly generate further, more widespread disaffection with the enterprise. There are times when having a public discussion of the relative value of learning a FL can be as sensitive an undertaking as any delicate topic in a personal, social and health education (PSHE) lesson. But, classroom management issues aside, how important is it for a languages teacher to access pupils' beliefs about what and how they are learning? Pupils' beliefs have the following roles in the process of FL teaching and learning:

1 as an opportunity for dialogue about the value and purpose of the lessons
2 as a way of co-constructing appropriate beliefs and attitudes
3 as a way of allowing the voice of the pupil to be heard in this context
4 as a way of airing and subsequently counteracting prejudices and stereotypes
5 as a way of acknowledging the personal dimension of the language learning experience
6 as a way of investigating pupils' perceptions of specific aspects of foreign language learning
7 as a way of encouraging pupils to articulate balanced views as part of a constructive process of metacognitive reflection on their own learning and understanding.

Beliefs about the nature of the TL

Pupils often hold strong convictions about the FL they are learning, and some of the influencing factors are external to the language itself. Each school tends to develop its own cultural attitude vis-à-vis the study of different FLs, created largely by pupil consensus. This pupil perspective of the value and interest of individual languages can spread through a school through peer group interaction. Often this consensus is built on the reputations of the different FLs teachers in the school. The language is closely identified, whether positively or negatively, with the teacher in the pupils' mind (especially in cases where a class has been taught the language by the same teacher in successive years). Similarly, teachers and researchers have commented on the pattern of pupil opinion about the nature of the FL. French is seen as a more 'feminine' language, and German more 'masculine'. There is, of course, no linguistic justification for this view – it is merely a reflection of stereotypes that themselves are historically and socially defined, as is indicated by this quote from a 'high-proficiency' Year 9 boy interviewed in a study on motivation: 'French is the language of love and stuff [and German is] the war, Hitler and all that' (Williams *et al.*, 2002, p. 520). Correspondingly, in many studies, such as the research carried out by Arnot and Gubb (2001, p. 81) in schools in West Sussex, girls in general have been found to prefer French, whereas boys have preferred German.

Beliefs about speakers of the TL

For many pupils their attitudes towards a FL (especially one they are learning at school) are closely bound up with their attitudes towards the native speakers of that language. Attitude is in part generated by beliefs. In their study of the conceptions of French, German, Spanish and Italian people of 216 5–10-year-old English schoolchildren, Barrett and Short (1992) found that strong attitudes and ideas about foreign peoples are formed even before the pupils receive any factual information about them. The researchers found that the rank order of frequencies with which the children claimed to have visited the four target countries was Spain > France > Italy > Germany; this closely paralleled the rank order in which the inhabitants of these countries were liked. The most frequently cited sources of information about these nationalities were television, parents and books. Teachers were rarely cited. This is not too surprising given the scarcity of FL teaching in primary schools at the time, but it does suggest that teachers of other subjects do not succeed in effective teaching about other nationalities and are perhaps still largely inward looking. Barrett and Short also found that the older children in the study tended to express more differentiated and more positive responses to the different nationalities; they also report a strong correlation between most well-liked nationalities and ones they had most information about (French and Spanish). For the secondary languages teacher, the significance of these findings is that the pupils they are teaching a language to *ab initio* more often than not have already formed a set of half-conceived notions and attitudes towards the culture and speakers of that language, which they are in the process of shedding or transforming through a process of maturation. The canvas in front of them is not entirely blank.

Beliefs about teaching

Pupils' acknowledgement of the role of the teacher in influencing their attitudes towards the study of a certain language has been reported by several researchers investigating pupil motivation. In her study of uptake of FLs post-16, Fisher (2001, p. 38) encountered several pupils who held the view 'that the teacher in MFL lessons was even more important than in other subjects'. When describing what they found most valuable about the 'good' language teachers they had been taught by, the pupils 'mentioned a friendly atmosphere in the class', and that the teachers were 'sympathetic and helpful'.

Pupils, including habitually reluctant learners, usually express strong views about how FL teaching should be done. Sometimes these views are coloured by previous experience of teaching. A new teacher taking over a class from someone else or a beginner teacher taking temporary responsibility for a class while on placement will invariably encounter comments such as: 'Miss Black used to let us use a dictionary in tests' or 'Can we play noughts and crosses, please? Mr White always did at the end of a lesson' or even 'Miss, speak in English! Mr Brown always did. I don't understand French!'. First, it is important to distinguish between comments that are made as a way of testing the new teacher's authority and signals of temporary allegiance to the familiar in the face of the new. However, it is also useful to recognise that pupils can also have some deep-seated and strongly held views about FL teaching that seem to transcend the influence of particular teachers they have encountered. Paradoxically, given that most KS3 pupils, at least, clamour for fun and interactive activities in FL lessons, the trend in pupils' explicit views on FL teaching methodology (as can be culled from studies that have elicited such commentary) is predominantly in favour of a conservative pedagogy. The following are the kinds of assumption that pupils studying MFL have expressed about language teaching and learning:

- *Girls are better than boys at languages*: This is partly a reflection of the widely held view, shared by many including some educationists, that on the whole girls favour the communicative dimension of language learning. This view is based on the assumption that girls are more 'wired up' for verbal processing and on the view that girls are more interested in participating in the sort of social and personal communication at the centre of FL syllabuses. There is no evidence, however, drawing for instance on comparative studies of FL performance in single sex schools, to support this claim.

- *Real learning takes place in writing tasks*: This belief is often expressed on the faces of many pupils towards the end of the initial whole class oral interaction stage of a lesson that characterises most FL lessons following the paradigm of 'introduction–presentation–practice–exploitation–assessment' (Pachler and Field, 2001a, p. 49). Even with those pupils who engage willingly in the whole-class oral interaction, one can frequently observe the relish or relief with which they open their exercise books and reach for their pens. Again, no in-depth study exists to help us interpret this belief, but one can suggest two possible explanations. First, writing has a symbolic significance for learners. Writing and study are seen as interdependent because that is the form of expression that is most widely used in other subject lessons and most frequently used in examinations. Second, and on a more psychological level, writing provides the language learner with a permanent record of data, which is absent from the ephemeral exchanges of oral presentation and practice.

Exploiting beliefs

What is the teacher to make of this undercurrent of beliefs that runs not far below the surface of the pupils' minds as background to their response to the teaching? It would seem misguided to ignore it, as these assumptions might impede effective learning. Finding out about pupils' beliefs about FL learning could contribute additional information for the process of differentiation. As well as accounting for learning styles and ability levels of different pupils, knowledge about their beliefs and understandings can help to provide the teacher with a fuller picture of the individual pupil. The following are direct methods of eliciting and developing pupils' views about FL learning.

1 through sometimes reflecting a little with the class when presenting the lesson objectives and, where appropriate, making reference to a comment that pupils have made previously about some aspect of language learning;

2 through surveys completed at the end of the year, or term or of a unit of work;

3 through a homework task: occasionally, as a summative reflection about the direction of their learning, pupils could be asked to write a page (in English) about their thoughts about what they have found easy and hard, what they have enjoyed and why, particular strategies they have tried, and about future goals;

4 through part of the concluding interchange between teacher and class before dismissal: as well as the routine question asked by many teachers, 'what have you learnt today?', more probing questions could be added: 'was it useful?', 'why?' etc.;

5 through notes and comments collected anonymously in a box on the teacher's desk;

6 through small-group activity (for instance, discussion around statements about task preferences in the TL);

7 through noticeboard displays by pupils about successful FL learning strategies.

The following are indirect methods:

8 through informal activities in a lunchtime language club, using a range of resources such as ICT, film, readings, drama etc.; a variety of language-related activities unfettered by syllabus requirements is more likely to lead to a more emancipated view of the purpose and potential of FL learning;

9 through planning occasional lessons that incorporate a degree of pupil choice from a menu of activities;

10 through being alert to opportunities for one-to-one exchanges with individuals about their views on their progress, and making discreet written comments in exercise books when marking about suggestions for improvement.

WHAT IS PUPIL METACOGNITION?

Relevance

The question of pupils' views about FL learning is closely linked to the question of pupils' views about their own FL learning. Indeed common sense tells us that pupils' broader views about language learning are best developed on the basis of successful thinking about their own personal experience of FL learning. The term 'metacognition' is used to refer to the process of self-conscious reflection about how one learns the FL and the strategies one consciously and subconsciously uses. The relevance of the issue of metacognition to the practical context of the languages classroom can be gauged from the following vignette.

From our experience as teacher educators, beginner teachers, who are asked by their tutors to observe the ways in which the NC MFL Order is effectively implemented in the FL lessons they observe at their placement school, often report back on the planned activities, the strategies used by the teacher for managing the activities and for helping the pupils meet the learning objectives, and the pupil response to the teaching. This analytical observation is cross-referenced with the relevant objectives from the PoS, although either the links can be consciously made by the teacher and explicitly announced to the pupils, or their presence is implicit in the lesson and it is only the observing beginner teacher who makes the connection. For instance, a beginner teacher (whom we shall call Steve Studious) observes a Year 7 mixed-ability French class, the main learning objective of which is the correct use of a set of expressions to describe the weather and to link this to different leisure activities. Here is Steve's 'reading' of the lesson:

1 In the opening phase of the lesson, the teacher engages the pupils in whole-class and individual repetition of the phrases, using flashcards as prompts. In his report Steve notes that, as the teacher focuses on pronunciation, the PoS objective being addressed here is 2b ('Pupils should be taught correct pronunciation and intonation').

2 In the next activity, the teacher focuses on the meaning of the phrases by eliciting correct recall of the phrase as she shows the different cards in turn while asking '*Quel temps fait-il?*'. This is followed up by pupil practice of the exchange through a guessing game where a pupil selects a card and asks another to say the correct weather. In his notes Steve cross-references this activity with PoS 2c ('How to ask and answer questions').

3 The next focus of the lesson is on revision of phrases describing different activities ('*je reste à la maison*', '*je joue au tennis*' etc.) and on linking these with reference to the weather: '*Quand il pleut, je reste à la maison.*' Steve notes that, as this sequence builds up to the pupils attempting to say what they really do

under different weather conditions, the PoS objective targeted here is 1c ('How to express themselves using a range of vocabulary and structures').

4 Later in the lesson, the teacher plays a tape of several French children talking about what they usually do at a weekend depending on weather conditions. The pupils are given a grid on which to tick the weather conditions and activities mentioned. In his report, Steve identifies this as the second half of PoS 2a ('How to listen carefully for gist and detail').

How accurate are Steve's links to the NC PoS? With 1 there seems little to argue about, but what can one notice in the case of 2–4? One point that Steve has missed is that each of the three PoS objectives he cites begins with the phrase 'how to'. Is there any evidence in the lesson that the teacher has taught her pupils 'how to', for instance, ask and answer questions in French? They may have engaged in this kind of discourse at a very simple level, but for her to have taught them 'how to' do it, she would need to draw their attention to some key principle which they could attempt to apply for themselves. In this case, it might be pointing to the inversion '*fait-il/il fait*'. Another way of teaching them 'how to' do something is to provide them with a brief list of alternative methods. for instance, turning a statement into a question by raising the final intonation ('*il pleut?*') or by adding '*est-ce que*' at the start. Similarly, in the case of the listening task, although the pupils were engaged in a valid comprehension and auditory recognition exercise, they were not taught 'how to listen'. This would have entailed some reference to strategies that they could apply in other listening contexts as well. What Steve appears to be doing is confusing or conflating two related but separate mental processes: cognitive engagement in learning and metacognitive reflection on the learning. These terms will be defined more explicitly below, but for the moment it is worth thinking of the difference as a focus on content or a focus on strategy. It is worth noting that of the eighteen PoS objectives listed under the first three headings ('Knowledge, skills and understanding', 'Developing language skills', and 'Developing language-learning skills'), no less than eleven are expressed as 'how to' objectives. A further two refer to 'strategies' and 'techniques', which can be read as equivalent to the 'how to' statements. No theoretical or pedagogical explanation is given for this prioritisation of focus on strategy. The same emphasis is repeated in the KS3 Framework objectives with only a cryptic signal by way of explanation: 'the words that introduce an objective need to be carefully noted: the requirement may be that pupils are taught **how** something is done, or **that** something is the case, or simply a fact or item of knowledge' (DfES 2003, p. 23).

Definitions

It is best to begin by considering the contrasting terms of 'cognition' and 'metacognition'. Both allude to mental processes: the first, simply put, refers to the process of understanding; and the second refers to the process of reflecting on that understanding. In a sense, metacognition is always at one remove from the learning objective. Metacognitive thinking is also described as operating within the parameters of long-term memory, where items are stored more permanently and can be retrieved relatively effortlessly. Cognitive thinking usually takes place in what is called working memory or short-term memory and therefore requires specific strategies to help assimilate the data and store it in long-term memory.

An example of cognition in the FLs context would be successful processing of the difference between the use of *por* and *para* in Spanish. An example of metacognition would be thinking about what one knows of this structure (metacognitive knowledge), thinking about what one is currently doing (metacognitive skill) or thinking about one's learning (metacognitive strategy). It is the latter process that writers on FL learning have sought to probe and develop.

Parallel, therefore, to the dual notions of cognition/metacognition, language theorists have attempted to define the distinction between cognitive strategies and metacognitive strategies employed by FL learners.

In an early, influential book that drew on a number of studies they carried out on this topic in the context of SLA, O'Malley and Chamot (1990, pp. 137–8) defined metacognitive strategies as 'thinking about the learning process, planning for learning, monitoring the learning task, and evaluating how well one has learned'. Among the examples given are 'proposing strategies for an upcoming task', 'checking, verifying, or correcting one's understanding ... one's language production', 'tracking use of how well a strategy is working'. Cognitive strategies, on the other hand, 'involve interacting with the material to be learned, manipulating the material mentally or physically, or applying a specific technique to a learning task'. Examples include the use of repetition, use of resources, note taking, deduction/induction, translation, inferencing.

Definitions and exemplification of these terms are by no means fixed, and several attempts to specify and add to O'Malley and Chamot's categories have been made since. One of the reasons for this indeterminacy is that researchers and teachers have difficulty accessing the mental processes of second-language learners, and especially of younger learners who are not accustomed or skilled in externalising their thoughts. The following section summarises three studies that give an indication of the kind of metacognitive processes that may be brought to the surface by a researcher or teacher. All three studies rely on the most commonly used instrument for data collection in language learning strategy research: the think-aloud protocol. This procedure involves subjects verbalising their thoughts as they complete a task. When analysing the recordings subsequently, researchers can look at the various mental strategies used by the learners in tackling the task.

There are shortcomings to the method as an accurate means of gaining insight into cognitive and metacognitive thinking. First, one can argue that the technique generates thinking that might otherwise not exist. After all, most of us complete mental tasks without producing a mental running commentary on what we are doing. Second, the technique relies on the assumption that subjects are sufficiently articulate and clear-sighted to be able to verbalise their thought processes when completing a language task. This may be especially true of younger and less linguistically able pupils. Further, for practical reasons, research using this technique is usually based around completion of a specific task (processing a reading text or writing in the TL). However, pupils also engage in cognitive and metacognitive thinking in other learning situations such as, for instance, while listening to the teacher explaining a grammatical structure.

Despite these caveats it is clear that the use of the think-aloud protocol is a useful tool for generating pupil thinking and that this provides us with some glimpse (however partial) of the metacognitive strategies pupils employ in making sense of the language they are learning. The three examples have been selected primarily because they are set in different contexts: adult learners of English as a second language in the US; A level students of French and German in the UK; Year 10 pupils of French in the UK. At the same time, and partly because of the different contexts, each study provides us with a different emphasis and types of insight to pursue further.

EXAMPLES FROM RESEARCH

EXAMPLE 1: Anita Wenden (2001) Metacognitive knowledge in SLA: the neglected variable

Research focus:
To examine the relationship between what learners know and how they self-regulate their learning. Wenden describes self-regulation as 'the processes by which learners plan how they will approach a task, their task analysis and how they actually monitor its implementation' (p. 50). A number of adult learners of English in the US were asked to complete language tasks using the think-aloud protocol and other methods.

The author identifies three main processes involved in self-regulation: planning, monitoring and evaluating.

Sample excerpt 1:
The following is an excerpt from one of the participants, Dina, who is planning her written task (an essay entitled 'Should immigrants be expected to return to their native countries?') prior to writing. Once she had written her first sentence, 'One of the biggest problems that exists today in the US is the problem of ILLEGAL IMMIGRANTS', she paused, and the researcher asks: 'You started writing right away. You didn't have to think about it?'. The reply provides the researcher with useful evidence of the thought processes:

> I was thinking of the way how to write and everything . . . I was thinking of the topic . . .
>
> I was thinking about the title. I decided it's a big problem and my idea is that I . . . think they don't have to go back to their native countries. But I'm going to give first why is the problem and then I'm going – uh – you know – the against – the plus and against but my opinion I will try to support my opinion that they don't have to go back to their countries. But now I'm just trying to put it in the way that I am thinking to give first a general idea to put everything I want . . . and maybe I'm going to change. Usually I change them you know. I wrote something then I put all the corrections I want . . .

Wenden interprets this extract as showing that Dina here first draws on her subject knowledge, 'I was thinking before of the topic . . .', then she is guided by her rhetorical knowledge (procedures for writing an essay), 'I'm going to give first why is the problem then I'm going . . . the against', and finally she draws on strategic knowledge, 'I'm just trying to put them in the way I am thinking to give first a general idea . . . Usually I change them'.

Sample excerpt 2:
Wenden argues that monitoring consists of five 'sub-processes: self-observation, assessment, deciding whether to take action, deciding how and when to take action, implementing the action' (p. 54). In this excerpt, Dina thinks aloud as she writes the second sentence of her essay:

> I always try to say out loud. I like to hear my ideas . . . In a minute I'm going to change something. But then I'm going to go over it and I'm going to change it again . . . I like my ideas but I don't like the place. I'm going to change the place . . . but now I'm just want to put down my ideas in the right order.

Wenden comments that Dina here displays self-observation ('I always try to say out loud . . . I like to hear my ideas') and assessment ('I like my ideas but I don't like the place'), and she decides to take action on the basis of task knowledge ('I'm going to change the place . . . but now I'm just want to put down my ideas in the right order').

Pedagogical implications:
It would seem from research that there is 'a reason for what [learners] choose to learn, the strategies and learning activities they prefer, and the manner in which they approach and complete a task'. She concludes that teachers should use similar techniques for probing their students' metacognitive knowledge in order to 'facilitate the process of second language learning within the classroom' and to help them develop independent learning skills in informal settings.

EXAMPLE 2: Suzanne Graham (1997) *Effective Language Learning*: Positive Strategies for Advanced Language Learning

Research focus:
To discover what learning strategies are employed by students to overcome the difficulties they experience in the FLs classroom. The study involved

interviews with twenty-four A level students at seven schools, as well as questionnaires distributed at forty-nine schools in England and Wales. Graham used retrospective interviews to identify the students' strategies in processing the four language skills. The think-aloud protocol was also used in connection with reading, listening and writing tasks.

Sample excerpt 1:
In processing a reading text which he found difficult, Student H displayed excessive reliance on contextual inferencing. After reading the initial sentence in the text on youth leisure in Hamburg, the student speaks his thoughts as follows:

> Hamburg – Eine neue Art von Anstrengungen raubt jungen Leuten den Schlaf: Der Freizeitstreß
>
> Hamburg . . . um, a new place I think from . . . a new place, um I'll miss that out cos I don't know what it is at the moment (+ 'Anstrengung'?) Yeah, and 'raubt'. Um, young people . . . 'schlafen' to sleep, oh, young people come and when they're free from stress . . . I guess it's an area that's been designed where young people can come where they don't have to do anything connected with school.

Graham comments that this student is showing top-down processing (inferring from context), but the problem is that this is not complemented by other processing strategies such as checking his interpretation with other aspects of the text, such as lexis and syntax.

Sample excerpt 2:
Student L, according to Graham, displays the converse weakness; namely, that of not seeing the wood for the trees. This A level French student is asked to verbalise his thoughts while processing a text about active working holidays for young people.

> Rencontres enrichissantes, confrontation avec les réalités, elle a pu se faire une vraie idée d'un pays du tiers-monde.
>
> Ok, 'rencontres enrichantes' . . . um, to meet rich people . . . + . . . um, well, cos it's got rich in it, I don't actually know what the word is, but it looks like that, um . . . to meet rich people, maybe it's some sort of work for rich people.

Pedagogical implications:
Graham provides a more nuanced conclusion than earlier studies, which report that more successful students used learning strategies more often, 'more appropriately, with greater variety, and in ways that helped them complete the task successfully' whereas 'ineffective students used fewer strategies and often used strategies that were inappropriate to the task' (p. 43). Her study showed that the types of way in which effective and ineffective language students differed in the way they employed meta-cognitive strategies varied according to the type of learning context: listening, reading, speaking, writing, vocabulary learning, grammar learning. There would seem to be a case for training students in metacognitive strategies in relation to these distinct areas.

EXAMPLE 3: Ernesto Macaro (2001) *Learning Strategies in FL Classrooms*

Research focus:
This study differs from the previous two in that it includes an interventionist element in the form of a series of lessons that focused on three main aspects of strategy training: making the right decision of when to use L1 and when to use L2 in planning and composing; dictionary-use strategies; self-monitoring strategies. Six Year 10 classes of French at six different schools in England participated, three forming the experimental groups (following the strategy training course) and three the control group.

Excerpt of transcript extract:
The following is the first section of a transcript of a think-aloud commentary by a pupil, Katie, who is in the process of completing a post-test writing task in the form of a description of a camping holiday in France. Macaro's interpretative comments are given alongside each segment.

Katie's think aloud	Macaro's commentary
I am staying . . . that's the present tense so that's one verb . . . *je rester dans une famille* . . . I'm staying in a family . . . oh sorry, I'll put 'with' . . . (changes *dans* to *avec*)	Translating strategy combined with tense prompt. Auditory monitoring and back-translation lead to a change.

137

'we are staying' so that's the present tense again . . . *nous rester* . . . need something for *rester* . . . it's one verb but it's *nous* . . .

Uses tense strategy correctly and is beginning to turn her attention to endings – the next stage in the interlanguage development.

. . . in a campsite . . . [checks in dictionary] it's masculine so I'll stay with *un camping*

Dictionary-checking strategy.

le mere no *la mere* [corrects to *la*]

Auditory monitoring results in a correction.

La mere est très sampas [pronounced like Sampras!] . . . a word I know . . . *sampas* . . . I'll just check . . . it's not the word that I know so I'll change it . . .

Interesting combination of strategies here. Recombination linked with auditory monitoring caused doubt (perhaps she really is confusing the word with the name of the tennis player – July is the tennis season) but she is undecided whether to pursue the dictionary route. Opts for more familiar word although does not remember to make it agree.

Pedagogical implications:

Macaro found that the strategy training he designed for the experimental group in his project resulted in overall significant gains in performance in the writing task, especially with regard to reduction in verb phrase error. The pupils in that group also reported on changes to their approach to writing, that they had become more independent and used the dictionary more selectively. They also considered themselves to be less sloppy in checking their written work. The evidence here, therefore, seems to be that explicit strategy training can have a positive impact on cognitive as well as metacognitive performance.

CONCLUSION

We have argued in this chapter that understanding the process of pupil FL acquisition is a complex and multifaceted enterprise. Any attempt at investigating the process needs to include the three interlinking factors that we have described: pupil cognition, metacognition and beliefs. The three processes are in turn shaped by the distinctive developmental profile of secondary pupils, which makes some of the methods and findings described by teachers and researchers in the adult second language learning context largely inapplicable here.

Ultimately, for FL teaching to thrive in our schools, teachers must be given the time and means to reflect on how their pupils construct their knowledge and skills. A prerequisite for this, of course, is for the teacher to create opportunities for the pupils themselves to reflect and express themselves on and through their FL learning.

QUESTIONS FOR DISCUSSION

1 What are the key dimensions of pupil cognition in the context of foreign language learning?

2 What is the relationship between declarative and procedural knowledge in language learning?

3 We have presented two examples of pupils' folk beliefs about language learning. Can you add more from the experience of your own students?

4 Which aspects of FL acquisition are most vulnerable to loss among your students? Do learners from different age groups have different retention patterns?

5 List the different language-learning strategies you have recently provided your students with.

Part III

Subject and professional development

The final part of our book focuses on what might be seen as a rationale for language teacher action or rather, to coin a phrase, 'pro-action'. The question we are asking in these pages is 'How can FL teachers have an informed influence on language education within the bounds of their own professional experience?' We ask this question because it seems important to us to view the role of a teacher as more than that of a passive agent of policies dictated from above. It is also our view that FL teachers in schools have as much a part to play in the process of educational development as those in other subject areas. However, engagement in central curricular debates and decision-making within a school is, we acknowledge, all the more daunting for newly qualified teachers. At the same time, to sit on the sidelines and to avoid playing a part is to delay one's own progress as teacher as well as to deny the FL discipline its voice in the dialogue between subjects. Our view of educational development, we hasten to add, is not one of waving banners or engaging in interdisciplinary power relations. Rather it is one of first understanding the context and the factors that are at play, and then taking measured steps.

The perspective outlined here is based on a triangular relationship between personal development as a newly qualified FL teacher, subject development in the sense of investigating the potential of FL teaching and learning beyond its relevance to the individual teacher, and professional development in the sense of an individual's work within the wider school community. This relationship is often visible in the form of tension, sometimes even conflict. For a teacher in their first few years in the profession, the pressures of adjustment to the job through developing new skills and responding to a new field of experience can be an added factor of tension. However, although short-term solutions might be gained through 'battening down the hatches' and focusing on private battles, more long-lasting and fundamental professional competence as a teacher can only be achieved through pro-active engagement with others. We argue that an essential ingredient of such engagement is that it is not based on subjective preferences but on rigorous critical thinking. Such thinking is at the heart of most ITE courses, and it is increasingly recognised that this criticality should be encouraged through the induction period and beyond. The rigour and direction of such thinking stem from the sort of research literacies we outline in Chapter 6 and which evidence shows that a growing number of teachers see as realistic and relevant to their practice. Finally, the wider professional setting is depicted in Chapter 7, where we argue that the professional development of a teacher evolves through influence from and on three types of culture: of the teaching profession, of the subject discipline and of the individual school.

In this way, we draw a link between the two meanings hidden in the term 'subject': the subject as I, the teacher; and the subject as the specialist field (FL learning) that is transformed and transmitted to pupils in our schools.

Chapter 6

Educational and research literacies

INTRODUCTION

The previous sections of this book have been mainly concerned with different dimensions of knowledge related to pupil learning. For all teachers, regardless of their level of experience, this is rightly their primary goal. We now look at a different order of knowledge construction, which, until recent years, has been relatively neglected by FL teachers at school level: namely, knowledge about the process of investigating the teaching and learning of languages.

Literacy, as some writers have pointed out, has a role to play in developing 'personal and social change' (Olson *et al.*, 1985, p. 2). We apply the term 'literacy' in this context to refer to the process in which the teacher learns to 'read' the signs in their own classroom (and that of others) in order to bring about personal and wider change in patterns of learning. In this chapter we provide a snapshot of recent moves taken by languages teachers to research their own classroom practice. We then present a case profile of the route an experienced head of languages has taken in acquiring research experience and expertise as her career path has progressed. Finally, the chapter provides preliminary guidelines for teachers embarking on systematic enquiry of their own practice.

The relationship between teaching and research has drawn the attention of educational planners and policymakers in the UK in recent years. Seen in the broad context of governmental thinking on this aspect of educational development, the relationship can be separated into two, potentially interlinking, dimensions. They are perhaps two sides of the same coin.

On the one hand, one can identify a traditional, hierarchical relationship between research and teaching, whereby the former informs the latter. This approach can be seen to influence the idea of 'evidence-based practice' (TTA, 1996), whereby teachers are encouraged to base their own pedagogical strategies on previously validated generalisations about 'what works'. However, within the context of the government's National Languages Strategy (DfES, 2002), the evidence base beneath the prescription is not immediately apparent. How far is the approach outlined in the policy based on findings from, say, research into the effectiveness of primary FL experience in England and Scotland, or more generally from research into FL acquisition? For opposing answers to this question see Pachler (2003) and Johnston (2003). What can be agreed, however, is that this approach assumes that findings are easily transferable across individual contexts and that the relationship is that of the 'external' informing the 'internal'. The flip side to this view of the relationship between research and teaching is the 'practitioner–researcher' model, whereby teachers take on the role of the researcher themselves and use their own practice or context as sources of research-based findings which in turn will inform their own and others' teaching. It is this increasingly popular conception of the role of research in language teaching that will provide the focus for this chapter.

TEACHER AS KNOWLEDGE CREATOR

In a controversial and ground-breaking paper delivered in a symposium on educational research at the British Educational Research Association (BERA) in 1998, David Hargreaves coined the term 'knowledge creating school' to refer to 'a radical re-conceptualisation of knowledge creation and its dissemination in education'. At the heart of Hargreaves's argument is the concept of a 'school's intellectual capital'. By this Hargreaves meant that, as well as being teaching institutions, or rather through that process, schools could become producers of knowledge about teaching and learning, in place of their more traditional roles as facilitators or secondary partners in externally conceived, managed and disseminated research. Hargreaves and others have argued that teachers can and should become the main source of the knowledge creation process and of its management and dissemination. This conception of professional knowledge is based on a model of the knowledge creation process in industrial firms.

The component features identified in this view of the school knowledge creation process are:

- *Knowledge audit* is where the collective intellectual capital of a school's staff is shared, and the gaps in a school's knowledge needs are identified. This strategy is also seen as a way of reducing the isolation of teachers within a school, who often are unaware of their own and their colleagues' developing professional knowledge.

- *Management of the process of professional knowledge creation* is defined by Hargreaves in terms of characteristics and dynamics. In his view, the characteristics of a knowledge creating school include there being a culture of continual improvement, a respect for diversity and difference of view, an awareness of, and readiness to assimilate, external knowledge, recognition by senior management of staff subject specialist expertise, decentralisation and flat hierarchies of staff, cross-fertilisation between teams and job rotation, a readiness to tinker and experiment with new ideas, a willingness to participate in partnerships and networks.

- *Knowledge validation* is the stage whereby knowledge is 'turned into a practice which demonstrably and repeatedly works'. Hargreaves distinguishes between a good idea 'which may be worthwhile but which has not been subject to any kind of test', a good practice 'which implies some kind of validation that it is sound and effective' and best practice 'which implies a practice that has been shown to be better than other good practices'. In an attempt to tighten this loose terminology, Hargreaves proposes five different types of knowledge validation: ipsative (when a teacher compares own present practice with past practice); social (when a professional group, such as subject association or teacher union, reaches, through analysis and discussion, a view on what is good practice on a particular issue); independent (parents', inspectors', academics', LEA, government views of good practice); judicial (rules of evidence about the effectiveness of specific practices); and scientific (practice that has been shown to be effective through formal research methods, including tests of reliability and validity).

- *Dissemination of knowledge*, in contrast to the 'centre-periphery' approach of traditional educational research initiated by a university or government agency whereby findings are sent out to schools and teachers as recipients, here focuses on dissemination of knowledge or practice within a school or from one school to another. Hargreaves introduces the notion of 'transposability' of knowledge or practice, meaning reiteration of practice between different places (classrooms, schools, school contexts).

David Hargreaves went on to influence UK government educational policy, first as Chief Executive of the QCA and then as Chairman of the British Educational Communications and Technology Agency (BECTA), where he continued to promote the value of lateral networking between teachers on a local and national scale. He saw ICT as a vehicle for this but argued that its potential as an effective infrastructure for the sharing of good practice and professional knowledge is as yet largely unrealised (Hargreaves, 2003b).

Despite the relative infancy of this view of the role of the teacher as creator and disseminator of professional knowledge, it is true that over the last decade or so some tangible efforts have been made to develop such a culture of thinking among teachers. Beacon and specialist schools are examples of initiatives whereby expertise from a lead school is shared with other schools through local networks. Similarly the National Grid for Learning (www.ngfl.gov.uk) is seen as an instrument for information distribution and as a 'gateway to educational resources on the internet'. However, although many initiatives remain institution-focused rather than teacher-focused, the Best Practice Research Scholarships (BPRS) scheme is the most tangible way in which, in recent years, government policy has promoted teacher research at grass-roots level. Although this scheme was wound up in 2003 after three years of implementation, it remains the most extensive state-funded promotion of teacher research in this country, and therefore provides us with some evidence, however unsystematic and unrepresentative of the cohort as a whole, of the current grass-roots research interests of practising FL teachers.

In the context of the prevailing research and educational climate in this country and of the diminishing status of FL teaching in schools, FL teachers need to take the initiative in relation to knowledge creation.

146

TEACHER RESEARCH

Interestingly, the wording in the title 'Best Practice Research Scheme' seems to have picked up on Hargreaves's notion of 'best practice' (though in reality the projects completed were mostly examples of 'good practice' in that they tended to be descriptive accounts with little reference to prior practice). Similarly, Hargreaves's thinking can be seen behind the linkage between research and professional development in the stated aims of the scheme which were 'to enhance teachers' own professional and personal development, to enable collaborative work with their colleagues and to raise their own profile amongst their peers'. Applicants had to appoint a research mentor, who would support them in 'establishing and completing a rigorous and successful research project'. The mentors could be drawn from 'universities, schools, professional associations, subject associations, LAs, research bodies, Excellence in Cities Partnerships, Education Action Zone coordinators or any other individuals suitable for the position'. What constitutes 'rigorous and successful research' was never spelt out, and, therefore, methodological rigour may not have always been consistent. However, lack of specification of focus of the project was a welcome development and resulted in a large number of applications from subject teachers, including from the hitherto research-reticent FL teaching community.

A search of BPRS project reports on the government website (www.teachernet.gov.uk) reveals a list of 100 titles relating to an aspect of FL teaching. Below is a list of the most common topic areas investigated by the completed projects. The most popular topics by some way are ICT-related projects (16 per cent of the total) and studies examining some aspect of boys' motivation or achievement in language learning (15 per cent).

- National Literacy Strategy and FL teaching;
- raising boys' motivation and achievement in FL;
- social barriers to achievement in FL;
- language learning and language skills strategies;
- ICT and FL learning or teaching;
- music and FL learning or teaching;
- teaching thinking skills;
- writing and citizenship;
- special educational needs learners and FL;
- primary/secondary MFL school partnerships;

- class management;
- grammar teaching;
- primary MFL;
- effective starter activities for KS3 German;
- vocational alternatives at KS4;
- motivation in MFL learning;
- visits and exchanges abroad for primary children;
- FL assistants for improving performance and confidence of learners;
- teaching other subjects in French;
- assessment and progression;
- the 'able linguist';
- reward systems in the FL classroom;
- QCA KS3 Schemes of Work;
- differentiation;
- multisensory approach in FL.

A closer look at the titles of the BPRS studies reveals some interesting patterns that may shed light on the kinds of subject teaching concerns of FL teachers in this country. First, a striking feature of the list is the lack of reference in any of the titles to languages other than French or German. Of course, some projects with generic titles referring to MFL do draw on Spanish classes. However, the absence of an explicit focus on Spanish, Italian or other languages being taught in schools is worthy of note. This no doubt is partly related to the continuing dominance of French and German in UK schools, but may also be related to other factors. Is there a perception or subconscious belief in FL teachers' minds that French and German are more acceptable languages in terms of public educational research? Does German grammar inspire proportionately more analytical interest in teachers and learners than other FLs? If either or both of these hypotheses are true then there is much still to be done to develop a more open and more multilingual consciousness among languages teachers in this country. Second, it is noteworthy that the majority of the BPRS titles focus on pupil learning (either in terms of learning or motivation) rather than on pedagogy. Few, for instance, seem to deal with analysis of the effectiveness of different aspects of teaching strategy. As well as reflecting teachers' natural and, in our view, totally justifiable primary concern for the quality of learning of their pupils, it may reflect a thirst for information and insights into the quality and level of that learning that are not currently available through the current machinery of assessment. Third, the titles reveal different types of emphasis between the projects. A recurrent word in many of the titles is that of 'improvement'. In these projects, research is seen as a pursuit of evidence of improvement in learning. In many cases, this improvement is defined in terms of better results in tests or in some form of visible performance. In other words, the objective of the enquiry is to examine outcome of learning rather than a qualitative examination of the process of learning. Is this a reflection of the culture of school improvement and target-led policymaking that has dominated education in the UK over the last two decades or so? The phrase 'raising standards' used in some of the titles is an unmistakable echo of the language used by the government and Ofsted. The content of many of the projects echoes national policy initiatives such as the National Literacy Strategy and the KS3 Strategy. It would seem, therefore, that although some of the BPRS projects emerge from internal concerns and objectives, others are influenced by externally formulated priorities. The extent to which the BPRS scheme favoured projects that linked up with officially established educational priorities is beyond the scope of this book and would require more systematic investigation.

Although valuable both as a promoter of teacher-led research in general and for the individual teachers and schools involved in the projects it funded, the experience of BPRS as a national scheme nevertheless points to one fundamental and inescapable reality. Without wishing to diminish the importance of external and institutional support, when all is said and done, the indispensable factors (which will be determinants in any approach to professional knowledge development) are the desire and motivation of individual teachers to engage in this activity. This desire will be kindled in different ways for different teachers, but without it a teacher will do no more than go through the motions of classroom investigation and will not see it as intrinsic to their professional development. The BPRS initiative has now ended, and the financial and public support it provided has been taken away. What cannot be taken away is the spirit and motivation of teachers to engage in action and reflection in relation to their classroom practice. How can this spirit be reconciled with the more immediate concerns of subject teaching? Although senior management and external agencies rightly seek organisational, philosophical and strategic solutions to this issue, for individual subject teachers more immediate and personal solutions are sought. And what for the FL teacher is the framework within which personal engagement in classroom research is possible?

In order to seek answers to these questions we look now at the experience of one highly successful FL teacher.

THE DEVELOPMENTAL PROFILE OF A FL TEACHER'S ENGAGEMENT IN RESEARCH

The exploded narrative presented in the following section, which we have interspersed with comments highlighting key themes of relevance to the general issue of language teacher research development is based on a recent interview with Rachel Hawkes, who at the time of the interview was head of modern languages at Comberton Village College, a mixed 11–16 comprehensive school in Cambridgeshire. By adopting an 'exploded narrative' format we are able to respect the original chronology of the narrative produced by the teacher at interview (which is important given the autobiographical content of the narrative) and to provide readers with direct access to her thinking and rationalising about the different stages of her development as a practitioner researcher:

Initially my first taste of research was on arrival at a new school where I had been appointed as head of languages in 1999. I walked into the job and one of the first things I remember was being told about an ongoing exchanges project, a link up with the University of Cambridge and I'd be expected to collaborate in some way and arrange for things to happen. I wasn't given more details than that and so I just waited to be contacted. And at the time I was very new to the job, had a lot of very urgent things to resolve not least of which were results and difficult staffing situation and getting to grips with my own timetable and my own classes and the idea of doing anything over and above was completely abhorrent to me and quite an imposition I felt. So I didn't approach it at all positively and essentially tried not to engage with it except in fulfilling my duties which were arranging for pupils to sit different kinds of tests before and after their exchange visit. Then I remember the researcher needing a room to come in for the day to do interviews and that had to be the departmental office and that pupils needed to come out of their classes. It seemed to me a logistical activity. A long time later, it seemed, I can't remember how much later it was,

I was invited to a meeting where some of the findings were presented. And I remember this was much more of a positive and interesting occasion not least of which because there were things that I could recognise and there were pupils that I knew who had clearly had some kind of change as a result of this experience and this was discovered and presented in a way that seemed very clear to me and the result being that I remember one pupil showing a clear difference between the language he produced after the exchange compared to what he did before the visit. There was a very obvious difference both qualitatively and quantitatively. I suppose because I knew the pupil concerned, I knew this to be the case. He was a pupil in my tutor group. Suddenly it seemed very real, what had been present or shown to be the case. I suppose my interest was sparked though I was still under a lot of pressure of work and so I did very little about it after that. So I thought: 'OK that's great. Wasn't that nice? Now I don't need to do any more work on that idea.' But nonetheless I felt positively about something that I had experienced there.

The story of Hawkes's active involvement in research begins with her arrival at Comberton Village College. Though as an intelligent, highly qualified and experienced teacher it would be wrong to assume that she had not reflected critically on her own or others' classroom practice beforehand or that she had not previously had an interest in practitioner research, it is nonetheless significant that her active involvement coincided with arrival at this school. First, the school as a whole, as her narrative reveals later on, had already established a strong culture and commitment to educational research through partnership with the University of Cambridge, through research networks with other schools and through widespread support of staff within the school to engage in such activity. Second, Hawkes's arrival at a critical point in the data collection stage of an ongoing research project to which her department had already committed meant that her first involvement in research was obligatory. The ice-breaking moment in Hawkes's research career was, therefore, that of unavoidable participation in an externally planned and managed research study. Her account here also underlines her perception at the time of a separation between this research involvement and her pressing teaching and administrative duties as newly appointed head of department. She saw the project as an imposition, someone else's initiative. Her role seemed purely 'logistical'. However, once the findings are discussed with her as part of the research team and once she sees that the findings reflect real features of her pupils' language learning, she begins to develop a genuine taste for the process.

> Then subsequently my school had a working group which we called the Gender Working-party. It was felt important that we got to grips as to why girls were doing much better than boys in most subjects including languages. I volunteered to sit on this committee and then there didn't seem to be any obvious way forward or anything proposed. I happened to have seen in a book a gender questionnaire that was languages related. In my enthusiasm I immediately decided to pilot this questionnaire with all of the Year 6s on the incoming open day and then find some way of analysing the results and feed that to the working party. Having suggested this it was then leapt upon by the other members of the committee. I then had to do it. It was a very unwieldy document; I didn't find anyone else who had used it successfully. With the benefit of hindsight I realise I should have piloted it with a few people to find out its pitfalls but I used it with 200 odd pupils. And then had a lot of data to do something with. Again it was a little dive-in, a little taster. There were things that I was told, that I found out in analysing the data that I already knew. But I suppose it confirmed certain things for me. However, the lack of quality of the instrument itself made me lose momentum. I fed back what I had which was impressive to the working party because I had done what I said I would do. But it really stopped there, it didn't take everyone forward, it didn't particularly help us to do anything in the languages department which we hadn't already been planning to do. But it did raise the profile of the department a little and did get people thinking that I was serious about looking at gender. And I suppose in some ways approaching something in a serious frame of mind and doing something quite active can be one way of getting things changed that you want to change in terms of your departmental agenda. But, as I say, it was not a great instrument. So I left that there.

The second phase of Hawkes's development as a practitioner researcher is marked by her involvement in a whole-school initiative. Again the initiative is not conceived by herself but by senior management or a corporate decision-making group. The experience here would seem to correspond to Hargreaves's notion of social validation. Hawkes again feels pressured to engage in the project, though this time it is peer group pressure. She feels under obligation to carry out a commitment made in public in a moment of enthusiasm. Hawkes attributes the weakness of the project mainly to the use of a ready-made and inappropriate questionnaire as her main research instrument. Her work here shows a continuing dependence on external support though to a much lesser degree than with the first project. The other interesting point in her comments here is the importance she felt at the time about the profile of the department within the school as a whole. Involvement in research, therefore, especially in a school where this is given a high priority, is a way of raising the profile of one's subject and of one's subject department within the institution as a whole.

The next project that I had anything to do with at all was the TICTALK project. It was again generated from within the university but drawing in several schools. It was a link up between schools in different countries on-line. It involved pupils airing their views with other young people from different Francophone and Anglophone countries in a sort of cultural exchange, an ideas exchange but also a language exchange as well. I loved the idea. Again because of pressure of work, I was half relieved but half disappointed that actually it wasn't going to be appropriate for me because I was teaching KS4 German and not KS4 French (the target group of the project) and that it was going to be another colleague who was going to be taking this on. I had very mixed feelings of 'thank goodness that's not going to require me to do anything more' but also how glad I was that it was going on in my department anyway and 'I'm going to be very interested in finding out how Alison was getting on with it'. So I was beginning to note I think now, looking back at myself, the gap between how much work you imagine a project is going to be and the peer benefits that projects and collaboration of any description I suppose can bring, certainly something that's set up properly, how positive that can be and how dynamic that can be for a department to be involved in. That was my development stage there.

The opportunity to collaborate on another university-led research project this time had the added benefit of involvement at the beginning and co-operation with different schools, including francophone schools abroad. As head of department, Hawkes shows a willingness to foster the collective, departmental research profile. She makes a telling reference to 'peer benefits', which accrue through teachers within the department sharing experiences related to their project work.

Then the formation of BPRS came on the horizon. My school has a person responsible for research who is on the senior management team who is very keen herself having got involved first herself in doing studies that were research related and then leapt on to the BPRS bandwagon. She got a lot of people to apply and a lot of people had projects approved in that first year. And then it seemed to me something that I really should do. Two people in my department had already embarked on one. I suppose I was waiting for something that was for me a burning issue. There were several possible but in order to invest the time I suppose I wanted that something a little bit extra of personal interest that would give me that kick to do it. And that came when I got thinking about pupils interacting and the balance of interaction within the classroom being very teacher-dominated and that we all struggle all of the time to get pupils to speak spontaneously in the target language to take the initiative and to join in. I suppose in some ways feeling the burden of always having to take the initiative with everything and always being so controlling and directing from the front that can be very reassuring because it means you are the only one making a decision but it can also be very, very tiring. And feeling that maybe there is another way and trying to think my way around that maybe money from the BPRS would be a very good way of moving forward to help me look at this idea. So I put in a proposal for which I was supported very well by the senior teacher. Also I think there is a climate now she has struggled over 5–6 years to develop a climate of acceptance for the notion of teacher involvement in research. It's not that teachers were anti the idea but they were, as I was, just anti the notion of extra work. 'What's in it for me?' She managed very successfully over time to help smoothe the way in a practical way by winning some money which people can use for requesting some time to do something; by also putting a lot of information our way; by modelling how positive this can be; and by talking to people one-to-one about their interests and what the possibilities are. She's done a great job but you have to come to it yourself as well. I think at the time I submitted the BPRS I was at the right place. All the little things over the last few years that had just shown me a little taster had then led me to this point. So I got a BPRS and almost simultaneously with that funding I felt that I wanted something bigger. I wanted something more than that and the project that I was envisaging just became bigger. After being HOD for 7 years and teacher for 9, I really felt like the need for a challenge that was very different but also was intimately related and would take me further. So there was a motivation to reflect some deep change in my teaching and in other people's teaching. This was also to do with influencing other people as well, you do that as HOD then you get to the point of thinking well actually maybe some of these ideas should go further than just the confines of the department. So there's the desire to discover something, to be at the centre of something fairly big and then to share it further. Which I think was just a reflection of where I was in my career. Having not mastered the role of HOD (because you never do that) having got to a certain place where the department was doing well but that MFL teaching still had so much further to go.

BPRS here too played a role in facilitating Hawkes's professional knowledge development. The role of school senior management in supporting and fostering teachers' research involvement and in preparing applications for funding is underlined. BPRS represented financial support that allowed her and the other teachers on projects to be freed from some teaching in order to focus on the project. What is interesting here also is that the BPRS is not viewed by Hawkes as an end in itself but that it 'almost simultaneously' triggered a desire for working on 'something bigger'. It is clear that this is a crucial phase in Hawkes's development. First, she refers to a distinction between the performance of the department and the performance (in a general sense) of FL teaching. Although the former is now in good shape, the latter is in need of her contribution and, by implication, that of all language teachers and educators. She seems here to be manifesting a greater sense of belonging to the wider FL education community and responsibility for the state of language teaching that transcends the local performance of language teaching in her school. Second, she identifies the 'something bigger' as a 'motivation to reflect deep change in my teaching and in other people's teaching'. Research here is pictured as a transformative practice.

So I applied to do an MEd at that point. Still with the same idea of focusing on spontaneous talk within the context of classroom interaction within languages. So I applied for that, and started that. In the meantime other things started happening. If you dabble you find that you can't do anything but investigate. Once you start looking, you can't stop looking. In the course of some of my reading, I came across something on pupil consultation that had just been published. And then the science teacher in my school revealed that he had been one of the people who had contributed to it. And then I read it and I read the accompanying materials. I had been for quite some time aware that pupil consultation was something that as a school we hadn't gone into. Certainly not in the department. So I then started designing a little project to investigate how pupils feel about their learning in languages and to involve pupils in the research. I produced a question-naire which was a lot better than the one I used a few years earlier. So at least there was proof that some development had taken place for me. I did those pupil consultations with all the pupils in Y8. I analysed the data; I haven't finished yet. I did an initial read through. There were some opportunities for them to comment as well as tick boxes. I analysed the 'easy' data, and read through the comments and fed back to them what seemed to be the salient points. And I have involved them from the beginning: I told them what was going to happen, that they were going to do this and then it was going to be discussed and I was going to give them some feedback and there would be several stages of feedback and we would probably go back and talk about it again but that there was going to be initially something quite concrete that would come back to them. And that there quite probably would be some changes and some things that I might try in reaction to their suggestions. In feeding back to them, several things were changed. For example, quite a lot of pupils had talked about not being asked a question when they hadn't got their hand up because they really didn't know the answer then. And they would put their hand up if they really did know it. Now whatever my misgivings about whether that's actually true, feeding it back to them was useful because we then embarked on a trial system whereby I had to feel that about two thirds of the class had their hand up, and that I wouldn't pick on anyone who hadn't got their hand up so long as that was the case. Interestingly enough, now I have roughly the level of volunteering that I would consider optimum at any one time. They also talked about the fact I reseat them for every lesson. They don't always like that; they sometimes like that, when they are sitting next to a friend. I talked about my misgivings about them working always with friends, particularly as I have tables where they are sometimes grouped together in six, it can look much more like a table in the canteen than in the classroom. We compromised by having a learning buddy that was a person they were always with, that they would do pair work with, and have a learning rapport with, that they were comfortable with, that they knew they could work well with. They would always sit with that one person but they would be on different tables with different other pairs. That way I could get my mixture and they would always have their learning buddy. Again, that's one of the things that has come out as a direct result of the pupils' consultation and they have responded very positively to it. For instance, there were 4 boys in the class who were very lethargic in terms of learning and were quite blunt in the questionnaire about how they didn't like the lessons. Since the dialogue has started and they've felt able to talk to me more about what they find difficult and easy, their attitude to learning the subjects has changed remarkably for the better. They're talking now about actually enjoying it. Really nothing has changed except for the dynamics of the classroom, except for the idea that they can now make some choices. That psychologically is very different for them but practically I'm still in control. I'm just responding to them, which I was always willing to do. I haven't gone through a personality change. I was always willing to be that kind of teacher, but they couldn't see a way in: they didn't necessarily know that those were the parameters, that they could intervene, that they could make decisions. That actually indirectly had an impact on spontaneous talk in the TL. Not only do we talk about the learning sometimes in English but they do participate more with me, taking initiative in the TL. That's been an interesting spin-off for me.

For Hawkes, at her current stage of professional development, clearly engaging with 'something bigger' has meant enrolment on a part-time M.Ed. course, which provides her with access to FL education theory and research, to generic and FL education research literature, and to the wider community of educational research students and academics. Perhaps there is a desire to link the local with the more universal.

The text here is also interesting in that it reveals the snowballing effect of a teacher's genuine involvement in research, which resembles a continual digging around a particular area of interest or concern: 'once you start looking you can't stop looking.' Hawkes's consultation project, although stimulated by readings and formalised by her studies, grows out of her previous investigations as a practitioner researcher. Moreover, as a languages teacher her concerns and focus are holistic, combining general behavioural objectives (pupil autonomy and decision making) and subject-specific objectives (increasing spontaneous TL output by pupils). Hawkes's model of the FL teacher–researcher, at least at her current stage of development, is based on a merging of both sides of the equation.

When asked about how a languages teacher can raise the profile of the subject within the school as a whole, she made a pertinent remark that draws on the principle of commonality through whole-school issues: namely, that teachers of other subjects will only sit up and be impressed by a language teacher's findings if elements can be extrapolated to their curricular context. Perhaps this is a variant of Hargreaves's notion of 'transposability', only this time between subjects.

> Teachers of other disciplines will find our offerings impressive only if they can take away something for their own discipline. As HOD, I can present something that I can show works particularly well in teaching languages. I can be very specific about how it works in languages but if they can just see an element that is adaptable to their discipline that would be the hook. If it's just an interesting story with nothing that they can then extrapolate and take to their curriculum area then it's less useful. I think we are very bound by our curriculum areas, we're bound by the job that we have to do and we want to glean all the ideas in the world that we can then nick for our subjects.

Finally, when asked to choose between 'improvement', 'change' and 'knowledge' as the main goal of her research activities, Hawkes provides a characteristically clear-sighted answer in which the three objectives are interrelated. Above all, the model that is presented here is that of a research-active classroom teacher who views the process of change, knowledge and improvement as a dynamic and personal process:

> I think your goal might always be improvement. You have to define improvement not just in the sense of just simple results improvement or achievement improvement, but improvement might be a whole range: in rapport, in motivation, in whatever. You are seeking to change but you're not ever seeking to change for the worse. Your goal is improvement. You may not always get that, though, with action

research. It doesn't guarantee you getting improvement. It certainly guarantees some kind of change because just by tampering with something, just by looking, just by investigating you've already changed before you've done anything differently, just by thinking about something in a way you haven't already thought about it before is change and you always get knowledge. Change and knowledge are the automatic by-products but your goal is probably improvement.

Change, by definition, includes change within yourself and knowledge about yourself as well as knowledge about pupils and about learning. It is very corny to say that it's about self-discovery, but it actually is. One of the big things that gets you hooked is that the change that you experience is very, very dynamic and very, very personal.

(Rachel Hawkes)

PLANNING YOUR OWN CLASSROOM RESEARCH

What follows is a framework of guidelines for FL teachers who are contemplating carrying out their own research into some aspect of their classroom practice. Much has been written about action research (Halsall, 1998; Hopkins, 2002) and about language-teacher action research (Allwright, 2003; Lamb and Simpson, 2003; Wallace 1998). Broadly speaking, definitions can be situated along a spectrum between maximalist and minimalist conceptions of this research strategy. Kemmis and Taggart (1988) have influentially argued that action research should consist of three key characteristics: first, it is conducted by classroom teachers rather than by external researchers; second, it is collaborative; and, third, it is aimed at changing some aspect of the educational system. The third characteristic marks the process out as being (at least in intention) more than just a private or individual study for the benefit of the individual practitioner researcher. A more minimalist view is adopted by Nunan (1992, p. 18), for whom collaboration and objectives aimed at institutional change are not essential, who instead argues that what counts as action research is 'if it is initiated by a question, is supported by data and inter-pretation, and is carried out by a practitioner investigating aspects of his or her own context and situation'.

It is also true that, in most cases, existing discussions and prescriptions imply an audience of experienced practitioners who have completed several years' teaching and who have the confidence, and perhaps the psychological space, to embark on research-based projects. Rachel Hawkes's narrative in the previous section is a case in point. However, it is also clear that beginner languages teachers have particular conditions, pressures, needs, objectives and other professional circumstances that both motivate and restrict their engagement in research. Our text now addresses the reader with the assumption that you are in your first year or two as a languages teacher in the UK and that you are considering carrying out some small-scale investigation into language teaching or learning.

Selecting a research focus

Despite the potential plethora of interrelated topics that present themselves to you as you prepare to take the plunge, it is wise to remind yourself that this could well be the first of several projects that you will engage in during your career. The sharper and simpler the focus of your research objective, the more systematic it is likely to be and therefore the more useful its findings for your professional development. Avoid dual or triple focuses where, for instance, you flick between investigating, say, pupil motivation, differentiation, TL use etc. Also it is advisable not to switch focus in midstream. If you find that the study you began on inductive grammar teaching is throwing up some interesting questions about formative assessment, then it is best not to switch within the same project, but either to complete the original one on grammar and reserve the one on assessment for a later date, or to abandon the original one and start again on the new focus, but thinking through the questions, objectives, data collection and so on according to the new topic.

A second criterion to apply in selecting a topic is the degree to which you are interested in it. However, it may be that you feel a need, for professional reasons, to engage in such research but are unsure what precisely to focus on. It may be helpful to think back to the assignment topics completed during your training or induction years and to select a topic now that builds on that initial work and reflection you did earlier. In this way, you would not be starting something totally new and you would have your own insights and your previous tutor's contribution to serve as a starting-point. Here is a list of initial questions suggested by Macaro (2003, p. 46):

1 What generally do I want to find out?
2 Why am I interested in finding this out?
3 What do I know already about the topic?

4 What *exactly* is/are my research question(s)? [. . .]

5 How am I going to go about carrying out the research?

6 How are the data to be analysed and who is going to do it?

7 Who will I tell about what I have discovered?

Deciding on a research strategy

The first key decision to work on is the formulation of your main research question. This should be the engine that drives your investigation. Avoid rushing too soon into decisions about research methods before you are clear precisely what you are intending to investigate. Practitioner research is, broadly speaking, distinguishable from externally led research primarily through its emphasis on detailed, in-house analysis of the case being studied (be it, for example, an individual, a class or some aspect of teaching in a particular school context). In this sense, all practitioner research is ethnographic as the teacher/researcher is a member of the school community in which the research takes place and therefore can draw on the evidence that is accessible on an ongoing, informal basis in addition to the systematic enquiry conducted within the parameters of the project itself.

The second characteristic of much practitioner research is that it is concerned with understanding or improving some aspect of learning or teaching in the researcher's own classroom. As 'action research' it seeks to achieve some insight into or change in, the effectiveness of the experience in this context.

To return to the issue of the research question, languages teachers may want to ask different types of questions:

1 Which methods of differentiation are most effective in the teaching of KS3 French classes?

2 What factors affect girls' willingness to communicate in Spanish GCSE lessons?

3 Does programmed independent study lead to improvement in language proficiency?

4 What strategies do A level German students use in extended oral tasks?

5 Why does boys' motivation in FL learning improve in ICT-based lessons?

Let us briefly look at each question in turn in order to see how each might entail a different methodological approach.

1 A question like this implies an element of intervention (you are going to introduce something new into your pedagogy) and comparison (you are looking for signs of change in learning, performance, motivation etc.). The focus here is on methods of differentiation (for instance, by outcome, by task, by feedback and so on). You would plan and use these different methods with the same class over a period of time. A second element of comparison might be a before-and-after evaluation (known as an A-B-A design). How will you know which methods are effective? You should decide your criteria beforehand. These might be:

   a) based on learning outcomes, i.e. a comparison of pupils' test performance before and after the 'intervention' (which might last a whole term); or

   b) your own impressions based on observations of pupil performance in the lessons; or

   c) your evaluation of the effectiveness of the strategies in terms of managing pupil differentiation rather than effects on enhanced learning.

2 This question can potentially elicit two types of information. First, it might be useful for you to obtain the girls' perception of what encourages and discourages them from communicating in Spanish in lessons. Their perception may not, of course, always be synonymous with what really happens, but this information may still be useful in that you can later test out some of what they say by adapting your teaching accordingly. These perceptions would normally be gained quantitatively, through a questionnaire that would include, for instance, multiple-choice questions referring to different factors (such as embarrassment, content of discourse, preferences in grouping – whole class, group, pair work). Second, you might need to try to see for yourself what these factors are that seem to have an influence. This direct, observational data would be difficult to gather independently while teaching the lesson. It would be best either to video sample lessons, or to ask a colleague to observe a few lessons, completing an observation grid designed by you that focuses on your research

objective. In addition, and bridging these two sources of data collection, would be interviews with a selection of pupils to follow up their responses on the questionnaire. The interviews could also ideally be conducted shortly after one of the lessons, which would allow you to ask probing questions about aspects of the lesson in question. The pupils' response would therefore be usefully grounded in reflection of the events in the lesson still fresh in the pupil's mind. This project's methodology would therefore consist of a mixed-mode (quantitative and qualitative) strategy.

3 Here, the question is looking for measurement of improvement in a dependent variable (language proficiency) as a result of the effect of an independent variable (completion of a programme of independent study), and therefore your research is going to be based on a quasi-experimental mode. First, you will need to define what you mean by 'language proficiency'. Which of the language skills will you examine, and, in relation to that skill, which criteria will you apply (grammatical accuracy, vocabulary acquisition, fluency etc.)? What systematic method will you use to measure these criteria? Second, in order to ascertain whether or not improvement results from your programme of independent study you need to introduce a comparative element to your methodology. This would normally be done through identifying an experimental group (which follows your independent-study programme) and a control group (which only follows the normal programme of learning). Differences in language proficiency between the two groups can be measured on a whole-group basis by analysing their performance in the same language test at the end of the programme. More refined analysis can also be obtained through a matched-pair design by which you can identify paired individuals across the two groups, based on similar levels of language ability. A comparison of their post-test results would indicate to you the degree of effectiveness of the programme and might show up different levels of effectiveness with different types of pupils. Types are here being differentiated by levels and preferred styles of learning.

4 As indicated in the examples from the literature on strategy research given in Chapter 3, this type of study is essentially a

qualitative one. Questions beginning with 'What strategies . . .?' are essentially equivalent to 'How . . .?' questions. These are qualitative and are aimed at providing an analytical description of teaching or learning: in this case, an aspect of pupil cognitive behaviour in completing an oral task. The strategies in this example might be public and private. The public ones might include recourse to dictionaries or to help from other pupils from the teacher. The more private ones might be the mental strategies used, such as recourse to L1, use of cognates, use of circumlocution, which can be easily missed during 'live' observation. Both sets of data might well be valuable to you as a teacher in that they might provide you with evidence of recurring strategies used by the students that you could then exploit or cater for in your teaching, but how to capture the more private strategies used by the students? One method would be to provide them with tape recorders on which to record their pair work or individual oral presentations, which you can later analyse.

5 'Why . . .?' questions are primarily used in interpretative studies and relate to some aspect of the social psychology of FL learning or teaching. They are concerned with capturing and interpreting attitudes, motivation, understandings or other psychological variables that affect outward behaviour. In this case, there is an assumption that boys' motivation does indeed improve in ICT-based lessons. This may well be a broad and inaccurate generalisation. Does it improve in all ICT-based lessons, irrespective of the way they are planned? Nevertheless the assumption here is that the hypothesis is generally true, based perhaps on common knowledge as found in the literature, or on your own prior experience. The aim in this study is to try to explain this phenomenon, not to test the hypothesis. Again, this would not be a purely academic investigation, as the findings could be useful to the development of your pedagogy both in the computer room and in the conventional classroom. The methodology in this study could be a mixture of survey technique (perhaps administering a questionnaire to all boys within a year group at the school) and ethnographic interviews with a small sample (allowing the pupils to talk freely about their reactions to different aspects of the ICT language-learning environment).

CONCLUSION

The note on which we would like to conclude this overview of the opportunities for research available to teachers of FL is that, despite the difficulties of the challenge, this is a very worthwhile enterprise that can enrich the quality of a teacher's professional work. So much of a language teacher's time is taken up with communicating, performing and instructing, that little opportunity is available for systematic reflection and professional learning leading to self-improvement or institutional change. Research, defined in the relatively modest terms of this chapter, is one way of doing this. Three key questions emerge that we advise you to consider before planning the detail of the study and after its completion.

Before:

- Is the research question worth investigating?
- Is the project feasible?
- Will the project involve a qualitative or quantitative research design or a mixture of both?

After:

- What are my main findings?
- How can I validate my findings?
- Who should I share them with?

The final question is particularly important in transforming an initially personal engagement in practitioner research into a wider professional experience. You can share your findings and research with other colleagues in your department or in other school departments, with outside agencies or through publication in professional journals such as the *Language Learning Journal*. As Rachel Hawkes reveals in her narrative, sometimes it can also be very productive to share the findings with the pupils themselves.

QUESTIONS FOR DISCUSSION

1. How does a school or college become a knowledge-creating institution?
2. What are the key stages in Rachel Hawkes's development as a practitioner researcher?
3. What opportunities exist at your institution for promoting research activities for its staff?
4. What research methodology would be most suitable for investigating the effectiveness of an inductive method of teaching grammar?
5. Which issues arising out of your classroom practice would you most like to investigate in an action research study?

Chapter 7

Wider professional knowledge and professional learning

INTRODUCTION

'Wider professional knowledge' is a frequently used term in educational officialdom that, as it is used as a yard-stick by Ofsted and the TDA to evaluate teachers' performance, has significant implications for a teacher's career development. Despite this significance, the precise definition of professional knowledge can be vague and can imply something generic and separate from the substantive pedagogical knowledge we have been describing in earlier chapters. Our argument in this final chapter is that, for a FL teacher, as much as for a teacher of any other subject, professional knowledge includes the following elements: knowledge about education; the place of FLs in the curriculum; aspects of government educational policy; and the FL teacher as a member of a professional body.

Since 1988 and the introduction of the NC, central government has moved beyond its traditional role of education policymaker and has progressively taken over much of the educational decision making that was formerly left to educators. The plethora of new initiatives that schools have been called upon to implement have made huge demands on teachers and, arguably, have required a far greater degree of conformity and compliance and less opportunity to develop as autonomous professionals. At the same time, however, never has there been greater formal guidance and support on offer, emanating both from central government, through the DCSF and the TDA, and from quasi-governmental organisations such as CILT. Informal networks of individuals, links between local schools and the professional development initiated by LA advisory services in response to local need and demand have been largely replaced by more centrally controlled and regulated opportunities aimed at individual teachers. Equally, relationships among staff in schools have changed, with frequent, formal team meetings at every level, to discuss the implementation of policy and curriculum initiatives, which have to some extent taken over from the perhaps more haphazard, though often very creative, staff room and departmental office discussions between colleagues. Teachers, especially those who are new to the profession, need to be able to 'navigate the system', be able to seek out appropriate support for their professional development, but more importantly, to examine the changing relationship between education and society in order better to understand the policy initiatives that they are subject to and to gain a more objective understanding of their own professional practice.

In this chapter, we will examine the place of the FL teacher within the teaching community and consider the role that outside organisations play in developing languages education and in the professional development of teachers. We will also examine the parallel issue of the place of FLs in the school curriculum and their relationship with wider curricular concerns such as citizenship education.

HOW IS TEACHER PROFESSIONALISM DEVELOPED?

In this book, we have considered the important fields of knowledge in the teaching and learning of FLs that are the essential foundation of teacher professionalism and we have at least signposted their theoretical bases. Classroom practice, developed experientially, necessarily draws on theory, whether directly or indirectly, and is most effective when we understand *why* we adopt particular practices to promote effective learning in our students; that is, we are aware of the theoretical underpinnings that inform our work as teachers. Although your primary concern, particularly as a beginner teacher, is with the development of practical classroom skills, these can only be truly effective if accompanied by theoretical knowledge that enables you to become an educational thinker and principled professional as well as a competent practitioner. Intellectual engagement with ideas about education in general and what research tells us about the teaching and learning of FLs in particular can be what sustains you in your career development when classroom skills have become routine. Indeed, an understanding of the historical, social and organisational contexts in which teachers work is an essential part of the professional knowledge of the teacher.

In an initial teacher education period that is essentially practice-based and focused on the development of practical teaching skills, it is not surprising that beginner teachers often see theoretical knowledge as marginal to their professional development because it may not be 'useful' or *directly* relevant to what they perceive as their needs. However, principled guidance on practice accompanied by the development of reflective practice is now being provided by the majority of Postgraduate Certificate in Education (PGCE) courses in the UK and this signals a shift in the way 'theory' is understood.

With the QAA announcement in April 2005 that, from either September 2006 or 2007, PGCE qualifications should be offered at either H level ('professional graduate') or M level ('postgraduate'), many institutions opting for the latter are developing courses with an enhanced theoretical and research-orientated dimension. (The H and the M refer to Honours and Masters level, respectively.) UCET reports that, in 2006–7, most universities in England are intending to offer both routes for their PGCE courses. In practical terms this means that for the M level route the content of the course will have a strengthened intellectual component, with Master's criteria used for assessing written work, the completion of a small-scale research enquiry during professional placement and generally more rigour applied to the development of critical reading of educational theory. Such courses would also provide successful students with credits towards a Masters degree completed part-time subsequent to the PGCE year.

If you are a FL PGCE student about to embark on such an M level course, how can you make this research focus useful to you? The box on p. 170 shows some possible starting guidelines.

Although it has become something of a slogan, it is 'reflective practice' rather than theory that underpins both policy and practice in teacher training and in education. Indeed, it has become *the* medium through which theory and practice can be reconciled. It was Schön who first popularised 'reflection' as a professional activity in his 1983 book *The Reflective Practitioner – How Professionals Think in Action*. He claimed to offer 'a new epistemology of practice' more appropriate to professional life than the traditional approach to knowledge. Schön's analysis of professional knowledge was based on his experiences as a consultant working in industry. This is important to note, as one might question the desirability

169

GUIDELINES

- Research should be integral to your training not separate, so find a connection between the issues you read about in the research literature and the experience you have as a teacher in the classroom.

- When you choose a topic for your small-scale enquiry, ask yourself three basic questions:

  1 What is the pedagogical purpose? (i.e. How will this strategy improve pupil learning?)
  2 What is the intellectual purpose? (i.e. What insights will this give you about a recognised educational topic such as learning style or learner motivation?)
  3 What is the developmental purpose? (i.e. How will this investigation develop aspects of professional competence as a FL classroom teacher?)

- Think of the relationship between published research and classroom practice not as that between theoretical knowledge and practical experience but rather that of prior knowledge that can be validated, questioned or transformed in the light of your own classroom-based evidence.

and even legitimacy of transferring ideas about the professional–client relationship in business and industry to the domain of education.

Although the value of reflection on experience in the classroom in order to improve one's own teaching and promote more effective learning is not denied, it can only apply a subjective definition of knowledge and theoretical understanding. The process of reflection as a psychological phenomenon is necessarily subjective, placing the responsibility to improve professional practice firmly on the individual, and as such does little to encourage a broader critical understanding of issues. McIntyre (1993) makes the valid distinction between theoretical and practical knowledge: that theoretical knowledge 'is knowledge formulated in such a way as to imply claims to some sort of generalisability', whereas practical knowledge is 'knowledge which is used to guide practice . . . but does not go beyond the particular' (1993, p. 48). Therefore, although the ability to reflect is a desirable skill for teachers to develop in order to improve classroom practice, it should not replace, or indeed be confused with, theoretical knowledge. Indeed, as McIntyre points out, the initial teacher education period is best used as a time when beginner teachers have access to the ideas of others, and learning to reflect is a goal.

Learning to teach, therefore, entails an initiation into a body of theoretical knowledge as well as the development of practical teaching skills. It is a complex process involving the synthesis of knowledge, ideas and experience that continues through professional life.

SUPPORTING THE FL TEACHER AND PROMOTING FLS

Support for FL teachers can be divided into three main categories. First, a number of organisations offer courses, information and guidance on approaches to FL teaching and learning and on the implementation of new initiatives. Second, there are a large number of dedicated websites that provide teaching and learning resources for FL. Third, the cultural institutes attached to embassies, mostly based in London and other capital cities, offer a range of facilities and cultural events that might be of broader interest to the FL teacher.

However, as important as it is for you as a FL teacher to keep abreast of developments in FL teaching and learning and maintain and develop your own linguistic and cultural knowledge, it is equally important for you to engage with wider educational debates. The temptation for subject specialists to focus on the narrow, albeit important, concerns of their discipline, is natural, but teacher professionalism extends beyond the classroom. What happens in the FL classroom must be seen in the context of broader educational principles and policy issues, which are often ignored or accepted uncritically. Where do these wider debates about education take place? Clearly, the educational press keeps a watchful eye on government policy and reports widely on the world of education. There are a number of forums that enable teachers to express their own views and engage in debate, although these are often sadly under-used by teachers. So-called 'think tanks' such as Demos, the Institute of Public Policy Research (IPPR), the Centre for Policy Studies (CPS) and Policy Exchange research into, and comment on, educational policy and offer differing perspectives on educational matters (see www.policylibrary.com/education/ for further details of these and similar organisations). The Institute of Ideas (www.instituteofideas.com) has an 'education forum' for teachers and other education professionals for discussion and examination of the intellectual currents that lie behind government initiatives. Such organisations enable teachers to step outside the day-to-day concerns of teaching and schooling and develop a deeper critical understanding of education and their professional role within the system upon which their particular professionalism as FL specialists is predicated. Nevertheless, the paramount concern of FL teachers is undoubtedly teaching and learning within their specialist field, and, in this respect, there are numerous organisations that provide a wealth of information, resources and professional development opportunities for FLs teachers.

The most well-known of these is CILT, the Government's recognised centre of expertise on languages. Based in central London, CILT (www.cilt.org.uk) has been in existence for over 40 years and has become perhaps the most influential organisation in informing and promoting the implementation of government policies on languages. CILT organises a range of conferences and courses for FL teachers in all sectors. It conducts and disseminates research into FL teaching and learning and is a rich source of information on all aspects of FLs. Its reference library is possibly the UK's largest collection of FL books, teaching materials and multimedia resources, including several specialist collections, notably on language teaching methodology as well as a substantial collection of periodicals and examination syllabuses. CILT also operates throughout the UK with its partner organisations, CILT Cymru, Northern Ireland CILT and Scottish CILT. It also sponsors the national network of Comenius Centres which in themselves are a rich source of information and support for FL teachers. Equally, CILT publishes a number of books and other publications, notably the extensive *Pathfinder* series of practical guides, which many teachers are familiar with, and the *Reflections* series, which provides more in-depth considerations of FL issues. Though immensely valuable, it has to be said CILT publications rarely stop to question the wisdom of government policy and tend not to reference research evidence very widely.

As our introduction indicated, the trend in supporting teachers' continuing professional development (CPD) is towards a high degree of centrally accredited CPD through the DCSF and the TDA, although the actual provision of training mostly takes place at a local level. One recent example of this has been the staff development provided in relation to the National Languages Strategy KS3 Framework. Comprehensive training packages were produced centrally, and a team of trainers was recruited to 'deliver' the training to groups of FL teachers all around the country.

The aim of this style of professional 'development' is to ensure the dissemination of a consistent 'message' and to promote conformity in the implementation of new policies. However, it might be argued that the purpose of CPD should be to engage teachers in discussion and debate about issues in order to create a dynamic, critical relationship between policymakers and practitioners, rather than encouraging them to be passive conduits for new initiatives (see e.g. Pickering, Daly and Pachler, 2007).

Nevertheless, there is extensive information and advice now on offer on the internet through the DCSF website regarding all new initiatives such as The Languages Ladder (www.dfes.gov.uk/languages/DSP_languages ladder.cfm), part of the National Languages Strategy. TeacherNet (www. teachernet.gov.uk/professionaldevelopment/), another part of the DCSF site, offers enormous opportunities to increase teachers' knowledge or understanding and their effectiveness in schools. From NQT induction, primary phase and KS3 pedagogic packs, through to whole-school CPD, support for LEA capacity building and Postgraduate Professional Development (PPD), the TeacherNet website provides banks of information, resources and guidance that frames teachers' CPD.

For a more independent source of support, the Association for Language Learning (ALL) is the major subject association for those involved in teaching all FLs at all levels. With a national network of active regional branches, ALL (www.all-languages.org.uk) organises language-specific events, courses and conferences for its members. It is an organisation that essentially relies upon the interest and enthusiasm of its members to share expertise and knowledge and develop approaches to FL teaching and learning in a collaborative spirit. The ALL also prides itself on its contribution to the professional development of teachers through its journals. The *Language Learning Journal* is the foremost professional journal for FL teachers in the UK. Articles are submitted from language education professionals in all sectors from the UK and beyond, on a wide variety of topics from practical experience to research and theoretical perspectives. The journal offers a rich source of information, discussion and dialogue for FL professionals created by FL professionals. Equally, the language-specific journals *Deutsch: Lehren und Lernen, Dutch Crossing, Francophonie, Rusistika, Tuttitalia* and *Via Hispánica* aimed at teachers of particular languages, focus primarily on classroom practice. In addition, *Language World Quarterly* provides a regular update on the ALL and its activities and ALL's responses to government initiatives. The ALL annual conference, *Languages World*, is the largest conference for FL teachers in the UK. While seeking to maintain its independence, ALL nevertheless meets with government agencies, aiming to inform policy, and has contacts with teaching organisations worldwide, such as the *Fédération internationale des professeurs de français* (FIPF) and *Der Internationale Deutschlehrerverband* (IDV).

Besides professionally orientated organisations that support FL teachers' development, it is important not to neglect linguistic and cultural interests that may be seen as personally enriching. Indeed, this aspect of FL teacher professionalism is often ignored, unless there appears to be some deficit in subject knowledge that needs attention to ensure effective teaching. Arguably, maintaining and developing one's own cultural and linguistic interests are as important as the continued development of classroom skills, pedagogical knowledge and a broad interest in educational developments, because these are a great source of inspiration and motivation to the FL teacher. Maintaining linguistic fluency is, for the non-native FL teacher, a serious concern, when the majority of classroom language use is at a basic level. Equally, to continue to develop cultural interests and stay up-to-date with the politics, current affairs and cultural life of a foreign country requires a conscious effort that is not always easy to make, in the midst of busy school life. Funding opportunities for teacher exchange and school linking programmes or attendance at international courses are available for UK teachers through the British Council (www.britishcouncil. org/education/teachers/). Apart from the obvious rich source of information and entertainment that the internet, satellite TV and radio offer, the various cultural institutes of foreign embassies offer programmes of cultural events throughout the year. Equally, establishing contacts with schools abroad, although having the primary goal of enhancing pupils' FL learning experience, also provides interesting opportunities for teachers as well, both in terms of social contacts and deepening cultural knowledge. For the native speaker, these issues might not seem of such immediate concern, but, as many native-speaker teachers of languages will testify, it is very easy to lose touch with what is happening in one's own country when one is immersed in the language and culture of another.

However, the real point of seeking out opportunities to maintain and develop cultural and linguistic knowledge is not an instrumental one, but an intellectual one. The passion that FL teachers claim for their subject when they are starting out in teaching needs to be sustained intellectually as well as professionally. Moreover, it is through continually developing our own subject knowledge that we reinforce our belief in the importance of FL learning and are able to continue to enthuse, motivate and inspire young people in the FL classroom.

PROFESSIONAL AND SUBJECT IDENTITIES

It is perhaps understandable that the bulk of the literature on professional development is articulated from the standpoint of a generic, vocational depiction of the role of the teacher. The phrase commonly used, i.e. 'wider role', has a paradoxical echo in references to 'core' studies (both for the beginner teacher and for the school student) in that such metaphors suggest a clear boundary between focus on subject-related work and focus on generic work. What is the implicit opposition here: centre and periphery, breadth and specialism, academic and pastoral?

The separation of subject and 'core' is understandable in that we know, through our experience as teacher educators on PGCE courses, that many entrants into the profession arrive primarily on the basis of a love of their subject and a desire to impart that knowledge and enthusiasm to school children. This is certainly true in the case of aspiring FL teachers. The discovery of the nature of the work outside the FL classroom, both in terms of the specific duties involved and of the day-to-day interaction with colleagues, pupils and parents, entail professional attitudes and actions that in most cases are unanticipated to any significant extent before first arrival at the school gates. This remains true despite the fact that many beginner teachers of FLs benefit from prior experience of work as a FLA in a school abroad. This may be owing partly to the fundamental differences between the nature of the work of a FLA and a subject teacher, and partly to the differences between the systems and cultures of schools in different countries. Therefore, clear guidelines, expectations and definitions of the 'broader' or 'whole school' professional role of a teacher are undeniably necessary and welcome.

However, when one looks a little more closely at some of the Ofsted standards in this category, it is difficult not to question the apparent assumption that there is a dividing-line between subject work and the wider professional role. It is difficult to see how, for instance, teachers can commit to 'raising the educational achievement' of their pupils other than mainly through their subject teaching. Similarly, their ability to 'improve their own teaching, by evaluating it, learning from the effective practice of others and from evidence' must surely be centrally tied to critical analysis of their subject teaching and understanding, in the way we have suggested throughout this book, particularly in Chapter 6.

CULTURE AND PROFESSIONAL GROWTH

An alternative framework for defining the different professional dimensions of a teacher's role, which avoids an artificial distinction between subject teaching and non-subject roles, is to talk instead in terms of an overlap of cultures. Teacher culture has been described in an ethnographic sense as a 'subculture with shared behaviours, shared language and shared understandings of the concepts referred to by that language' (Woods, 1996). Hargreaves sees this culture as a scaffold for professional learning, consisting of:

> beliefs, values and assumed ways of doing things among communities of teachers who have had to deal with similar demands and constraints over many years. Culture carries the community's historically generated and collectively shared solutions to its new and inexperienced membership. It forms a framework for occupational learning. Cultures of teaching help give meaning, support and identity to teachers and their work.
>
> (Hargreaves, 1992, p. 217)

In our view, in order to define the formative contexts in which the professional development of the subject teacher takes place, it is important to identify at least three dimensions of professional culture that influence a teacher's development (see Figure 7.1).

Culture of the teaching profession

To some extent this culture consists of an abstract identity that is symbolically highlighted through professional qualifications (the first of which being the award of QTS), through membership of the General Teaching Council (GTC), and through membership of teaching unions and other similar generic professional associations. In most cases, this culture serves to provide legal and social reinforcement of the role of teacher. On a more interpersonal level, this culture is built up through networking, at conferences and regional training events, as well as by

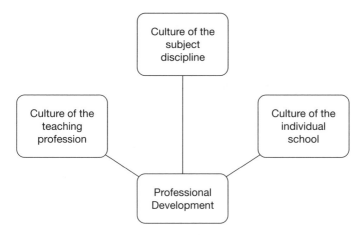

Figure 7.1 *Cultural dimensions of the professional development of a teacher*

developing a common language and sharing of concerns and objectives with the teaching community. The community of teachers is different to that of doctors or architects: a different language is spoken, and different sets of priorities are assumed.

Culture of the individual school

Here, teachers develop their professional identity by adapting and contributing to the life of the school they work in. This work represents more than salaried employment; it entails membership of the community of the school and solidarity with colleagues in the educational and pastoral support of the pupils at the school, participating in discussion and decision making and other practices that define the community. This contribution goes beyond physical involvement in, for instance, extracurricular events, form tutoring and teaching of personal and social education, ancillary work such as lunch-time supervision or bus duty, and involvement in staff meetings and training events. The adaptation required within this culture is partly triggered by interaction with the dominant mode of behaviour and thinking among staff at the school. The FL teacher is partly defined here by how other staff see them (whether through the lens of the vertical hierarchy of the headteacher and senior management team or the flat hierarchy of colleagues in other departments). There is a balance to maintain

177

between conformity to the dominant school culture (on, for instance, dress, discipline or curricular priorities) and contributing to evolution and change in that culture.

Culture of the subject discipline

As stated earlier in this chapter, subject culture is perhaps the one frame of reference that new teachers (and certainly beginner teachers at the start of training) bring with them as they embark on their career. For FL beginner teachers, this culture is primarily grounded in subject knowledge and the pleasure they have experienced in their own study of the TL and encounters with the target culture. By reflecting on the theory and methodology of FL teaching, and through contact with other FL teachers (experienced and fellow beginner teachers) and educators, as well as through the development of their own classroom practice, beginner teachers gain entry into the community of FL teachers. They begin to share an identity and a culture with other FL teachers in their school, a culture that is further fostered through affiliation to external agencies such as the ALL and through support from national sources of information and training in FL teaching such as CILT.

PROFESSIONAL DEVELOPMENT AS A DIALOGUE OF SUBJECTS

'You are how others see you': most subject teachers are labelled and defined by their subject specialism in the eyes of pupils. For most pupils at a secondary school, teachers are defined functionally as well as individually: Miss Jones is the French teacher, Mr Smith is the history teacher. Equally, in the staffroom and in the wider topography of the school site, teachers normally occupy separate curricular spaces that reinforce perception of their subject identity in the eyes of colleagues. To counter this apparent source of divisiveness, there is a natural tendency to see professional development as a means of breaking down barriers and of strengthening a sense of corporate belonging. We would strongly encourage the breaking down of barriers between subjects.

However, corporate bonding need not entail abandonment of subject identity; indeed, we would argue that professional development and integration within a school community can be helped by the teacher's effective and diplomatic application of their role as subject specialist. The following two examples are aimed at illustrating this very important principle. We use the metaphor of the bridge in both cases, because this implies that the space between can be crossed in both directions.

Literacy: the bridge between L1 and L2

The relationship between the teaching of FLs and of literacy is double-edged. On the one hand, both focus explicitly and intensively on the workings and practice of language. On the other hand, unlike literacy and all other subjects on the curriculum, they are separated by the fact that the FL taught (L2) is not English. The paradox, therefore, is that, although the formal and strategic objectives of both are often similar and some-times identical, the mutual benefits are indirect in that they involve transfer-ence from the domain of one language to another. This latter point of difference partly explains the government's hesitations over attributing a more central role to the study of FLs within the broad framework of literacy development in school. However, this difference is also a source of (as yet under-exploited) strength. Cultural and linguistic diversity need not be seen as an obstacle or as an irrelevance to L1 literacy development. The current framework of the NC MFL Order (based on a combination of communicative and grammar-focused principles) allows scope for a close meshing of FL and literacy objectives.

Areas for further development in FL methodology

The development of FL teaching in this country might be informed by literacy-related curricular thinking in the following ways: The following are some practical, policy-related suggestions for national development on this issue that FL teachers might reflect on productively and develop in their debates with teachers from other subject disciplines, not in an adversarial way but in order to locate FL (and, therefore, by implication, we would argue, their own professional status as educators) on a serious platform of curricular dialogue:

- The primary MFL initiative (DfES, 2002) needs to consider the place of literacy and knowledge about language within the primary MFL curriculum. The Nuffield Languages Inquiry (2000)

FL CONTRIBUTION TO LITERACY AT KSS 3/4:

- revision at KSs 3/4 of more elementary word/sentence level work (e.g. reinforcement of tenses, agreements etc.) ('helping to rescue children who might otherwise have been left behind');
- formal, concentrated focus on:
  - patterns/rules of spelling;
  - patterns/rules of pronunciation (phonic work: choral repetition, songs etc.);
  - sentence construction.
- opportunities for interactive, communicative discourse (including real text exchanges with peers from the target cultures through letters, emails, computer-mediated communication etc.);
- development of independent language-learning skills (e.g. practice in how to use dictionaries and other reference materials (PoS 3d), how to memorise vocabulary and phrases (PoS 3a), how to use context and other clues to interpret meaning (PoS 3b) and other language-learning strategies).

THE CONTRIBUTION OF LITERACY TEACHING AT KSS 1/2 TO FL TEACHING AND LEARNING:

- improved grounding in grammar terminology and understanding of grammar;
- opportunities to compare the L2/3 with L1 provide the basis for developing pupils' language awareness and knowledge;
- helps pupils to 'use their knowledge of English when learning the L2' (PoS 3c);
- reinforces the link between reading and writing, between communicative intent/content and written/oral expression.

recommended that, 'The national action for early learning should (inter alia): introduce the national Literacy Strategy programme modules of language awareness, the content of which would be designed to bridge the gap between English, literacy and foreign languages.'
- FL teaching methodology needs to give more attention to the development of text-based work.

- Greater integration of form-focused and meaning-focused perspectives of pupil work (e.g. at GCSE, fluency, content and accuracy are assessed separately).

- FL teachers' knowledge of the similarities and differences between the language(s) they are teaching and English should be strengthened.

- The current dominance of the genres of transactional and personalised language use in FL courses should make way for greater practice in other genres as well.

Citizenship: a bridge too far?

In a recent book exploring extended reading in history for 11–14-year-olds, Counsell (2004, p. iv) offers the following answer to the question 'What are subjects for?':

> Within a particular field of enquiry, a subject provides rigour in the quest for knowledge or truth. By making sense of a subject's practices, pupils gain a way of enquiring, an understanding of the conditions under which valid claims can be made and a sense of the scope and limits of enquiry. A subject is not a collection of information. Subjects are different ways of thinking and knowing.
>
> (Counsell, 2004, p. iv)

If history teaching connects with citizenship education goals by developing pupils' understanding of the concept of 'becoming informed, active and responsible citizens' through finding out 'where the concept came from' and revisiting it in different settings as part of the process of 'tracing the roots of British identity' and seeing 'how it is re-shaped' at different moments in time (Wrenn, 1999, pp. 7–9), how are these goals defined within the specifically FL perspective of thinking and knowing? The following are some suggestions:

- Learning a FL at school involves thinking about otherness in substantively simple yet cognitively complex ways. Social topics (daily living, customs, schooling) and social issues (healthy eating, the environment, youth culture) are explored in a languages classroom through explicit focus on the target country (France, Germany, Spain) or through comparison with the same topics

181

and issues as they affect the lives of the pupils in the UK. Even when the lesson is ostensibly eliciting personalised use of the TL by referring to the pupils' own experience of, say, daily routine, the French teacher can exploit the situation to draw out the French parallel from the background. As a citizenship education goal, the pupils are engaged in reflecting about their context and a parallel European context, and, in this way, their thinking about difference and identity can be built up from a comparative, cross-national perspective.

- Learning a FL at school is (especially at KSs 3 and 4) primarily a first-person experience. The process of learning here consists largely of a subjective expression and perception of life. The point of view is mainly adolescent. The texts they process are regularly produced, whether real or simulated, from the perspective of a teenager. In this way, a generational dimension is introduced into the learning that can be exploited for intercultural and communal purposes. These broader citizenship goals (membership of a European and global community) can be incomparably strengthened through real contact in the form of exchange visits, email correspondence and similar means.

- Learning a FL at school allows the learners to 'get under the skin of a foreign culture'. The 'skin' in this case is the language. By reading, listening, speaking and writing the language, pupils adopt an insider's view of the ways of thinking of the people of the target country. Even encountering and applying simple pragmatic rules about the use of *tu* and *vous* in French tells the pupils something about the conventions of interpersonal relations in France, which they would not otherwise be able to glean from non-linguistic forms of study. Pachler and Field (2001a, pp. 147–74) and Pachler, Barnes and Field (2008) provide different illustrations of the way FL learning provides opportunities for the four stages of acculturation whereby a learner's cultural awareness is developed: excitement, alienation, recovery and acceptance.

- Learning a FL at school is a sustained effort. Unlike international references in other subjects, studying a FL, if taken through to A level, lasts on average 7 years. If planned effectively (by everyone involved in this process, including the DCSF, syllabus designers, examiners and teachers), the experience offered to the pupil is potentially one of in-depth knowledge of the social and

PROGRAMME OF STUDY: CITIZENSHIP

1 Knowledge and understanding about becoming informed citizens

Key Stage 3

Pupils should be taught about:

b) the diversity of national, regional, religious and ethnic identities in the United Kingdom and the need for mutual respect and understanding

i) the world as a global community, and the political, economic, environmental and social implications of this, and the role of the European Union, the Commonwealth and the United Nations

Key Stage 4

a) the legal and human rights and responsibilities underpinning society and how they relate to citizens, including the role and operation of the criminal and civil justice systems

j) the wider issues and challenges of global interdependence and responsibility, including sustainable development and Local Agenda 21

2 Developing skills of enquiry and communication

Key Stage 3

Pupils should be taught to

a) think about topical political, spiritual, moral, social and cultural issues, problems and events by analysing information and its sources, including ICT-based sources

b) justify orally and in writing a personal opinion about such issues, problems or events

c) contribute to group and exploratory class discussions, and take part in debates

cultural fabric of the country being studied and the diversity of its people, at the same time as the pupil develops a communicative proficiency in the FL.

We end this discussion with two examples of ways in which the experience of FL learning echoes Young's notion of 'connective specialisation' (discussed in Chapter 4) and which we have described here as a form of outreach to aspects of the wider world. Both examples suggest ways in which citizenship education can be embedded within the processes of FL learning and FL use; they differ in that one example refers to authentic communication interaction, whereas the other takes the form of explicit, classroom-based teaching and learning.

Dress and identity

The theme of the ban on the wearing of headscarves in schools throughout Europe in recent times has its origins in the controversial ruling by Jules Ferry, prime minister of France in the 1880s, which declared state schools as '*écoles sanctuaires*', thus establishing secular education in the country, which has continued to this day. Although originally conceived in relation primarily to the influence of the Catholic Church in state schools, it has since the 1980s been invoked in the context of the debate surrounding the wearing of headscarves by Muslim schoolgirls. Originally the principle of '*laïcité*' was conceived in the name of citizenship, eliminating ostensive affiliations to different religions in order to strengthen ties of citizenship between all children in France despite their diverse backgrounds. Many today see the law as an infringement of civil liberties and, post-September 11, the issue has gained added controversy; disputes over the wearing of hijabs and veils at school have spread to other European countries including the UK.

At A level, the topic has featured on French specifications (for instance, in the context of the topics of immigration and multiculturalism). With younger learners, the theme touches, inter alia, on more familiar topics such as national identity ('*tu es britannique ou anglais?*'), and place of birth ('*je suis né à*'), acquisition of adjectives (*tolérant, agressif* etc.) and practice of the modal verbs *pouvoir*, *vouloir* and *devoir*. A related topic, commonly visited at KS3 and 4 is that of school uniform: it takes little to turn this issue from a purely informative snippet about whether or not a uniform is worn in France and descriptions of uniform worn in England into a vehicle for developing arguments related to equality. As the following extract (presented in unedited form) of a bilingual computer mediated conference discussion between teenagers in England, France and Canada indicates, pupils are prepared to handle such issues in a FL communicative context:

Vindra: *Selon moi, l'uniforme de l'école n'est pas une mauvaise chose. J'ai porter l'uniforme pendant tout mon primaire et secondaire et je suis encore vivante. L'uniforme ne change pas t'a personnalité ni ta façon de penser, elle permet d'égaliser les élèves entre eux. Ce n'est pas par les vêtements qu'on ressort notre personnalité, mais plustôt par la façon de parler, socialiser et agir. C'est vrai, quel ressort notre côté créative, mais on peut sortir notre créativité par la coiffure, bijoux et autres accesoires. Bref, selon moi l'uniforme est cool.*

Amanda: Hello!!!! I wear a school uniform, and always have done!! I hate it, it's a blue long navy pleated skirt, with a shirt and jumper, but I am grateful for it, because I don't spend ages deciding what to wear, and because everyone wears it, apart from the teachers and sixth form! It doesn't matter! So, I don't think school uniforms should be abolished!

Leaig: *Pour ma part, je pense que les uniformes sont une bonnes chose car il permait de ne pas faire de differences entres les élèves bien que les chaussures – le permettent mais à la limite les differences. En revanche, il n'y a pas la liberté de s'exprimer. J'aimerais bien essayé pendant juste une semaine pour voir ce que se la fait.*

Vindra: *Tu a raison Leaig, les uniformes limitent les gens de s'exprimer, mais ce n'est pas juste les vêtement qui degageant qui tu es, mais plûtot ce que tu degage en parlant. En tout cas, moi qui a porter uniforme pendant tout mon primaire et secondaire, ce n'est pas si pire et en plus tu ne passes pas des heures le matin à choisir ce que tu veux porter.*

What this brief exchange indicates is that a managed framework of independent discourse between pupils communicating in a FL (Vindra in this exchange is an anglophone and Leaig is a francophone speaker) can spontaneously entail reflection on questions of social equality and identity.

Poverty in Central America and the present tense of regular -*ar* verbs

In her article, published in *Vida Hispánica*, Malarée (2004) describes a project funded by the Department for International Development that aimed at raising pupils' awareness of poverty through subject-based teaching. The class was a Year 9 Spanish group.

The teachers involved in the project designed a unit of work with the objective of teaching about a 'subject-based (Spanish) worldview of poverty with particular emphasis on banana plantations in five Spanish speaking countries'. This involved giving the pupils an awareness of the connection between their daily lives (shopping for Fair Trade fruit) and the economic conditions of workers in Latin America. Through practising verbs such as *comprar*, *trabajar*, *dañar* and looking at simple texts and statistics about the working conditions, the teachers succeeded in drawing the pupils' attention to 'the interaction between [themselves] as consumers and the producers in faraway countries'. In her conclusion to the article, the author states:

> When creating and trialling the teaching materials for development education in the Spanish classroom the intention was not to influence drastically pupils' views of the less privileged in the world but to inform so that students can develop skills in critical thinking.
>
> (Malarée, 2004, p. 6)

In this instance, a FL teacher has benefited from collaboration with teachers from other disciplines, supported and funded by an outside agency, and thereby raised the profile of her subject by connecting with a common educational goal.

CONCLUSION

> As a PGCE student you feel on the safe side. If anything ever goes horribly wrong you know that you are only a trainee and everybody will understand. As an NQT you feel more as a professional and you want to be able to cope yourself. You want to do this as a trainee too but when you have completed your PGCE you think of yourself as a proper teacher now.

Inevitably, much of the discussion in this book, including in this chapter, has drawn on models provided by experienced teachers of FL. New FL teachers cannot all be expected to engage in ground-breaking activities and approaches to FL teaching, although we continue to be pleasantly surprised by those former beginner teachers of ours who make rapid progress in their careers, taking on responsibilities, sometimes as head of languages, within three years or so. On the other hand, the quote from a recent NQT above does highlight a recognisable distinction in the transition from beginner teacher to NQT. For many FL teachers, the first year of employment is a time for staking one's claim as a professional, able to cope for oneself and unsupported by the family of the training system. It is a time for asserting or finding one's individuality as a teacher vis-à-vis the pupils and the peer community. What we have been arguing throughout this book, however, is that, in the longer term and at a deeper level, the effective FL teacher must participate in the collective culture of teaching and learning.

QUESTIONS FOR DISCUSSION

1 How would you define the wider professional role of the teacher?

2 How are individual teachers affected by the different cultural dimensions of professional development?

3 What opportunities for professional development exist at your institution?

4 We have provided examples of how aspects of literacy and citizenship can be enhanced by the specific experience of studying a FL at school. How would you make a similar case for the contribution to Special Educational Needs?

5 What form of cross-disciplinary collaboration would contribute to your own professional development at this stage of your career?

6 Besides the specific applied theory of FL teaching and learning, what other areas of broader educational theory are important to a teacher's all-round professional development?

Recommended books

Allford, D. and Pachler, N. (2007) *Language, Autonomy and the New Learning Environments*. Oxford: Peter Lang.

Allwright, D. (1988) *Observation in the Language Classroom*. London: Longman.

Bialystok, E. and Hakuta, K. (1994) *In Other Words: the science and psychology of second-language acquisition*. New York: Basic Books.

Block, D. (2003) *The Social Turn in Second Language Acquisition*. Edinburgh: Edinburgh University Press.

Byrnes, H. (ed.) (1998) *Learning Foreign and Second Languages. Perspectives in research and scholarship*. New York: The Modern Language Association of America.

Chaudron, C. (1988) *Second Language Classrooms: research on teaching and learning*. Cambridge: Cambridge University Press.

Cook, G. and Seidlhofer, B. (eds) (1995) *Principle and Practice in Applied Linguistics*. Oxford University Press.

Cook, V. (2001) *Second Language Learning and Language Teaching*, 3rd edn. London: Arnold.

Davies, A. and Elder, C. (eds) (2004) *The Handbook of Applied Linguistics*. Oxford: Blackwell Publishing.

Dörnyei, Z. (2001) *Teaching and Researching Motivation*. Harlow: Pearson Education.

Eckman, F., Highland, D., Lee, P., Milcham, J. and Ruthkowski Weber, R. (eds) (1995) *Second Language Acquisition Theory and Pedagogy*. Mahwah, NJ: Erlbaum.

Ellis, R. (1994) *The Study of Second Language Acquisition*. Oxford: Oxford University Press.

Ellis, R. (1997) *Second Language Acquisition Research and Language Teaching*. Oxford: Oxford University. Press

Field, K. (2000) *Issues in Modern Foreign Language Teaching*, London: Routledge.

Gass, S. and Selinker, L. (1994) *Second Language Acquisition: an introductory course*. Hillsdale, NJ: Lawrence Erlbaum.

Graham, S. (1997) *Effective Language Learning*. Clevedon: Multilingual Matters.

Grauberg, W. (1997) *The Elements of Foreign Language Teaching*. Clevedon: Multilingual Matters.

Green, S. (ed.) (2000) *New Perspectives on Teaching and Learning Modern Languages*. Clevedon: Multilingual Matters.

Larsen-Freeman, D. and Long, M. (1991) *An Introduction to Second Language Acquisition Research*. Harlow: Longman.

Lightbown, P. and Spada, N. (1999) *How Languages Are Learned*, 2nd edn. Oxford: Oxford University Press.

Macaro, E. (1997) *Target Language, Collaborative Learning and Autonomy*. Clevedon: Multilingual Matters.

Macaro, E. (2003) *Teaching and Learning a Second Language. A guide to recent research and its applications*. London: Continuum.

McDonough, S. (2002) *Applied Linguistics in Language Education*. London: Arnold.

Mitchell, R. and Myles, F. (1998) *Second Language Learning Theories*. London: Arnold.

Nunan, D. (1992) *Research Methods in Language Learning*. Cambridge: Cambridge University Press.

Pachler, N. (ed.) (1999) *Teaching Modern Foreign Languages at Advanced Level*. London: Routledge.

Pachler, N., Barnes, A. and Field, K. (2008) *Teaching Modern Foreign Languages*. 3rd, revised edition. London: Routledge.

Pachler, N. and Field, K. (2001) *Learning to Teach Modern Foreign Languages*. London: RoutledgeFalmer.

Pachler, N. and Redondo, A. (eds) (2007) *Teaching Foreign Languages in the Secondary School: a practical guide*. London: Routledge.

Richards J. and Rodgers, T. (2002) *Approaches and Methods in Language Teaching: a description and analysis*, 2nd edn. Cambridge: Cambridge University Press.

Sharwood-Smith, M. (1994) *Second Language Learning: theoretical foundations*. London: Longman.

Stern, H. (1983) *Fundamental Concepts of Language Teaching*. Oxford: Oxford University Press.

Stern, H. (1992) *Issues and Options in Language Teaching*. Oxford: Oxford University Press.

Swarbick, A. (ed.) (2002) *Teaching Modern Foreign Languages in Secondary Schools: a reader*. London: RoutledgeFalmer.

Towell, R. and Hawkins, R. (1994) *Approaches to Second Language Acquisition*. Clevedon: Multilingual Matters.

Widdowson, H. (1990) *Aspects of Language Teaching*. Oxford: Oxford University Press.

Williams, M. and Burden, R. (1997) *Psychology for Language Teachers*. Cambridge: Cambridge University Press.

Yule, G. (1996) *The Study of Language*, 2nd edn. Cambridge: Cambridge University Press.

Recommended journals

Annual Review of Applied Linguistics (http://journals.cambridge.org/action/display Journal?jidAPL).

Applied Linguistics (http://applij.oxfordjournals.org/).

German as a Foreign Language (www.gfl-journal.de).

Foreign Language Annals (www.actfl.org/i4alpages/index.cfm?pageid3320).

Language Learning (www.blackwellpublishing.com/journal.asp?ref0023-8333 &site=1).

Language Learning Journal (www.tandf.co.uk/journals/titles/09571736.asp).

Language Learning and Technology (http://llt.msu.edu).

Language Teaching (http://journals.cambridge.org/action/displayJournal?jid= LTA).

Language Teaching Research (http://tr.sagetub.com).

Studies in Second Language Acquisition (http://journals.cambridge.org/action/ displayJournal?jid=SLA).

System (www.elsevier.com/wps/find/iournaldescription.cws_home/335fdescription #description).

TESOL Quarterly (www.ingentaconnect.com/content/tesol/tq; www.tesol.org/tq).

The Canadian Modern Language Review (www.utpjournals.com/cmlr/).

The Modern Language Journal (http://polyglot.lss.wisc.edu/mlj/).

Zeitschrift für den interkulturellen Fremdsprachenunterricht (http://zif.spz.tu-darmstadt.de).

Also, from time to time, non-specialist journals will run special issues of FL themes, e.g.

Cambridge Journal of Education (4/36), 2007, 'Choices in language choice' (www.informaworld.com/smpp/title~db=all~content=g773400222).

or

Support for Learning. The British Journal of Learning Support (3/20), 2005, 'Inclusive approaches to teaching foreign languages' (www.blackwell-synergy. com/toc/sufl/20/3?cookieSet=1).

References

Allwright, D. (2003) 'Exploratory practice: rethinking practitioner research in language teaching', *Language Teaching Research*, 7(2): 113–41

Alptekin, C. (1993) 'Target-language culture in EFL materials', *ELT Journal*, 47(2): 136–43

Arnot, M. and Gubb, J. (2001) *Adding Value to Boys' and Girls' Education*. West Sussex County Council.

Bailey, R. (2004) 'Why does truth matter?', in D. Hayes (ed.) *The Routledge Falmer Guide to Key Debates in Education*. London: RoutledgeFalmer, pp. 202–6.

Baker, C., Cohn, T. and McLaughlin, M. (2000) 'Inspecting subject knowledge', in J. Arthur, and R. Phillips (eds) *Issues in History Teaching*. London: Routledge.

Ball, D. (1991) 'Research in teaching mathematics: making subject knowledge part of the equation', in J. Brophy (ed.) *Advances in Research on Teaching*, Vol. 2, *Teachers' knowledge of subject as it relates to their teaching practices*. Greenwich, CT: JAI Press, pp. 1–48.

Banks, F., Leach, J. and Moon, B. (1999) 'New understandings of teachers' pedagogic knowledge', in J. Leach, and B. Moon (eds) *Learners and Pedagogy*. London: Paul Chapman, pp. 89–110.

Barret, M. and Short, J. (1992) 'Images of European people in a group of 5–10-year-old English schoolchildren', *British Journal of Developmental Psychology*, 10: 339–63.

BBC (2002) *Teacher Numbers Hit '20 Year High'*, 5 August 2002. Available at http://news.bbc.co.uk/1/hi/education/2173253.stm.

Bennett, N. (1993) 'Knowledge bases for learning to teach', in N. Bennett and C. Carré (eds) *Learning to Teach*. London: Routledge, pp. 1–17.

Block, D. (2002) 'Communicative language teaching revisited: discourses in conflict and foreign national teachers', *Language Learning Journal*, 26: 19–26.

Bourdillon, H. and Storey, A. (eds) (2002) 'Subject knowledge and preparation for teaching', in *Aspects of Secondary Education – Perspectives on Practice*. London: RoutledgeFalmer, pp. 43–62.

Broady, E. (2002) 'Changes, challenges and complexity: recent debates in English language teaching', *Language Learning Journal*, 26: 62–7.

Broady, E. (2004) 'Sameness and difference: the challenge of culture in language teaching', *Language Learning Journal* (29): 68–72.

Brown, S. and McIntyre, D. (1993) *Making Sense of Teaching*. Milton Keynes: Open University Press.

Burn, A. (2005) 'Teaching with digital video', in M. Leask and N. Pachler (eds) *Learning to Teach Using ICT in the Secondary School*, 2nd edn. London: RoutledgeFalmer.

Calderhead, J. and Shorrock, S. (1997) *Understanding Teacher Education*. London: Falmer Press.

Canale, M. (1983) 'On some dimensions of language proficiency', in J. W. Oller, Jr. (ed.) *Issues in Language Testing Research*. Rowley, MA: Newbury House, pp. 333–42.

Chambers, G. (1999) *Motivating Language Learners*. Clevedon: Multilingual Matters.

Chapelle, C. (1998) 'Multimedia CALL: lessons to be learned from research on instructed SLA', *Language Learning and Technology*, 2(1): 22–34. Available http://llt.msu.edu/vol2num1/article1/index.html.

CILT/ALL (2004) *CILT/ALL Language Trends Survey 2004*. Available www.cilt.org.uk/key/trends2004.htm.

CILT/ALL (2006) *CILT/ALL Language Trends Survey 2006*. Available www.cilt.org.uk/research/languagetrends2006.htm.

Cochran-Smith, M. and Lytle, S. (2001) 'Beyond certainty: taking an inquiry stance on practice', in A. Lieberman and L. Miller (eds) *Teachers Caught in the Action: professional development that matters*. New York: Teachers College, Columbia University, pp. 45–58.

Cogill, J. (2006) 'Pedagogy, models of teacher knowledge and the use of the interactive whiteboard', *Education Today*, 56(3): 6–13.

Coleman, J. (1995) 'The evolution of language learner motivation in British universities, with some international comparisons', in R.G. Wakely (ed.) *Language Teaching and Learning in HE: issues and perspectives*. Edinburgh: University of Edinburgh/CILT, pp. 1–16.

Coleman, J. (1996) *Studying Languages: a survey of British and European students: the proficiency, background, attitudes and motivations of students of foreign languages in the United Kingdom and Europe*. London: Centre for Information on Language Teaching and Research.

Coleman, J. (1999) 'Looking ahead: modern foreign languages in higher education', in N. Pachler (ed.) *Teaching Modern Foreign Languages in the Sixth Form*. Routledge, 1999: 322–41.

Cooper, P. and McIntyre, D. (1996) 'The importance of power-sharing in classroom learning', in M. Hughes (ed.) *Teaching and Learning in Changing Times*. Oxford: Blackwell, pp. 88–108.

Council of Europe (2001) *Common European Framework of Reference for Languages: learning, teaching, assessment.* Cambridge: Cambridge University Press. Available http://culture2.coe.int/portfolio/documents_intro/common_framework.html.

Counsell, C. (2004) *History and Literacy in Y7.* London: John Murray.

Dearing, R. and King, L. (2006) *The Languages Review: consultation report.* London: DfES. Available www.teachernet.gov.uk/_doc/10690/6869_DfES_Language_Review.pdf.

Dearing, R. and King, L. (2007) *Languages Review.* Available www.teachernet. gov.uk/_doc/11124/LanguageReview.pdf.

DES/Welsh Office (1990) *Modern Foreign Languages for Ages 11–16.* London: DES/Welsh Office.

DfEE (1999) *Citizenship. The National Curriculum for England.* London: DfEE and QCA.

DfES (2002) *Languages for All: languages for life. A strategy for England.* London: DES. Available www.dfes.gov.uk/languagesstrategy/pdf/DfESLanguages Strategy.pdf.

DfES (2003a) *Subject Specialism: consultation document.* London: DfES. Available www.dfes.gov.uk/consultations/downloadableDocs/222_2.pdf.

DfES (2003b) *Framework for Teaching Modern Foreign Languages: Years 7, 8 and 9.* London: DfES. Available www.standards.dfes.gov.uk/keystage3/respub/mflframework/.

DfES (2004a) *The Languages Ladder – steps to success.* Available www.dfes. gov.uk/languages/DSP_languageladder.cfm.

DfES (2004b) *Putting the World into World-Class Education. An international strategy for education, skills and children's services.* London: DfES. Available www.globalgateway.org.uk/PDF/World%20Class%20Education.pdf.

DfES/TTA (2002) *Qualifying to Teach.* London: DfES/TTA.

DfES/TDA (2007) *Professional Standards for Teachers: qualified teacher status.* Available www.tda.gov.uk/upload/resources/pdf/s/standards_qts.pdf. (accessed 24 September 2007).

Dörnyei, Z. (2001) *Teaching and Researching Motivation.* Harlow: Pearson Education.

Doughty, C. (2001) 'Cognitive underpinnings of focus on form', in P. Robinson (ed.) *Cognition and Second Language Instruction.* Cambridge: Cambridge University Press.

Doughty, C. and Long, M. (2003) 'Optimal psycholinguistic environments for distance foreign language learning', *Language Learning & Technology,* 7(3): 50–80. Available http://llt.msu.edu/vol7num3/pdf/doughty.pdf.

Driscoll, P. (1999) 'Modern languages in the primary school. A fresh start', in P. Driscoll and D. Frost (eds) *Teaching Modern Foreign Languages in the Primary School.* London: RoutledgeFalmer, pp. 9–26.

Duranti, A. (1997) *Linguistic Anthropology.* Cambridge: Cambridge University Press.

East, P. (1995) 'He she it, das "s" muss mit! Who formulates a learner's rule?', *Language Learning Journal,* 12: 44–6.

Ellis, R. (1997) 'SLA and language pedagogy. An educational perspective', *Studies in Second Language Acquisition,* 19: 69–92.

Ellis, R. (2003) *Task-Based Language Learning and Teaching*. Oxford: Oxford University Press.

Eraut, M. (1994) *Developing Professional Knowledge and Competence*. London: Falmer Press.

Fisher, L. (2001) 'Modern foreign languages recruitment post 16: the pupils' perspective', *Language Learning Journal*, 23: 33–40.

Freeman, D. (1994) 'Knowing into doing: teacher education and the problem of transfer', in D. Li, D. Mahoney and J. Richards (eds) *Exploring Second Language Teacher Development*. Hong Kong: City Polytechnic, pp. 1–20.

Freeman, D. (1996) 'Redefining the relationship between research and what teachers know', in K. Bailey, and D. Nunan (eds) *Voices from the Classroom*. Cambridge: Cambridge University Press, pp. 88–115.

Freeman, D. (2002) 'The hidden side of the work: teacher knowledge and learning to teach. A perspective from north American educational research on teacher education in English language teaching', *Language Teaching*, 35: 1–13.

Freeman, D. and Freeman, Y. (1994) *Between Worlds: access to second language acquisition*. Portsmouth, NH: Heineman.

Gatbonton, E. (1999) 'Investigating ESL teachers' pedagogical knowledge', *The Modern Language Journal*, 83(1): 35–50.

Golombek, P. (1998) 'A study of language teachers' personal practical knowledge', *TESOL Quarterly*, 32(3): 447–64.

Graham, S. (1997) *Effective Language Learning*, Modern Languages in Practice 6. Clevedon: Multilingual Matters.

Graham, S. (2002) 'Experiences of learning French: a snapshot at Years 11, 12 and 13', *Language Learning Journal*, 25: 15–20.

Graham, S. (2003) 'Learner Strategies and Advanced Level Listening Comprehension', *Language Learning Journal*, 28: 64–9.

Grauberg, W. (1997) *The Elements of Foreign Language Learning*. Clevedon: Multilingual Matters.

Green, P. and Hecht, K. (1992) 'Implicit and explicit grammar: an empirical study', *Applied Linguistics*, 13: 169–84.

Groot, P. (2000) 'Computer assisted second language vocabulary acquisition', *Language Learning and Technology*, 4(1): 60–81. Available http://llt.msu.edu/vol4num1/groot/default.html.

Grossman, P., Wilson, S. and Shulman, L. (1989) 'Teachers of substance: subject matter knowledge for teaching', in M. Reynolds (ed.) *Knowledge Base for the Beginning Teacher*. Oxford: Pergamon Press.

Halsall, R. (ed.) (1998) *Teacher Research and School Improvement*. Buckingham: Open University Press.

Hargreaves, A. (1992) 'Cultures of teaching: a focus for change', in A. Hargreaves and M. Fullan (eds) *Understanding Teacher Development*. London: Cassell, pp. 216–36.

Hargreaves, D. (1998) *The Knowledge-Creating School*. BERA Annual Conference. Belfast.

Hargreaves, D. (2003) *Education Epidemic: transforming secondary schools through innovation networks*. London: Demos.

Harris, V. (1997) *Teaching Learners How to Learn: strategy training in the ML classroom.* London: CILT.

Hawkins, E. (1981) *Modern Languages in the Curriculum.* Cambridge: Cambridge University Press.

Hawkins, E. (1987) *Modern Languages in the Curriculum,* revised edn. Cambridge: Cambridge University Press.

Hawkins, E. (ed.) (1996) *30 Years of Language Teaching.* London: CILT.

Hayes, D. (2002) 'Non specialists reach "disturbing" level', *TES,* 4 July. Available www.tes.co.uk/search/search_display.asp?section=Breaking+News+Stories&su b_section=Breaking+News&id=366007&Type=0.

Hayes, D. (2003) 'The truths about educational research', in J. Lea *et al.* (eds) *Working in Post-Compulsory Education.* Maidenhead: Open University Press, pp. 153–67.

Hyland, T. (1993) 'Competence, knowledge and education,' *Journal of Philosophy of Education,* 27(1): 57–68.

Hyland, T. (1994) *Competence, Knowledge and NVQs: dissenting perspectives.* London: Cassell.

Johnson, K. (2001) *An Introduction to Foreign Language Learning and Teaching.* Harlow: Pearson Education.

Johnstone, R. (2003) 'Evidence-based policy: early modern language learning at primary', *Language Learning Journal,* 28: 14–21.

Jones, B. (1994) 'Modern languages: twenty years of change', in A. Swarbrick (ed.) *Teaching Modern Languages.* London: Routledge.

Jones, N. (2006) 'Assessment and the National Languages Strategy', *Cambridge Journal of Education,* 36(4).

Kemmis, S. and Taggart, R. (eds) (1988) *The Action Research Planner.* Geelong: Deakin University Press.

Kern, R. and Warschauer, M. (2000) 'Introduction: theory and practice of network-based language teaching', in M. Warschauer and R. Kern (eds) *Network-Based Language Teaching: concepts and practice.* New York: Cambridge University Press. Available www.gse.uci.edu/markw/nblt.html.

Klapper, J. (2003) 'Taking communication to task? A critical review of recent trends in language teaching', *Language Learning Journal,* 27: 33–42.

Kramsch, C. (1996) 'The cultural component of language teaching', *Zeitschrift für interkulturellen* Fremdsprachenunterricht, 1(1). Available www.ualberta. ca/~german/ejournal/archive/kramsch2.htm.

Krashen, S. (1985) *The Input Hypothesis: issues and implications.* London: Longman.

Kress, G. (2000) 'A curriculum for the future', *Cambridge Journal of Education,* 30(1): 133–45.

Lamb, T. and Simpson, M. (2003) 'Escaping from the treadmill: practitioner research and professional autonomy', *Language Learning Journal,* 28: 55–63.

Lambert, D. and Pachler, N. (2002) 'Initial teacher education in the UK', *Metodika. Special Issue: Changes in education of teachers in Europe,* 3(5): 221–33.

Lawes, S. (1996) 'Preparing student teachers to teach a second foreign language', *Links* (15). London: CILT.

Lawes, S. (2003) 'What, when, how and why? Theory and foreign language teaching', *Language Learning Journal*, 28: 22–8.

Lawes, S. (2004a) 'Practice makes imperfect', in D. Hayes (ed.) *The Routledge Falmer Guide to Key Debates in Education*. London: RoutledgeFalmer.

Lawes, S. (2004b) 'The end of theory? A comparative study of the decline of educational theory and professional knowledge in initial teacher training in England and France', Ph.D. thesis, Institute of Education, University of London.

Leinhart, G. and Smith, D. (1985) 'Expertise in mathematics instruction: subject matter knowledge', *Journal of Educational Psychology*, 77: 247–71.

Lightbown, P. (1985) 'Great expectations: second language acquisition research and classroom teaching', *Applied Linguistics*, 6: 173–89.

Little, D. (2006) 'The Common European Framework of Reference for Languages: content, purpose, origin, reception and impact', *Language Teaching*, 39: 167–90.

Littlewood, W. (1981) *Communicative Language Teaching*. Cambridge: Cambridge University Press.

Lomas, J. (2000) 'Connecting research and policy', *Isuma*, 1(1): 140–4. Available www.isuma.net/v01n01/lomas/lomas_e.pdf.

Macaro, E. (2001) *Learning Strategies in Foreign and Second Language Classrooms*. London: Continuum.

Macaro, E. (2003a) *Teaching and Learning a Second Language. A guide to recent research and its applications*. London: Continuum.

Macaro, E (2003b) 'Second language teachers as second language classroom researchers', *Language Learning Journal*, 27: 43–51.

McCallum, B., Hargreaves, E. and Gipps, C. (2000) 'Learning: the pupil's voice', *Cambridge Journal of Education*, 30(2): 275–89.

McLaughlin, B. (1990) 'Restructuring', *Applied Linguistics*, 11(2): 113–28.

McLaughlin, B. (1992) *Myths and Misconceptions about Second Language Learning: what every teacher needs to unlearn*. Educational Practice Report 5, National Centre for Research on Cultural Diversity and Second Language Learning. Available www.ncela.gwu.edu/pubs/symposia/reading/article6/mclaughlin93.html.

Maclure, S. (1988) *Education Reformed: a guide to the Education Reform Act*. London: Hodder & Stoughton.

McPake, J. (2002) 'The impact of languages research on classroom practice', in A. Swarbrick (ed.) *Teaching Modern Foreign Languages in Secondary Schools: a reader*. London: RoutledgeFalmer.

McPake, J., Johnstone, R., Low, L. and Lyall, L. (1999) *Foreign Languages in the Upper Secondary School*. Edinburgh: Scottish Council for Research in Education. See also *Interchange 59*. Available www.scotland.gov.uk/hmie/pdf/ers/interchange_59.pdf.

Macrory, G. and Stone, V. (2000) 'Pupil progress in acquisition of the perfect tense in French: the relationship between knowledge and use', *Language Teaching Research*, 4(1): 55–82.

Malarée, C. (2004) 'Development education in the Spanish classroom', *Vida Hispánica*, 30: 4–11.

Mamiala, T. and Treagust, D. (2003) 'Characteristics of explanation in school physical science textbooks', European Science Education Research Association, Research and the Quality of Science Education Conference, The Netherlands. Available www1.phys.uu.nl/esera2003/programme/pdf%5C276S.pdf.

Meighan, R. (1988) *Flexi-Schooling. Education for tomorrow, starting yesterday*. Ticknall: Education Now Publishing Cooperative.

Milton, J. and Meara, P. (1998) 'Are the British really bad at learning foreign languages?', *Language Learning Journal*, 18: 68–76.

Mishra, P. and Koehler, M. (2006) 'Technological, pedagogical content knowledge: a new framework for teacher knowledge', *Teachers College Record*, 108(6), pp. 1017–54.

Mitchell, M. (1994) 'Investigating the communicative approach', in A. Swarbrick (ed.) *Teaching Modern Languages*. London: Routledge, pp. 33–42.

Mitchell, M. (2003) 'Rethinking the concept of progression in the National Curriculum for modern foreign languages: a research perspective', *Language Learning Journal*, 27: 15–23.

Mitchell, R. and Martin, C. (1997) 'Rote learning, creativity and "understanding" in classroom foreign language teaching', *Language Teaching Research*, 1(1): 1–27.

Mitchell, R. and Myles, F. (1998) *Second Language Learning Theories*. London: Arnold.

Modern Languages Review Group (2004) *A Systematic Review of the Characteristics of Effective Foreign Language Teaching to Pupils Between the Ages 7 and 11*. London: EPPI-Centre.

Moore, A. (2000) *Teaching and Learning: pedagogy, curriculum and culture*. London: RoutledgeFalmer, pp. 1–25.

Moss, G., Jewitt, C. and Levacic, R. (2005) *Interactive Whiteboards, Pedagogy and Pupil Performance Evaluation: an interim report*. Evaluation of Schools Whiteboard Expansion Project (London Challenge). London Knowledge Lab/ Institute of Education.

National Recognition Scheme for Languages (2004) *Languages Ladder*. Available www.dfes.gov.uk/languages/DsP-languagesladder.cfm.

Neuner, G. and Hunfeld, H. (1993) *Zur Entwicklung der Methoden des fremdsprachlichen Deutschunterrichts*. München: Langenscheidt.

Noss, R. and Pachler, N. (1999) 'The challenge of new technologies: doing old things in a new way, or doing new things?', in P. Mortimore (ed.) *Understanding Pedagogy and its Impact on Learning*. London: Sage, pp. 195–211.

Nozick, R. (2001) *Invariances: the structure of the objective world*. Cambridge, MA: Harvard University Press.

Nuffield Languages Inquiry (2000) *Languages: the next generation*. London: The Nuffield Foundation.

Nunan, D. (1992) *Research Methods in Language Learning*. Cambridge: Cambridge University Press.

Nunan, D. and Lamb, C. (1996) *The Self-Directed Teacher: managing the learning process*. Cambridge: Cambridge University Press.

Nutley, S., Walter, I. and Davies, H. (2002) *From Knowing to Doing: a framework for understanding the evidence-into-practice agenda*. Research Unit for Research Utilisation: University of St Andrews. Available www.st-andrews.ac.uk/~cppm/discussion_papers.htm.

O'Malley, J. and Chamot, A. (1990) *Learning Strategies in Second Language Acquisition*. Cambridge: Cambridge University Press.

Olson, D., Torrance, N. and Hildyard, A. (1985) *Literacy, Language, and Learning*. Cambridge: Cambridge University Press.

Pachler, N. (ed.) (1999) *Teaching Modern Foreign Languages at Advanced Level*. London: Routledge.

Pachler, N. (2000) 'Re-examining communicative language teaching', in K. Field (ed.) *Issues in Modern Foreign Language Teaching*. London: Routledge Falmer, pp. 26–41.

Pachler, N. (2002) 'Foreign language learning in England in the 21st century', *Language Learning Journal*, 24: 4–7.

Pachler, N. (2003) 'Foreign language teaching as an evidence-based profession?', *Language Learning Journal*, (27): 4–14.

Pachler, N. (2005a) 'Internet-based approaches to foreign language teaching and learning', in N. Pachler and A. Redondo (eds) *Teaching Modern Foreign Languages in the Secondary School*. London: RoutledgeFalmer.

Pachler, N. (2005b) 'Who are our students and what do they bring from previous experience?', in J. Coleman and J. Klapper (eds) *Effective Learning and Teaching in Modern Languages*. London: Kogan Page.

Pachler, N. (2007) 'Choices in language education: principles and policies', *Cambridge Journal of Education*, 36(4): 1–15.

Pachler, N. and Field, K. (2001a) *Learning to Teach Modern Foreign Languages in the Secondary School*, 2nd edn. London: RoutledgeFalmer.

Pachler, N. and Field, K. (2001b) 'From mentor to co-tutor: reconceptualising secondary modern foreign languages ITE', *Language Learning Journal*, (23): 15–30.

Pachler, N. and Watson, G. (1996) 'School-based initial teacher training: the implications for the role of university staff in the training of teachers', in N. Ephraty and R. Lidor (eds) *Proceedings of The Second International Conference Teacher Education: Stability, Evolution and Revolution*, Vol. B. The Zinman College of Physical Education and Sport Sciences, Wingate Institute, Israel, pp. 1269–84.

Pickering, J., Daly, C. and Pachler, N. (eds) (2007) *New designs for teacher's professional learning*. Bedford Way Papers. London: Institute of Education.

Plato (360BC/1987) *Theaetetus*. Translated by R.A.H. Waterfield, Harmondsworth: Penguin Books, pp. 170a–1e.

QAA (2002) *Languages and Related Studies. Subject benchmark statements*. Gloucester: QAA. Available www.qaa.ac.uk/crntwork/benchmark/phase2/languages.htm.

QCA (2004) *Modern Foreign Languages in the Key Stage 4 Curriculum*. London: QCA. Available www.qca.org.uk/libraryAssets/media/7563_mfl_in_ks4_curric. pdf (accessed 24 September 2007).

QCA (2007) *The Secondary Curriculum Review*. Available www.qca.org.uk/ secondarycurriculumreview/.

Rowan, B., Schilling, S., Ball, D., Miller, R., *et al.* (2001) *Measuring Teachers' Pedagogical Content Knowledge in Surveys: an exploratory study*. Available www.sii.soe.umich.edu/documents/pck%20final%20report%20revised%20B R100901.pdf.

Rowlinson, W. (1994) 'The historical ball and chain', in A. Swarbrick (ed.) *Teaching Modern Languages*. London: Routledge.

Rudduck, J., Chaplain, R. and Wallace, G. (1996) *School Improvement. What can pupils tell us?* London: David Fulton.

Rudduck, J. and Flutter, J. (2000) 'Pupil participation and pupil perspective: "carving a new order of experience"', *Cambridge Journal of Education*, 30(1): 75–89.

Schmenk, B. (2004) 'Drama in the margins? The Common European Framework of Reference and its implications for drama pedagogy in the foreign language classroom', *German as a Foreign Language*, 2004(1): 7–23. Available www.gfl-journal.de.

Selinker, G. (1972) 'Interlanguage', *International Review of Applied Linguistics*, 10(3): 209–39.

Sharpe, K. (2001) *Modern Foreign Languages in the Primary School: the what, why and how of early MFL teaching*. London: RoutledgeFalmer.

Shulman, L. (1986) 'Those who understand: knowledge growth in teaching', *Educational Researcher*, 15(2): 4–14.

Shulman, L. (1987) 'Knowledge and teaching: foundations of the new reform', *Harvard Educational Review*, 57(1): 1–22.

Shulman, L. and Shulman, J. (2004) 'How and what teachers learn: a shifting perspective', *Journal of Curriculum Studies*, 36(2): 257–71.

Siegel, H. (1987) *Relativism Refuted: a critique of contemporary epistemological relativism*. Dordrecht: D. Reidel.

Skehan, P. (1996) 'Second language acquisition research and task-based instruction', in J. Willis and D. Willis (eds) *Challenge and Change in Language Teaching*. Oxford: Heineman.

Stern, H. (1983) *Fundamental Concepts of Language Teaching*. Oxford: Oxford University Press.

Stoller, F. (2004) 'Content-based instruction: perspectives on curriculum planning', *Annual Review of Applied Linguistics, Advances in Language Pedagogy*, 24: 261–81.

Tabberer, R. (1996) *Teachers Make a Difference*. Slough: NFER.

Thomas, G. (2002) 'Theory's spell – on qualitative inquiry and educational research', *British Educational Research Journal*, 28(3): 419–34.

TTA (1996) *Teaching as a Research-Based Profession*. London: TTA.

TTA (1999) *The Use of ICT in Subject Teaching. Identification of training needs: secondary modern foreign languages*. London: TTA.

Turner-Bisset, R. (2001) *Expert Teaching*. London: David Fulton.

Van Ek, J.A. (1976) *The Threshold Level for Modern Language Learning in Schools*. Strasbourg: Council of Europe.

Vasseur (2000) 'Apprendre à être professeur de langue étrangère dans un pays étranger', *Recherche et Formation* (33): 45–61.

Wallace, M. (1998) *Action Research for Language Teachers*. Cambridge: Cambridge University Press.

Wenden, A. (2001) 'Metacognitive knowledge in SLA: the neglected variable', in M. Breen (ed.) *Learner Contributions to Language Learning*, Harlow: Pearson Education.

White, J. (ed.) (2004) *Rethinking the School Curriculum: values, aims and purposes*. London: RoutledgeFalmer.

Whitty, G., Furlong, J., Barton, L., Miles, S. and Whiting, C. (2000) *Teacher Education in Transition: re-forming professionalism?* Buckingham, Open University Press.

Wicksteed, K. (2005) 'Primary languages: will it work?', *The Linguist*, 44(11): 2–4.

Widdowson, H. (2002) 'Language teaching: defining the subject', in H. Trappes-Lomax and G. Ferguson (ed.) *Language in Language Teacher Education*. Amsterdam: John Benjamins Publishing, pp. 67–81.

Williams, K. (2000) *Why Teach Foreign Languages in Schools? A philosophical response to curriculum policy. Impact No. 5*. Ringwood: Philosophy of Education Society of Great Britain.

Williams, M. and Burden, R. (1997) *Psychology for Language Teachers*. Cambridge: Cambridge University Press.

Williams, M., Burden, R. and Lanvers, U. (2002) '"French is the language of love and stuff": student perceptions of issues related to motivation in learning a foreign language', *British Educational Research Journal*, 28(4): 503–28.

Woods, D. (1996) *Teacher Cognition in Language Teaching*. Cambridge: Cambridge University Press.

Working Group on 14–19 Reform (2004) *14–19 Curriculum and Qualifications Reform: Final Report of the Working Group on 14–19 Reform*. London: DfES. Available www.14-19reform.gov.uk/docs_general/_52/Final%20Report.pdf.

Wrenn, A. (1999) 'Build it in, don't bolt it on: history's opportunity to support critical citizenship', *Teaching History*, 96: 6–12.

Young, M. (1999) 'Knowledge, learning and the curriculum of the future', *British Educational Research Journal*, 25(4): 463–7.

Index

87; hidden 86, 99; informal 86; local 86; national 86; negotiated 94; past 87; planning 83–7, 96; policy exemplification documents 112–13; post-16 84–85, 101

Development: personal 141; subject 141
dictionaries 88

education: frames of 92–3; Reform Act (1988) 9
elitism 1, 8; enjoyment 100
European Languages Portfolio 35
European Union (EU) 15, 16
examination specifications 42

failure: socio-pragmatic 73; L2 29
FL(s) (L2) 123; aims and purposes of 7, 73; attainment in 16; attitudes to(wards) 8, 13; beliefs about 57, 124–9; cognitive demands of 13; competence-based 18; curriculum content for 10; decline in interest in 7; entitlement to 1; learning experience 20; instrumental arguments for the learning of 21; knowledge about 47–8; knowledge of 24, 48; learning experience 20; myths about 20; personal beliefs about 25, 26; playful approaches to 100; policy 1, 2; political interest in 9; politics of 7, 8–10; primary 15, 105–11, 179; proficiency in 16; in schools 13–15; as subject discipline 19–22; status of 1, 2; transformational capacity of 19; utilitarian rationale for 98; value and purpose of 2, 8
fluency 174
focus on form(s) 67, 69
focus on meaning 69
foundation disciplines 65
functionalism 21–2

GCSE 13, 88, 91, 99, 100
General Teaching Council (GTC) 176

good teacher 61
Graded Objectives 9, 18
grammar 31–3; teaching 66–8

Higher Grade 120

ICT 74–9, 91
identity 93, 175–6, 184
independence 121
induction 173
Initial Teacher Education (ITE) 64
input: comprehensible 66, 121; hypothesis 66; TL 30–1, 66
'inquiry as a stance' 63
instrumentalism 3, 5, 21–2
interaction modes 72
Interactive Whiteboard (IWB) 77–9
interlanguage 26, 67
interviews: retrospective 136

Key Stage 3 (KS3) 14, 100
Key Stage 4 (KS4) 1, 14, 98
'know-how' 58
knowing: about 62; how to 62; what 62; who to 62; why 62
knowledge: audit 145; beginner's 121; comparative linguistic 25; construction 57; content 25, 54, 59, 60, 65, 78; creation 144, 145; cultural 11, 24, 73; curriculum/curricular 59, 81–113; declarative 62, 116–17; dissemination of 146; domains 115; about education 167; of educational contexts 60; educational policy 167; explicit 62; of FLs in the curriculum 167; implicit 62; instrumental view of 19, 21, 22, 41; intercultural 73–64; of learners 60; lexical 100–1, 102; metacognitive 132, 134–5; pedagogical 53–80, 115, 116; perspectives 81; for/in/of practice 63; practical 58; prior 123; procedural 116–17; professional 53–80, 167–71; propositional 58; pupil 114, 115, 116, 121–4; socio-cultural 73;